PICAFLOR

By

Matthew J. Pallamary

Mystic Ink Publishing

Mystic Ink Publishing
San Diego, CA
mysticinkpublishing.com

ISBN 10: 0-9986809-5-8 (sc)
ISBN 13: 978-0-9986809-5-8 (sc)

Library of Congress Control Number: 2021912301
Mystic Ink Publishing, San Diego, CA

Book Jacket and Page Design: Matthew J. Pallamary/San Diego CA
Cover artwork: Alfredo Zagaceta C /Pucallpa Peru
Author's Photograph: Matthew J. Pallamary — Gibbs Photo/Malibu CA

DEDICATION

This book is dedicated to M.A. the face of the Cosmic Feminine who nurtured me in this life and the spirit of the Cosmic Feminine she connected me with in the revelation of Santa Teresa de Avila. By proxy this dedication includes Ayahuasca the mother of all the jungle plants and the voice of Madre Tierra who nurtures all life in this three dimensional realm at the junction of unconditional love with the Cosmic Father.

Together they bless us with the Great Mystery of existence.

Acknowledgements

The author would like to thank Rob and Kim Gubala, Ken Symington, Mary Conrad, Jacques Olivier, and M. A. whose support made this book possible .

.

TABLE OF CONTENTS

INTRODUCTION

I am a storyteller who was taught by gifted writers that information is the enemy of drama. This tale, which is the second installment of my passage through this dream we call life has plenty of drama and it is also a map I am leaving behind for those who might follow. Unlike classic story structure the terrain of this deep inner and outer journey often defies logic. The fact that much of it *is* nonrational doesn't invalidate the dense gems hidden within its alien, nonlinear symbolic language. The information will get dense, nonsensical, and hard to follow at times, but this is in the service of accuracy. The chaos of my recorded dreams and visions may often come across as excessive, but I felt it important to record my deeply personal subjective experiences, particularly when my dreams and their interplay with my visions were stimulated by the teacher plants of the Amazon that bring life changing revelations in the isolation of shamanic plant dietas.

Remembering dreams and visions comes out of sequence, typically though not always moving backward from the most recent memories. While analyzing them I realized that the nonrational creative side of my brain was putting on plays and telling stories in its own unique language of metaphor and symbolism which is what we do with our art, books, music, and movies. Instead of communicating by stringing thoughts in linear sentences, our right hemisphere uses this symbolism as its own unique language to convey its concerns.

As far as my human interactions with the "external" world go, the names have been changed to protect the guilty.

ONE

The Song Remains The Same, But Hopefully The Dance Has Improved

At the time of this writing I have spent more than a quarter of a century traveling the mountains, deserts, and jungles of North, South, and Central America pursuing my studies of shamanism. The majority of that time has been focused on hunting the most cunning, treacherous, predator known to man deep in the primal heart of the Peruvian Amazon. I am cognizant of the fact that the act of hunting makes *me* a predator, but I am also the prey and I sense my quarry stalking me, ready to pounce and overwhelm me at the first sign that I am not paying attention.

There's a tacit agreement in the back and forth of my predator/prey dance where they mirror each other so precisely that the predator becomes the prey and the prey becomes the predator, often from instant to instant. Although opposites they are complementary and inexplicably bound to each other until it becomes indistinguishable as to who is who.

Many of us like to think that we are beings of the highest light; "hue-man" beings, but if you take an honest look at the human condition and our relentless drive to consume more at the expense of fellow human beings, plants, animals, and all other forms of life along with the natural resources that we exploit to our detriment, the sad truth is that we are far from the light.

We are ravenous beasts that destroy practically everything we come in contact with, driven by greed and senseless addictions to what we think of as power. The irony of this makes it a futile attempt to fill an emptiness that can never be filled, and the more "things" we acquire in this transitory blip in the Cosmos that we call life, the more attached we become to them and the more acute our emptiness becomes. Our collective instinct is to deny and distract ourselves from these obsessions to obscure the truth of our existence at the expense of everything else.

All anyone needs to do is examine the state we find ourselves in amidst the aftermath of an environment that we have destroyed in our rampant quest for *more*, regardless of the cost to what sustains us and all of the life that we share our planet with.

We are living a lie, or better still a canon of lies, and the sad state we live in with our supposed brothers and sisters, and the widespread death, suffering, extinction, and destruction of all living things cannot be denied. The catastrophic events we are living through and perpetuating are the results of our own actions. Our self destruction is self induced and the collapse of our environment is manmade even when these events appear to be "natural disasters" like hurricanes, floods, tsunamis, pandemics, and tornadoes. More often than not these are the result of the damage we have done to our environment by destroying the natural world we were born into.

We all share variations of the same demons of self-deprecation, self-destruction, martyrdom, stubbornness, greed, arrogance, and impatience. Some of these are in greater proportions than others depending on individual manifestations, but collectively the path of the inner work is the same, although the terrain can be radically different for each of us.

If you have not figured it out by now, the demonic predator that I so desperately seek in my inner and outer jungle is myself, or better still my shadow, which is of my own making. We all harbor the same denied abandoned monsters and we all try to deal with them in our own unique ways of distraction, which adds to the collective madness we are all drowning in.

From as far back as I can remember I have never been comfortable in a world of lies and hypocrisy in a system that is doomed to failure pursuing fleeting gratification to the relative few by taking advantage of the larger exploited masses.

Many of us love to think of ourselves as spiritual beings of light, but the bigger truth is that we are beings of light *and* darkness. We deny the darkness we have created in ourselves as defensive egoic personalities huddling in the darkness, abandoned as unloved children *we* have fostered. We refer to them as our shadow, which is both intensely personal and collective.

How can we become whole when we ignore our dark, "hidden" nature by cultivating endless lies and distractions designed to keep our attention focused outside of ourselves when the real work of self discovery lies within where the terrifying truth hides in the darkness?

From my very first inklings of awareness I have longed for and dedicated my life to searching for Truth in a lie filled world. A quote from my first published book, a short story collection titled **The Small Dark Room of the Soul** shares this sentiment.

"Through the ages, countless spiritual disciplines have urged us to look within ourselves and seek the truth. Part of that truth resides in a small, dark room -- one we are afraid to enter."

This has turned out to be the driving force of my existence, literally to the detriment of all else.

What is it like to seek out the place where your deepest fears are amplified and there is nowhere to hide, and no one to save or protect you, forcing you to face the darkness head on and embrace awe and terror? Where is such a "place" where the predator becomes the prey and the prey becomes the predator? In ancient South American shamanic cultures this is called being swallowed by the jaguar. In other ancient cultures it is referred to as being decapitated and/or being dismembered.

Looking back, I was amazed to discover my dawning awareness evident in my first published collection of short horror stories. I didn't realize it at the time, but all of the monsters in my stories are human and collectively the writing of them turned out to be an examination of humanity's shadow.

What you are reading now is titled **Picaflor**, meaning "bite or sting flower", the Spanish name for Hummingbird used in Peru. It is the continuation of my life's journey chronicled in my memoir **Spirit Matters** which ended in the year two-thousand at the turn of the century. I am gratified to see after more than two decades that "the song remains the same", and though I have reached higher and more refined levels of awareness, I am comforted by the fact that I will never become fully enlightened because spirit is infinite. Any delusion of enlightenment implies boundaries and limitations to what is ineffable, incomprehensible, and infinitely beyond any conception of what I or anyone else can ever conceive of within the boundaries of the three dimensional dream that we share.

Though it is more than twenty years later with lifetimes of experience behind me, the starting point is the same, as everything does come full circle, something the ancients knew on many levels. Infinitely expanding circles take the form of spirals that begin at a point, which by definition has no dimension and which also defines spirit as it has no limitations and no place in three dimensional reality, except as a starting point of spirit into matter. This expanding circle coming into existence from the no dimensional point of beginning is the essence of the word in*spir*ation, which is what my life and my work have been.

In the spirit of this sacred, inspired circle of existence that encompasses birth, death, rebirth, and the ever expanding journey of the gift of this adventure we call life, I am resuming this journey of my passage through three dimensional "reality" with the beginning and end of my memoir ***Spirit Matters***.

In many respects this opening from ***Spirit Matters*** is where it all begins and where it all ends.

It is returning, at last it is coming home to me — my own Self and those parts of it that have long been abroad and scattered among all things and accidents.

--Nietzsche
Thus Spoke Zarathustra

A WAKING DREAM

I am outside of time and space where the normal rules of perception no longer apply. Colors with hues that defy description bombard me, then unfold in multicolored geometric progressions that could be microcosmic quantum expressions, or unfolding galaxies. Within these realms I have lived as an insect devoured by still bigger insects, which have in turn been devoured by lizards and snakes with long ethereal stomachs that have passed me into nonrational dimensions that both amaze and terrify.

Outside of my physical body the frogs, birds, insects, jaguars, and other creatures of the Peruvian Amazon fill the night air with their calls, cries, twitters, and buzzes. For me there is no difference between the infinity expressing itself outside of me and the infinity that I soar through inside of me. It is all one. Outside of time and space a noise from deep in the jungle sounds as if it is right beside me, startling me. Sometimes I feel myself fully present and aware in two places at the same time, often in different times and dimensions.

After experiencing the consciousness of predator and prey in the lower worlds, I have flown first as a Condor, then as a Hummingbird into sublime and exquisite high frequency realities exploding with neon luminescent pastel manifestations that defy rationality. While my spirit soars, my body quivers and my insides teeter on the verge of both vomiting and shitting.

I soar between agony and ecstasy as each experience awes my soul with a palette of emotions that range from heavenly bliss to a hellish, maddening terror that cannot be articulated, much less comprehended. I am vaguely aware of others sitting around me in the humid jungle night inside a circular open air hut called a maloca. Many of them vomit and sometimes cry out in fear or bliss as they pass through their own visions. I feel my soul connected to theirs.

Our visions are directed by the music of a white clad *mestizo* shaman who sings magical songs, plays different flutes, and a stringed mandolin like instrument called a charango. He is the keeper of a vast body of knowledge of Amazonian healing plants that dates back to prehistoric times. His specialty is a unique combination of plants that have brought me to this visionary state that continues to unfold outside of three dimensional reality.

In this waking dream where time and space become fluid, I not only soar through alien vistas of sight, sound, and feeling, I also travel through events of my life, both good and bad, often reliving them and their emotional content. Throughout my journey, I often confront hidden aspects of myself that have been ignored and denied because of the negative emotional charge that they hold. I sometimes vomit when confronted with something particularly unpleasant, which clears it out energetically in what is called a purge.

I have come a long way to this remote spot deep in the primordial rain forest, far from civilization to spend extended time isolated in nature to learn what the plants have to teach me, especially about myself. To be healed I must confront the forces that have driven and tortured me throughout my life so that I can understand the lessons that they have to teach me. To get to their root, I must travel back to my beginnings so I can come to terms with the energies that brought me into this life.

EPILOGUE

If I ever had any doubts about the reality of my jungle experiences, my conversation with my mother proved to me deep in the recesses of my heart that spirit *does* matter. In my inner journeys I have discovered that I am a warrior with my many selves who has hunted the darkness where the lost and forgotten aspects of my Self have raged in fear and hopelessness. Fear and death have been my greatest teachers, but it is the spirits of the plants who have shown me the many faces of Mother Earth, Father Sky, and the Oneness that binds them all to the infinite Cosmos that lie beyond this narrow and fragile dream we call reality.

My story is a myth, a word whose original meaning meant, "One's truest and deepest story", and it is in this spirit that I have laid my life before you to show the many paths I have walked in search of truth, meaning, and my endless fascination with the boundaries, real or imagined, that blur, define, or redefine what each of us thinks of as real.

We all have personal truths that we carry in our hearts through the agony and ecstasy of each transitory moment of our existence that transforms who we are from moment to fluid moment. These inner truths made manifest in our conscience are proof of a greater reality made painfully evident in the fear and helplessness that grip us in the face of our own inevitable deaths.

My path has taken me from early, lost innocence in a civilized "jungle", to the real jungle where spirit did indeed touch my soul and show me the infinite teaching of the limitless expanse of consciousness that *Spirit* truly *Is*.

My inner and outer sojourn from splintered dissonance has led me toward an evolving wholeness that is itself evolving toward an even greater Oneness encompassed by All That Is, so that my divided and chaotic selves can continue transforming from a dark chrysalis of selfishness into a magical butterfly of selflessness that will wing its way homeward, back to the One.

My explorations into inner worlds have shown me that we are far more than we ever imagined. In them spirit has revealed to me that I am star dust, manifest in the wind, the rain, the rivers, the lakes, and the oceans. I am the rocks and the mountains and the ground that gives life. I am the grasses in the fields, the flowers, trees, vines, bushes, funguses, mosses, and molds. I am all of the creatures of the earth; my brothers and sisters who fly, walk, crawl, slither, and swim, for I am a keeper of the cosmic fire that burns within every one of them. I am in all of the plants and all of the animals because I come from the heavens, but I am of the earth. I am all of these things and all of these things are within me, because I am a child of the stars, born of the earth. Though I come from spirit, I will never forget that I am my mother's child, and I would not have come into this magical place we call the earth were it not for the union of my mother and father.

The gift of their complementary wounds polarized me, forcing me to rise above the paradox of anger and sorrow to a transcendent, emotionally balanced perspective. It is truly a miracle that I survived the darkness and difficulties that I faced in my early life. SomeOne loves me. SomeOne has been watching over me, guiding me, and protecting me each step of the way, and as it turns out, I wasn't unloved and abandoned after all. I got lost. Now me and my shadow are finding our way home.

TWO

Row Your Boat

Stories from the jungle tend to carry a more profound impact when you hear them in an altered state and more often than not they contain valuable pointers in navigating Ayahuasca journeys and life in general. I think this comes from the fact that you are far more subjective to what you hear because you are listening with more parts of you being opened. What follows is written in this same spirit of openness.

In the lore of the jungle, Ayahuasca is broken down into colored varieties which are primarily red, black, white, and yellow with variations. In terms of botanical classification there is no difference, but there are big differences at the energetic level. They say that yellow Ayahuasca comes on slowly and the visions are celestial and angelic. Red Ayahausca is more physical and purgative and brings no visions. Black Ayahuasca is much stronger, comes on quicker and lasts longer, and white Ayahuasca is reputed to facilitate light or dark magic.

Within this lore it is said that after experiencing deep and profound life changing effects on his psyche and the drastic behavioral changes it engendered, a man asked an old wizened vegetalista about the nature and validity of what Ayahuasca shows you.

After considering the question for a moment, the elder shaman said, "One third of what Ayahuasca shows you is the truth, and one third of what Ayahuasca shows you is not the truth."

The man waited for the old man to complete his response until it became apparent that nothing more was forthcoming, so he finally said, "What about the other third?"

The old shaman shrugged and threw up his hands.

This is an indisputable truth that I discovered both in the messages from spirit that Ayahuasca opened me to in my dreams and visions, and what I learned the hard way in the life's lessons that came to me in the years following my first Ayahuasca experiences.

This is what American Indians call Coyote.

Spirit Matters ended in the Peruvian Amazon at the turn of the century in a profound life changing experience that proved to me unequivocally the reality at the core of it in spite of the remaining questionable two thirds.

Spirit Matters.

One of the fascinating aspects of inspiration, epiphanies, visions, revelations, and realizations is the fact that they are subjective experiences. Jesus, Buddha, Mohammed, shamans, and anyone living and breathing in the world of consensual reality as we know it can be consumed in total rapture, deeply communing with God, a saint, far flung ancestors, entities from alien cultures, or any number of other non-physical beings while embracing a reality that to them is far more real and profound than the physical world. To the outside observer of their physical state they can appear nonresponsive to the point of being comatose, twitching, or wracked with spasms, and in the case of Ayahuasca, vomiting, drooling, and shitting their pants, which can be a disturbing sight to behold to uninitiated external observers.

In modern times those who exhibit these conditions are often drugged into submission and institutionalized, sometimes by necessity, but in ancient indigenous cultures people in these states were revered and taken care of out of respect for the divine that they were thought to be in communion with.

In light of *this* truth I find it humorous to hear or give reports of deep inner transformation facilitated by Ayahuasca or other entheogenic experiences to a fascinated listener who will ask, "Did you hallucinate and see colors and patterns?"

When the person who had the experience confirms this, sometimes the questioner will invalidate and discount the deep inner shifts that occurred because the person who had them admitted to seeing colors and patterns in their visions. On one occasion when someone asked me about this a woman who was listening in became indignant and said, "It's all just hallucinations!"

I responded with, "You are correct!", and with a sweeping gesture with my hand said, "And so is all this! As a matter of fact, I'm just a figmentation of your imagination and in the next few moments, none of this will exist anymore and tomorrow it will be nothing but a memory."

She stood up in a huff and stormed off.

Now that I have expounded on what I consider to be deep wisdom I want to stress that everything I share here is a reality that exists in *my* universe, and everyone is entitled to their own version of what constitutes theirs. I give my perspective here as an offering from my experiences that have resulted from my personal search for Truth, not as an argument or a point to prove. By its very nature an offering can be taken or left which is up to the person presented with the choice.

In reflecting back on these personal revelations, it fascinates me to see how my beliefs, hopes, and attitudes have evolved over the two decades of life challenges that befell me at the very moment I thought I had a achieved some life goals and arrived at happiness and stability. The deeper truth proved to me that nothing is permanent, validating the wisdom of the old nursery rhyme most of us have learned and possibly sung.

"Row, row, row your boat gently down the stream.

Merrily, merrily, merrily, merrily, life is but a dream."

On that same note, (pun intended) icaros are medicine songs sung to the spirits of the plants and animals in Ayahuasca ceremonies to appeal to and flatter them into helping guide, heal, and facilitate the journey. Ayahuasca is thought of as the river and the icaros are the boats that carry you along it.

In many indigenous cultures, dreams, visions, and every day "waking consciousness", including any number of altered states are not separate states of awareness, but are considered one continuum that once embraced includes death. With that realization the imaginary veils that we create and believe in become progressively transparent until they dissolve completely.

In my personal experience of pushing the limits of my consciousness as far as possible through every altered state that has become available to me, my transformation has been quickened by entheogenic experiences, particularly through 5MEODMT and even more so with Ayahuasca and other teacher plants I have embraced in the many shamanic plant *dietas* I have endured in the Peruvian Amazon.

The never ending result is that my dreams and visions have spilled over into each other and these in turn have seeped into my waking life making it all one continuum for me. The beauty of this iconoclastic and unifying shift in consciousness is that the magic of my dreams and visions are now an integral part of my "waking life", making my dreams and visions more real and meaningful, and my waking life more magical and dreamlike.

In shamanism and other spiritual practices, particularly Buddhism, the gift of this magic brings with it the tremendous power of nonattachment. This is a state of overcoming attachment to desire for things, people, or concepts of the world that results in a heightened perspective that holds its own challenges and increased responsibilities, among them the ability to relate to most people in a meaningful way.

By its very nature a heightened perspective goes beyond rationality and the limitations of logic. Any effort to articulate it forces us to go beyond these strictures and express the concept by bridging it with more expansive perceptions of archetypes in the form of the visual, self-apparent Universal language of geometry, one of the primary dialects of Ayahuasca.

To make the point, (pun intended, but not really), in the preceding chapter I touched upon the starting point in reference to infinitely expanding spirals that begin at a point that defines spirit which is actually indefinable. Spirit has no boundaries or limitations making it infinite with no place in three dimensional reality, except as a point of beginning that comes into existence from no dimension, and the essence of the word in*spir*e.

In an effort to "straighten things out" in a linear manner and literally and figuratively reinforce this infinite point that impinges on three dimensional reality, there can be no argument that everything that evolves must have a beginning. This nexus is defined as the point of origin where the intangible becomes tangible and the first duality that defines our existence comes into play. This infinity point is the basis for our dualistic three dimensional world view that plays out endlessly in the way we perceive it.

Spirit-matter, subject-object, positive-negative, yin-yang, male-female, day-night, sleeping-waking, and life-death are a small sampling of the dual archetype that provides the basis for life. It manifests in the inhale-exhale of our lungs, the beating of our hearts, the ticking of our clocks, our music in the primal beats of a drum, and the notes which would not be differentiated without the spaces between them. Two is also the basis for our world wide web of information, based on the simple binary notation of yes and no symbolized by ones and zeroes. The permutations of duality are endless, but to understand its origins we need to get to the point where it all begins.

A point has no size and can only be imagined. It fixes a location in space and has a dimension equal to zero. If you take a point and move it from its original location straight to another location, this moving point creates a line which constitutes the first dimension known as length.

This movement is a manifestation of energy, which is the essence of consciousness. When we move a line that has no thickness straight from its original location to another location, it leaves the first dimension and becomes a plane which has two dimensions, length and width.

When we move a plane, it leaves two dimensions and creates a solid body with three dimensions; length, width, and height. If each of these dimensional shifts cover the same distance, the result is a cube, the basic representation of three dimensional reality. When you move a three dimensional body in space it remains a three dimensional body and does not leave the third dimension.

If you can imagine yourself without dimension, you would be formless spirit or essence. Zero dimension is represented by the point, the first dimension indicating energetic movement is the line, the second dimension is the surface, and the third dimension is the solid body. If you imagine yourself as a being who can only move within the first dimension of a straight line, all you would see is points, not your own dimensionality. When we attempt to draw something within a line, points are the only option.

A two dimensional being moving through a plane would encounter lines and thus distinguish one-dimensional beings, but not their own two dimensions. By this same progression a three-dimensional being would encounter planes and perceive two dimensional beings, but not the dimension they occupy.

A one dimensional being can perceive only points, a two-dimensional being only one dimension, and a three-dimensional being only two dimensions. By the logic of this progression it becomes apparent that the perception of each dimension necessitates being one dimension above it, so human beings who can delineate external beings in three dimensions and manipulate three dimensional spaces are four dimensional beings and just as in the example above, human beings cannot perceive the fourth dimension that we live in.

The *point* of these intellectual gymnastics is to demonstrate that we have to occupy the dimension above to perceive the dimensions below, but if our consciousness resides in lower dimensions, the higher dimensions are incomprehensible because of the boundaries and limitations of where our awareness is focused.

My original memoir **Spirit Matters** ended at the close of the twentieth century. This continuation of that adventure is being written more than two decades into the twenty-first century in a brave new world, or better still a strange new world that validates the words of Terence McKenna, when he said, "The weirder it gets, the weirder it gets."

With these words I share the continuing dream of my brief passage through the transitory, magical dream of *my* three dimensional reality where instead of working toward the center and finding transcendence by overcoming the paradox of opposites, the majority of my fellow humans perpetuate an unsustainable, splintered, chaotic, polarized, war mongering society driven by fear, selfishness, and greed.

At this point in space and time I feel so far removed from the obsessions and collective insanity of the masses that I cannot in good conscience contribute any of my precious energy to it, yet my heart goes out to the pain, suffering, and confusion of my brothers and sisters that we have brought upon ourselves and currently find ourselves trapped in.

I find myself saying more and more that I'm not from here and don't belong here. I can only look within, and the further I look within, the further out I go and the more removed I feel from this ball of confusion where we currently exist. I am in no hurry to hasten my death, but I have to admit to looking forward to that portal out of these three dimensions and the possibilities that the great mystery holds for me.

It is my sincere hope that whoever or wherever you are, reading or listening to what follows might provide a map of some sort left behind by an intrepid explorer that could point to some shortcuts through the jungle of life on earth, and that my many missteps and hard won lessons will provide insight to help you avoid the traps that I endured so you can take it to the next level.

THREE

Shadow Dancing In The Mirrors

When I was getting ready to leave for my first shamanic plant *dieta* in the Peruvian Amazon in October of 2000 where *Spirit Matters* ended, my mentor who I will refer to as Yoda told my friend Lorenzo who created the Psychedelic Salon podcast, "Say goodbye to him, he's not coming back."

We had a good laugh over that.

I had a sense of what he meant, but had no idea of how prophetic this statement was, and how multilayered and far reaching those simple words would be on levels I could scarcely comprehend. I captured the essence of that shift in consciousness at the beginning of this book and it is detailed in *Spirit Matters*.

Not only did my inner world become transformed by the massive shift in perspective I experienced, it made it flexible and adaptable, a key to survival for any organism. In line with that my outer world changed completely, much of it due to the bigger external events of the world around me.

Looking back, I see that those spirit journeys taken with sincere intention prepared me for what was coming in so many unexpected ways that I might not have survived without the "dress rehearsals" my visions gave me, something that continues to unfold for me. I think of this opening as precognition. Whether I experience it in visions or not, that door is now open to me all the time and as is true in the world of psychonauts and consciousness expansion, once certain doors are opened there is no turning back.

The first notion of visionary precognition goes back to prehistory and the ancient beliefs and intentions of Ayahuasca traditions. In jungle lore, by sharing in the vibratory field of an animal's spirit energy in a state of surrender on that entity's terms, that animal learns from the human by seeing things through human eyes while the human learns other modes of perception from seeing things through the animal's eyes.

In this manner, by mutual agreement and the understanding that comes from sharing the energetic field and perception of specific animals, the shaman hunts the animals in spirit first, then follows through in the actual physical hunt.

This learned ability to tune in to and commune with these diverse plant and animal energies allows them to experience it all in a definitive subjective manner that helps them understand other perspectives. This cultivates empathy which is the ability to understand and share the feelings of another, and it opens them up in ways that only direct experience can while aiding them in developing the skills necessary for what is defined as soul retrieval.

This concept became a guiding light for me and has aided me in finding compassion for every entity I encounter, be it plant, animal, insect, politician, criminal, clergy, junkie, crackhead, racist, and any other manifestation of consciousness which in ancient thought are all equal in each of their own unique ways.

This "consciousness equality" is connected to the concept of what I call shamanic mirroring which has exploded in this recent turn of the century while demonstrating for me how the Greater Cosmos *always* seeks balance.

In this "new age" of the twenty-first century we have instantaneous internet access with our technological mirrors known as digital cameras, cell phones, and all manner of communication. Editors and censors are being bypassed, and the mirror of truth is being revealed showing the lies of governments and the atrocities of war as well as the lies and propaganda of diverse agendas. This exposure has gotten to the point where we have gone overboard in the name of political correctness, essentially erasing history from the shame of our past collective sins.

We have brought a worldwide covid pandemic upon ourselves and environmental chaos through greed, ignorance, and disrespect for our planet and the elemental forces of nature that sustain us. Our consumer culture has laid bare our collective shadow swallowing us in darkness and confusion. Everyone is buzzing about the latest scandals, not to mention the numerous incidents of police brutality, racial conflicts, mass murders, political corruption, wars, and more. The list is endless. The phenomena of Facebook allowed Egyptians to plan out and execute the overthrow of an oppressive government, and the violence that occurred was transmitted out to the World Wide Web for the entire world to see.

On a larger front, many believe that our erratic weather patterns, floods, wildfires, and earthquakes are a reflection of the turbulence going on within human consciousness, and many believe that this turbulence is the chaos that precedes the birth of something new.

When I proved to myself that we are all connected I saw each of us as a mirror to each other in a holographic manner from the macrocosm of the collective, down to the microcosm of our individual selves, down to the sub-personalities that make up what we think of as "I", or as I like to say, a cast of thousands. Some of my sub-personalities I take out to show to the world and others that I don't like I resign to my shadow.

Mirrors often show us what we do not want to see, but I discovered that if I summon the strength to be honest with myself while striving to be an integrated person, then the work focuses on reintegrating my hidden shadow(s). This work never ends and I never "arrive".

It is relentless.

These subpersonalities aren't called shadow for nothing. They are cunning, elusive, and some would rather see the death of me as I discovered the hard way, rather than be found out. Many of my demons think that if they are discovered they will die, which contains a grain of truth because in order to be reborn, a death is necessary.

We deny our shadows and the trick that the shadow plays is to project itself onto others trapping us in self-righteousness and judgment to muddy the waters and distort the reflection from our mirror. If we can bear the reflection we will realize that what we dislike and hate in others is a reflection of what we do not want to acknowledge or take responsibility for inside of us.

Take a good look at everyone in your life. Some of them are drawn to and support our darker unconscious nature, and some are drawn to and reflect our lighter more conscious side, while some are drawn to both the light and dark aspects of our many selves.

If you believe that we are all one, then the mirrors are reflecting back from everywhere we look. Any time we feel self-righteous, judgmental, and superior, we can be sure that we are seeing our shadow reflected back to us, but the reflection is not always clear.

Once we acknowledge and embrace these abandoned, infantile ego creations with compassion, we will realize that we don't want to kill them, which is a popular modern day pop culture spiritual admonition. We need to give them a new job. We created them and in spite of their misguided actions they are trying to protect us at all costs. Our true selves reside at the center of their universe so we need to take a good look at who is in our lives and what feelings they engender in us.

I described what happened to me in **Spirit Matters** which was my personal experience of descending into the underworld to undergo transformation by dismemberment, or to be, "swallowed by the jaguar". I was swallowed by my shadow in a psychological dismemberment that nearly took my life in the "ordeal, death, and rebirth" described in Joseph Campbell's Hero's Journey.

In the more revealing and sometimes fantastical parts of my life's journey my shadow appeared in dreams, visions, and other forms, including human. Its appearance and role depended on my personal circumstances as well as my part in the collective unconscious, proving to me what many Jungian psychologists believe when they say that the shadow contains the personal shadow and the shadow of society fed by neglected and repressed collective values.

Jung also suggested that more than one layer makes up the shadow with the top layers containing the meaningful flow and manifestations of personal experience made unconscious by the change of attention from one thing to another, forgetfulness, or repression. Underneath these layers are archetypes that form the psychic content of all human experiences. Jung described this deeper layer as psychic activity that goes on independently of the conscious mind and is not dependent on the upper layers of the unconscious, and perhaps untouchable by personal experience. This bottom layer of the shadow Jung referred to as the collective unconscious.

These encounters with shadow are what happens in the soul retrieval of subpersonalities that play a central part in the process of transformation. Jung said that this course of individuation exhibits a formal regularity and its signposts and milestones are archetypal symbols marking its stages, the first of which leads to the experience of the shadow.

In Jung's words, "The shadow personifies everything that the subject refuses to acknowledge about himself" and represents "a tight passage, a narrow door, whose painful constriction no one is spared who goes down to the deep well." This tight passage is in fact the birth canal that must be passed through, the road back in the Hero's Journey that leads to resurrection, which is rebirth coming from the transformative death of the ego.

The dissolution of the persona and the launch of the individuation process brings with it the danger of falling victim to the black shadow that everybody carries with them as inferior and hidden aspects of the personality. In Obi-Wan-Kenobi's vernacular from Star Wars, it is the dark side of the force.

The shadow can overwhelm a person's actions when the conscious mind is shocked, confused, or paralyzed by indecision. Jung said that, "A man who is possessed by his shadow is always standing in his own light and falling into his own traps ... living below his own level. In terms of the story of Dr. Jekyll and Mr. Hyde." It must be Jekyll, the conscious personality who integrates the shadow and *not* vice versa. Otherwise the conscious becomes the slave of the shadow.

If we follow this path the road home is back through healing *spirals* where the struggle is to retain *awareness* of the shadow without identifying with it. Non-identification or nonattachment demands tremendous effort to prevent falling back into the darkness. Though the conscious mind can be submerged at any moment in the unconscious, understanding or witness consciousness, meaning awareness acts like a life-saver by integrating the unconscious and reincorporating the shadow into the personality, producing a stronger, wider consciousness than before.

FOUR

The Coming Crash

My inner transformation and beacon of Truth I experienced through my soul searching culminated in the Peruvian Amazon in a ten day Ayahuasca dieta enhanced by a second healing plant called Bobinsana, a tree that grows by the water with roots that go deep into the earth and wide reaching branches that grow high into the sky. Its purpose, like its form, is to ground you solidly into the earth while lifting you into the spirit world above.

I was aided by plant baths with sweet scented Guayusa, a holly tree native to the Amazon whose harvested leaves have been used since ancient times for their health benefits, including antioxidant and anti-inflammatory properties. I didn't know it at the time, but Guayusa is one of three known caffeinated holly trees whose leaves are dried and brewed for their stimulative effects. I was pleasantly surprised when I saw it grow in popularity in the years since my first encounter with it as I consider it a powerful ally which I can now commune with in another form.

As a result of my first challenging plant dieta I connected with my long denied feminine shadow at the end of the year two thousand, leading me to believe that though the path is endless, and with full knowledge of the cliché, it is the journey and not the destination. My heart was opened wide and filled with a love I had only experienced through the blessing of my birth mother confirmed by the exquisite blessings of Santa Teresa De Avila, who to the best of my knowledge I had never heard of and who I now understand to be one of the many faces of The Divine Cosmic Feminine; something I had lost touch with.

My stunning moment of validation came after returning from the jungle when I found a telephone to call my mom and let her know I was all right. I didn't want to freak her out in my babbling excitement, but I couldn't contain myself and before I knew it, I told her about my visions and rapture with Santa Teresa. She remained quiet and I sensed something tangible on the other end of the phone line, then I thought, now I've done it. I told her too much and she thinks I've gone off the deep end. If she wasn't worried about me before, she's scared out of her wits for me now.

Finally I said, "Ma, what's wrong? Was it something I said?"

She hesitated, then said, "You're the first person I ever told this to in my entire life. As you know, your grandmother raised me Catholic. I was never a big believer in the church, but I always believed in God. Growing up as a little girl she assigned us saints to pray to, and every time I ever prayed I always prayed to my saint; Saint Teresa of Avila."

Largely in part to my newly opened heart, in early two thousand I began dating a troubled woman I met at work who I will call Penny. She had two kids, a boy aged seven and a nine year old girl. In the summer of that year I was invited to a beach birthday party for the girl's ninth birthday. When the party ended I saw the three of them gathering up the remains of the party by themselves so I offered to help when I saw them laboring up a sand dune with their belongings to pack them into their car.

I was attracted to Penny and when I saw her struggling with her kids it reminded me of my mother who raised four of us by herself in Dorchester, Boston's largest neighborhood, not an easy place to grow up in. In that moment my heart opened in empathy and I fell in love with the three of them, swept up in the myth I had been living most of my life of "riding in on the white horse and saving the day". I had done this many times over in some form or another, particularly with my traumatized older sister and her two abused little girls who I had sacrificed and given a considerable part of my life and resources to.

The trauma affecting Penny's kids came from her divorce. Their father was well off and at the time of their divorce owned fifteen houses that he shuffled out of his name to others. He ended up with the houses, an airplane, and other possessions while the kids while with their mother were crammed into a one bedroom apartment which enraged me to the point where I was determined to do something about it.

Penny was prone to drastic emotional acts, among them a failed suicide attempt and she had a history of court ordered therapy, but I was enraptured with the love she had for her kids which reminded me of my mother who sacrificed everything for me and my siblings, so I was fully and foolishly committed to the cause. I had many close friends in Dorchester who were in and out of prison along with parents, other family members, and my own father as well as my evil, former brother in law, the source of my sister's trauma, so for me dealing with the courts was not an issue.

I have tried throughout my life not to judge anybody by their past actions, but how they were at the time I met them, so my new found openness and the love and sacrifice I saw from Penny for her kids blinded me to deeper psychological issues that would be my undoing. In my blinded love I did an unofficial wedding ceremony with just me and Penny and for the sake of her kids. I was reluctant to do anything official as I did not want to get caught up in the financial battles she was enmeshed in with her ex-husband.

One of the indicators of her issues that I soon became aware of was an addiction to Fiorinal, a combination of aspirin, butalbital, and caffeine. Aspirin is in it as a pain reliever, an anti-inflammatory, and a fever reducer, and butalbital is a barbiturate used to relax muscle contractions, while caffeine is a central nervous system stimulant to relax muscle contractions in blood vessels and improve blood flow. She took Fiorinal for chronic tension headaches and drank on top of that as well as smoking cannabis which was one place where we bonded, and though it has its own addictive qualities, I have always considered it a lesser evil and take periodic breaks from it when I find myself becoming dependent.

Fiorinal is a drug of abuse and an overdose of butalbital can be fatal. Overdose or death can occur when alcohol is combined with butalbital and alcohol increases the risk of stomach bleeding.

I almost left her when she got drunk at a writers conference where I was honored with a man of the year award, and I was puzzled a few years later when she didn't come to the awards ceremony when *Spirit Matters* won a San Diego Book Award for best spiritual book. Her complete lack of energetic support troubled me after all I had done for her and I was too naïve to see these episodes as symptoms of something far more insidious.

After a few more uncomfortable and embarrassing episodes with her drinking I told her I would not tolerate it and would leave if it continued. She toned it down, but was sneaking beers every chance she could. Her nine year old daughter who had been playing the parent role in their relationship saw my intentions and became my ally, letting me know when she caught Penny sneaking drinks and between the two of us we managed to get that under better control. I also did some painful deep tissue massages on Penny's neck muscles that felt like steel cables which helped wean her from her headaches and addiction.

I shared psychedelic experiences with her in hopes that the insights from them could foster a healthier shift in perspective, which it did to some degree, but it also brought a different set of problems to the surface. Although not as life-threatening, they indicated deeper issues which became apparent when she developed a holier than thou spiritual attitude that I didn't recognize at first, combined with wanting to do mind altering substances every weekend.

I discouraged doing so much and stressed the need for integration to incorporate those experiences into day to day living. Constantly doing those substances made something special become boring and mundane, reinforcing the old psychonaut's adage, "You've gotten the message, you can hang up the phone now."

I discovered the hard way how so many people thought mind altering substances that engendered blissful and insightful glimpses into higher states of consciousness were mistaken for true spirituality; something I would witness first hand in a tragedy at the hands of a self-appointed spiritual leader who embodied a delusion I call guru-itis.

The core of the trauma I walked into the aftermath of came from a critical point in the divorce when Penny kidnapped her kids and drove to Belize where she was turned away at the border. Her little boy was two years old and his older sister was four. With nowhere to go but back to the United States Penny was met at the border by child protective services who put her in custody and took the kids away, realizing her deepest fear.

When the dust settled from this criminal act Penny was not allowed to see her kids for some time after that until a court appointed guardian was present. When the kids finally could see their mother they were often dragged away from her. I heard stories of her little boy hysterically clinging to the leg of a table to keep from being forced away from his mother. As traumatic and damaging as this was, it paled in comparison to the violence and trauma my sister and her kids went through, so I was undaunted and ready to help.

After the older girl's birthday beach party I went back to their one bedroom apartment to help unpack and felt hostility from the girl who was playing the protective mother role and the withdrawn little boy who became that way from his abandonment trauma at such an early age. I had already struggled with the trauma from my older sister's abuse and that of my nieces at the ripe old age of twenty two and I wanted to make a difference for these kids.

When I returned from my first Amazon adventure in October of two thousand all of my vulnerable open hearted feelings were amplified and my "new found love" that I felt and thought were being reflected back to me were aching for expression. I thought it no coincidence that my inner transformation came at this point in time. My new found life of love, family, and happiness were primed to unfold in the bright new, burgeoning twenty-first century because my inner reality had changed drastically through my obsessive search for Truth and all the work I had done to find it. My world had changed and I was on the cusp of bigger changes, so surely the outer world I lived in must have also been in the midst of massive transformation, and it was; but not in any way I ever could have imagined.

I was turning forty five and I had a great job along with one of my best friends with the largest employee owned technology company in the country overseeing twenty five technicians in eighteen buildings who took care of the networks, cables, computers, servers, software, and everything else related to Information Technology, referred to as IT.

I owned an amazing three bedroom house with an added family room with a fireplace and a screen porch on the edge of a canyon in San Diego that I took a second mortgage out on to publish and promote *Land Without Evil*, my critically acclaimed historical novel that was gathering momentum after expending considerable time and resources on book tours throughout the North Eastern United States and Southern California.

I also had a healthy stock portfolio, and thinking of my new found family crowded in to a one bedroom apartment bothered me. They could not join me at my bigger house because of complications from the custody situation between Penny and their father that required them to live where they went to school.

Penny found a cute half of a duplex condo near the kid's school, so with the advent of the twenty-first century and the newly expanded emotions of my open heart, I made the decision to commit and in January of two thousand one we moved in. I loved my bigger house which was close to work and did not want to lose it, so we moved back and forth between the two places to accommodate the custody schedule for the kids. It felt good to be in their lives in a way that I could provide a stable environment for them when they were in their mother's care.

With the much appreciated help of my brother and nephew, those first few months were spent renovating the inside of the condo to better accommodate four of us living in the smaller space, which though small, was much better than the three of them crowded into a one bedroom apartment.

When we had the kids I spent a lot of time with the withdrawn little boy, gradually coaxing him out of his shell. I played sports with him and took him to movies and a few sporting events, and as other neighborhood kids came into the picture I helped him develop friendships beyond the slowly developing one we had.

A single flame can light a room and one pinch can snuff it out and plunge the room into darkness, driven by fear of an unknown that cannot be seen. Toward the end of that year the blazing fire in my heart felt the snuff from the bigger flame of September eleventh two thousand one, known historically as 911 – the three digit number called for emergencies.

Though hobbled by an unethical publicist, I had an amazing publisher and **Land Without Evil** was gaining momentum from my ongoing book tour and promotional efforts. I owned two houses and had a new adopted family that I loved in spite of the challenges and a great job.

All of that and my life's accomplishments to date teetered on the precipice of unprecedented change when I walked into work that morning greeted by a stunned employee who urged me to go to a conference room where I joined a group of shocked people watching the iconic image of the burning World Trade Center tower in New York City, the second jet slamming into its twin, and the attack on the Pentagon.

The technology company I worked for was a government contractor that had seventy percent of their work coming from government and defense contracts and thirty percent from health care, and was in the midst of shifting to a fifty-fifty balance between the two. We lost a few employees in the Pentagon attack and the federal government came looking for help in the form of more defense work, tipping the majority of the company's work out of health care into defense.

The world and life as I knew it stopped on that day. All air traffic in the United States was grounded and I found myself running errands at lunch looking at anyone who looked vaguely foreign or middle eastern with fear and suspicion. At that time the epicenter of publishing was in New York City and everything book related froze. Best selling writer friends on promotional book tours were sent home and their tours cancelled. One writer friend had just published in hard cover had her book die an anonymous death before ever hitting any bookstores. Needless to say, after a challenging birth and a hard won slow growth in sales, **Land Without Evil** suffered its own extinction, spurring a sad spate of often damaged returns.

Penny worked in our company's travel department and had gotten us a paid five day trip to Hawaii for the cost of air fare. Our reservations were already paid for, so when air travel resumed we decided that it was probably safer than before the terrorist attack.

An indelible image in my mind is standing in a long line awaiting a heightened security check in at LAX while National Guardsman walked up and down patrolling the line with automatic weapons at the ready, reminding me of jungle encounters with similar checkpoints by the Guatemala border with Mexico, and in the Peruvian Amazon.

When we arrived in Hawaii, Waikiki was a ghost town which turned out to be a boon for us and a bust for them as we were treated like royalty.

Air travel and border crossings were never the same after that horrific attack and the repercussions continue.

FIVE

The Waking Dream Revisited

Like our Hawaii adventure, I had already signed up and paid for my second dieta in the Amazon, scheduled to leave out of LAX on October 12th, 2001, one month after the 911 attack. Once more I would be isolated in the middle of the jungle, fully out of touch with civilization, technology, and its trappings, which felt appropriate. Not only had my inner reality changed in unimaginable ways, but my outer one had its own cataclysmic transformations on both micro and macrocosmic scales.

Yoda's comment to Lorenzo, "Say goodbye to him, he's not coming back," became even more prescient. I was about to learn that each time I surrendered to the timeless supernatural world of the jungle with plant teachers who ruled the ordeals of these ancient dietas, I could gauge how much I had changed from the year before.

I have been writing most of my life in a variety of genres and as I have hinted at, the biggest challenge I have is trying to convey multifaceted nonrational experiences that shatter the boundaries of conventional communication. Limited by one word written or spoken at a time, this serialized string is taken in by the listener or reader and reconstructed one word at a time, strung into phrases, sentences, and paragraphs necessary to find coherence between the transmitter and the receiver. This act of bridging is hopefully not misinterpreted by the bias of personal filters, lapses of attention, or other distractions, making it a verbal "high wire act", *especially* when it comes from nonrational subconscious material in dreams and visions.

This is what I do in my every day life as a writer, so to fully embrace the experience of a prehistoric jungle dieta, the last thing I wanted to do is journal. To this end I brought a cassette recorder and dictated my experiences to get them fresh in the predawn hours in the aftermath of intense Ayahuasca experiences. This proved to be rewarding when I completed *Spirit Matters.* When I transcribed those experiences from my recordings it brought them vividly back to memory. I continued that practice on each successive jungle adventure and for close to twenty years, first copied from cassette tapes to MP3 format, then transcribed into editable documents.

I mentioned earlier how indigenous cultures consider dreams, visions, and waking consciousness as one continuum, and how the veils we create become progressively transparent until they dissolve. Nowhere is this concept more apparent than in the cumulative unfolding of a ten day Ayahuasca dieta where the interconnectedness of dreams, visions, and nightmares become more real, meaningful, and magical. While often being nonsensical, and what sounds and feels like absolute truth and conviction in the moment of their expression, these events often come across absurd and embarrassing in their retelling.

This ambiguity confirms the old vegetalista's wisdom of one third truth, one third untruth, and the incoherent mystery of the last third, something that will become increasingly apparent as this narrative progresses. There are complex psychological and physiological reasons for how this multifaceted cornucopia of jumbled subjective emotional and intellectual bombardment assaults our sensibilities. I am elaborating on those dynamics here to serve as a guidepost of sorts in an effort to help make sense of the confusing amalgam of rational and nonrational eruptions arising within the context of this passage, enhanced and amplified by the dieta and the teacher plants that bring nuanced, sometimes incomprehensible elements to the experience.

Spirit Matters opened with a prelude titled **A WAKING DREAM** which I added to the beginning of this continuation with the statement that this is where it all begins and where it all ends. Among other considerations, my primary reason for titling it this way is an attempt to define the nature of experiences that defy logic.

In "reality", nothing is ever defined in black and white like the ones and zeros of binary logic, yet many of us define and control our individual realities in this way, especially those who are intellectually centered. The greater truth is that everything in the realm of our experience is in degrees with lots of overlap.

Our infinitely complex human brain weighs about three pounds and this holographic universe contains roughly one hundred billion neurons and one hundred trillion connections that constitute the command center of everything we think, feel, and do. This miracle is divided into two hemispheres and within each half, particular regions control certain functions. These two sides look identical, but there's a huge difference in how they process information and despite their contrasting styles these two sides don't work independently of each other.

If you're intellectually centered you are mostly analytical and methodical in your thinking, and said to be left-brained. If you are emotionally centered, you are considered creative or artistic, and thought to be right-brained. I have found these distinctions to be true in my own experience, particularly when it comes to my observations of Ayahuasca experiences with myself and with others.

Scientific research indicates that the left brain is more verbal, analytical, and orderly than the right brain. It is sometimes called the digital brain because it excels at reading, writing, and computations, and is associated with logic, sequencing, linear thinking, mathematics, facts, and thinking in words.

In contrast the right brain is visual and intuitive. It is sometimes referred to as the analog brain because it has a more creative, less organized way of thinking. It is also connected to imagination, holistic thinking, intuition, arts, rhythm, nonverbal cues, feelings, visualization, and daydreaming.

The two hemispheres are tied together by bundles of nerve fibers, creating an information highway, and although the two sides function differently, they complement each other whether you're performing a logical or creative function. As an example, the left brain is credited with language and the right brain helps to understand context and tone. In the same manner the left brain handles mathematical equations while the right brain helps with comparisons and rough estimates.

The waking dream where I stated that it all begins and ends characterizes the Ayahuasca experience where this interaction comes into play, and it holds the key to integrating the overwhelming onslaught of perception that it engenders. This neuropsychological blitz coupled with the active dreaming that accompanies visionary states is heightened by the jungle dieta and its associated neurochemical enhancements.

Aside from the visionary experiences brought on by ingesting

Ayahuasca, the cumulative effect of the strict dietary regimen combined with the daily ingestion of other teacher plants influences every state of consciousness experienced during the dieta, especially dreaming, which dovetails with the visions. These two similar neurological states become extensions of each other as well as filtering into the waking state. In many respects plant dietas can be thought of as one extended Ayahuasca session as the normal rules of cognition and perception are increasingly challenged with each passing day.

The most well known indication of dream sleep is rapid eye movements, or REM. Most dreaming occurs during REM and is associated with brainstem arousal, right hemisphere activation, and low-level left hemisphere arousal.

Scientific studies show that the brainstem activates the right hemisphere during dream sleep, and dream content has its source in memories and impressions stored within the right half of the brain. Additionally the right hemisphere not only dreams the dream, which the left hemisphere, being at a low level of arousal passively observes, but it stores the dream in right hemisphere memory which is why it becomes harder to recall. When you awaken with high left hemisphere and low right brain activation the question arises; are dreams really forgotten, or are they locked away in a code not easily accessible to the speaking left hemisphere?

With Ayahuasca the answer lies somewhere in between because both hemispheres of the brain are turned on at the same time and the floodgates are opened creating the nonrational visionary state of consciousness I call the waking dream.

REM is characterized by high levels of activity within the brainstem, occipital lobe, and other nuclei. Electrophysiologically the right hemisphere becomes highly active during REM, whereas the left brain becomes more active during NON-REM. Similarly, measurements of cerebral blood flow show an increase in the right temporal and parietal regions during REM sleep, and in subjects who report visual, hypnagogic, hallucinatory and auditory dreaming on waking; these are also the effects that come from Ayahuasca in its waking dream state.

Enhanced activity in the right temporal and temporal-occipital area happens when drinking Ayahuasca and can increase dreaming and REM sleep. Similarly, REM sleep increases activity in this same region more than in the left hemisphere which indicates a complementary relationship between REM sleep and right temporal-occipital activity.

In a normally functioning brain, everyday memories appear to be stored unilaterally rather than laid down in both hemispheres because each hemisphere is specialized to perceive and process certain types of information unilaterally stored in the right or left half of the brain.

If the left temporal lobe is incapacitated, verbal memory functioning and the ability to recall words, sentences, conversations, and written material becomes impaired. The right cerebrum does not readily store this type of information, so if the left temporal lobe is incapacitated, verbal information is forgotten. Conversely, the left has difficulty storing or remembering nonlinguistic, visual, spatial, and emotional information. Visual, personal, and emotional memories are the province of the right temporal lobe which is one of the primary reasons why accepting and integrating visionary Ayahuasca experiences is so challenging, especially for intellectually centered people.

In contrast, right temporal impairment hinders recognition memory for tactile and recurring visual stimuli like faces and meaningless designs, memory for object position and orientation, and visual-pictorial stimuli as well as short-term memory for melodies. Similarly, memory for emotional material is also hindered with right versus left cerebral impairment, including the ability to recall or recognize emotional faces. Individuals with right hemisphere impediments also have more difficulty recalling personal emotional memories.

The left hemisphere is responsible for encoding and recalling verbal, temporal-sequential, language related memories, and the right is dominant in visual-spatial, non-verbal, and social emotional memory functioning. Each hemisphere stores the type of material it is best at recognizing, processing, and expressing. Consequently, during right hemisphere REM-dreaming, visual and emotional memories and images predominate.

In the normal brain during sleep and dreaming when one hemisphere learns, has certain experiences, and stores information in memory, this information is not always available to the opposing hemisphere. One hemisphere cannot always access memories stored in the other half of the brain, but under the influence of Ayahuasca both sides are turned on at the same time, so the full extent of the bewildering experiences defy logic and overwhelms everything.

To gain access to these lateralized memories, one hemisphere has to activate the memory banks of the other through the corpus callosum which is part and parcel of the integration experience. In many respects for true consciousness expansion this is more important than the visionary experiences themselves. If you do not put into practice what you have been shown, then you have only glimpsed this "truth" and have not arrived at "enlightenment". These revelations are meaningless unless you put them into practice in your everyday life where the real tests of your commitment to growth will challenge you.

The right hemisphere of the brain provides the physiological foundation where dreams derive their source, but because the left hemisphere is at a low level of arousal during dreaming and REM sleep, it is often unable to "remember" the dream upon waking.

In addition to dream production, the right brain also appears to be the dominant source for complex non-linguistic hallucinations. Tumors or electrical stimulation of the right temporal lobe is more likely to result in complex visual, musical and singing hallucinations, and left cerebral tumors or activation brings hallucinations of words or sentences.

Since the right hemisphere utilizes a visual-spatial, emotional language that the left hemisphere does not speak, dream imagery is often incomprehensible to the language dependent half of the brain, even when providing an accompanying narrative or dialogue. The non-temporal gestalt nature of dreams appears to require that they be consciously scrutinized from multiple angles to discern their meaning, for the last may be first and what is missing can be just as significant as what is present because the right hemisphere analyzes and expresses information in a manner radically different from the left.

As a result of my personal and scientifically documented research, I have observed that those who are intellectually oriented, particularly those who have been highly educated have suffered with the darkest, most excruciating Ayahuasca experiences. I believe this comes from the fact that they have spent their lives controlling what they perceive as reality with their logical minds and find themselves in terror and panic when their lifelong coping mechanism no longer work, leaving them in an unprecedented state of panic and terror in the face of something outside of their control. Instead of accepting what has confronted them making them powerless, they flounder, struggling to make sense of their helplessness while immersed in a nonrational situation where the rules they have lived by no longer apply, and like a fly trapped in a spider's web, the more they struggle, the worse it gets.

The key to overcoming this conundrum lies in acknowledging this repressed part of themselves which has become a core part of their shadow and learning how to dance with this "stranger" while absorbing the experience that the rational mind cannot keep up with.

In my experience the essence of integrating this multifaceted non-ordinary state of consciousness is to accept what it has to show you in ways you can scarcely comprehend in each moment of its unfolding.

It is in the less frenetic time in the wake of the neuropsychological fireworks that the overwhelmed linear logical mind can pick up the shattered pieces in its aftermath which is the true definition of psychological integration.

Although the majority of this work is done in the left brain dominated state of waking consciousness, much of it continues in the dreaming state.

SIX

The Journey And Passage Into The First Launch

During the course of an Ayahuasca dieta dreams, visions, and waking consciousness occur as one continuum the way indigenous cultures experienced it, making the veils we believe in progressively transparent. If we can withstand the barrage of "non-ordinary reality", our struggles to make sense of it can develop into learning and mastering psychological navigation, regardless of the state of consciousness we find ourselves in. With our dreams and visions impinging on our waking state, the passing moments of everyday life become increasingly flexible, transient, and magical.

Everything preceding this recorded journal and my editing of it is an effort to bring coherency to the rambling, sometimes nonsensical jumble that follows within the context and circumstances surrounding it, particularly when referring to my dreams and visions.

At 7:00 on Friday morning October 12th 2001 I once again passed through locked and loaded National Guard troops and boarded a propeller driven "puddle jumper" from San Diego and arrived at LAX at 10:00 nursing a sore throat, then I boarded an eight hour fight to Lima arriving at 12:40 on Saturday morning October 13th.

Feeling more under the weather, I saw a big sign with Yoda's name on it in a jostling line of people waiting at the customs exit and we got hustled off to a waiting cab. The hotel was supposed to pick us up, but we made the unfortunate discovery when we arrived at the hotel at 2:00 in the morning that our cab driver had copied the sign from our original driver and cut in front of him in line. Yoda was angry with me for picking this sneak, but I didn't know any better. After an unpleasant scene in front of the hotel we checked in, but I couldn't sleep with my runny nose and sore throat.

After a few miserable sleepless hours we went back to the airport for an early morning flight to Pucallpa where we met the shaman José who we had worked with the year before and Ronaldo, a second shaman, and one of their mentors Don Guillermo a slight, older dark-haired man with intense penetrating eyes who came from Tarapoto, referred to as the City of Sorcerers. He told one person he was seventy-two, another he was sixty seven, and no doubt other ages other people, which I got a kick out of.

I had paiche, the world's second largest freshwater fish which is indigenous to the Amazon for dinner and we planned our upcoming ceremonies for Monday, Wednesday, Friday, Sunday, and the last on Monday night. I held off my growing cold the best I could with aspirin while we ate a cheese sandwich and a glass of papaya juice to discuss our dieta that night. After a breakfast of scrambled eggs, toast, and a little coffee the next morning we left for the shaman's camp deeper in the jungle. We had fifteen people in our group on my first visit the year before and nine this time out, the attrition no doubt due to the uncertainties of 911.

We took a two hour ride in battered cabs along dusty, muddy, jungle roads, and after a couple of bone jarring hours came to the village we had been to the year before. Once again we became the main attraction to a group of kids, so we bought some candy and handed it out. Some cute little girls sang to us while we boarded canoes in thunder and sprinkling rain.

Nine of us and all of our gear filled two long canoes, each one carved out of a huge tree trunk. Outboard motors with long drive shafts projected the propellers a dozen or so feet behind the boats that churned bubbling white water behind us, powering us two hours upstream to an unmarked tributary of the Amazon in virgin rain forest to the shaman's hidden camp.

The river looked low when we arrived, so we disembarked on the shore of the main river and hiked a half a mile or so through the jungle while smaller canoes navigated the shallow tributary and brought our gear up to the main camp.

Our shirts and pants clung to us, thoroughly soaked from sweat in a matter of minutes while the jungle carried on its cacophony of sight, sound, and scents that I consider a symphony to my soul. Birds, animals, and insects buzzed over the gentle white noise of water that rose and faded as we moved toward and away from it, while trees, vines, bushes, and other exotic plants and beautiful flowers bloomed in strange places.

I could not get my spot from the prior year because of our reduced numbers, so I pushed for the last tambo in line along the river bank. There were two more further out, but this one was as far as they would let me go. The year before, my open air tambo and all the others had dirt floors with thatched roofs, rough hewn tables, stools, a small set of shelves, a hammock, and a bed built from logs covered with a piece of foam, a sheet, blanket, pillow, and a mosquito net. Each one had five gallons of fresh water, a roll of toilet paper, a cigarette lighter, and a small package of candles. I later discovered that my prior year had been the first year the camp was opened, and this year saw improvements, among them wood floors instead of dirt and new tambos made with finished wood making a pallet bed, a desk/table, and a small cupboard. The old tambos had collapsed and the ceremonial maloca now had a wooden floor instead of the dirt floor of the old one.

We met at 7:00 for our last dinner of salad, olives, cheese, avocado, bread, rice, soup, and something like coleslaw in the communal kitchen which was off limits after the dieta started to enforce the required isolation. After dinner we discussed the phenomenon of dark shamans who did things like inviting young ladies down to the water's edge for special midnight initiations and stories of enslaving these poor trusting innocents. The people I was lucky to be working with stayed disconnected from them and I eventually learned that there is suspicion and petty jealousy among many who starry-eyed seekers revered.

Traditionally shamans were never called that back in South American prehistory. That moniker came from the Siberian Manchu-Tungus word šaman. The noun **is** formed from the verb ša- "to know", so a shaman is literally "one who knows." The "plant men" of the Amazon and many other places did things for their tribe like determine the weather, hunting procedures, crop harvesting, and protection against enemies.

Dark shamans were not part of that, but as travel increased and tribal elements broke up from encroaching civilization, many became more "civilized" which ended in the misuse of power, which is neutral by nature, but guided by the intention behind it. I felt blessed to be with the best of the best where integrity ruled.

After our discussion we stated our intentions. My friend Penrose was in remission from cancer and hoped to be rid of it. At the time I did not know much and hoped to heal lipoma lumps forming under my skin due to an overgrowth of fat cells and I wanted to try and heal a chronic heat rash on my ass. I also intended to try and find healing for Penny and her kids. Finally, I wanted to explore shapeshifting and pay close attention to my dreams and attempt to interpret what they tried to tell me.

As I mentioned earlier, I was discovering how I could gauge how much I had changed from the year before. Once back in the solitude of my tambo I sensed how much the monkey mind chatter of my ego had diminished since my first dieta giving me a kind of psychic barometric indicator of growth. Even though I knew the work ahead of me was only beginning and would go on infinitely, overall I felt more together and more aware. As hard as I knew it would be, I also knew deep down that there was no way I could not do what I was doing.

It had become my life.

Mother Earth, spirit energy, and the spirits of the plants was not only for me, but for everyone connected with me. I thought about the Ayahuasca brew, a mixture of two plants. The Ayahuasca vine that carries its name, Banisteriopsis Caapi, also known as The Vine of Death, The Vine of the Soul, Caapi, Yajé, and many other names, and Chacruna, classified as Psychotria Viridis, the primary psychoactive component of the brew that carries N,N-*dimethyltryptamine*, commonly referred to as DMT.

I pondered what José said about the DMT carrying Chacruna bush and the Ayahuasca vine that empowers it. The vine is the power and the Chacruna is the light, so one did not work without the other. No power. No light.

It was also determined that in my second year doing a dieta I would be working with Chuchuwasi, a wide tree with a thick trunk with its active part within the bark which is taken for strengthening partially because it is a big tree. Along those same lines Chuchuwasi is considered physically, spiritually, and energetically fortifying. Classified as Maytenus laevis, the bark, roots, and leaves are used as medicine taken by the mouth for arthritis, back pain, broken bones, diarrhea, complications after childbirth, joint disorders, sexual arousal, and as a tonic. It is also applied to the skin for skin cancer. I would be getting a full pitcher of it every day of the dieta.

As I described in detail, when examined in the light of waking logical thought, dreams and visions are often nonsensical, yet they contain rich emotional and conceptual content. There are tons of books written about dream symbolism, and there is no doubt that they contain universal archetypal symbols, but the deeper truth is that dream imagery and its complex amalgams of thought and emotion are intensely personal based on the subjective reality and unique history of the dreamer, so there are no cookie cutter interpretations.

The ten day dieta is an extended journey of continuous altered states. I have included my remembered dreams in italics no matter how chaotic and disjointed they may be, and follow them with my own attempts at what they might mean in the context of the dieta as a whole, hopefully bringing more insight into the process. The technology company I worked for as a manager over computer technicians clearly influenced this first jungle dream.

The technicians working for me were trying to fix a printer the wrong way when someone asked for help unloading a car fixed up like a little room. I tried to get something out of a vending machine until someone else brought me a big blue Volkswagen diesel truck that looked like an older square step delivery van.

I couldn't figure out the printer problem, then I was talking to the stomach of a big technician who worked for me, but he kept pushing back at what I tried to tell him so I bit him in the stomach.

After that a more seasoned technician and someone else tried to help me find the way to someone's house, but I wasn't fully functioning. He pushed me in a shopping cart and down a hill fast, past some woman, through a field, a basketball court, and other people before stopping where a door was wide open that I couldn't close.

This dream reflected my concerns and frustrations over the performance of some of my technicians and my abilities to keep the technology and staffing running successfully with decreasing resources. As it turned out, this dream and its concerns were prophetic as the people involved were the ones who created the situation that triggered the actual downfall of my organization.

I ended up sleeping all day and woke up pre-dawn from this

chaotic dream and experienced the magical time between the worlds, the gradual change from the night time animals and insects to those of the day in a passage from total darkness to gradual outlines, forms and colors that became more defined until becoming crystal clear. I had slept long, on and off, fitfully waking to a dull headache.

As if to drive home the point of the dream and my frustration, later that following morning I was eating and a wasp flew straight into my mouth and stung me repeatedly until I managed to spit out.

SEVEN

Immersion

That evening the cicadas gave their shrill announcement exactly at 6:00 signaling another magical time between the worlds and the coming darkness. We had been instructed to meet at 7:00 to talk about our session which would begin at 8:00.

José said the brew was not cultivated and came from virgin jungle and it was very powerful. I felt tapped out and sick with my cold, so I had to push hard to get there with a dull headache and choke down the brew battling major inner resistance, then the candle was extinguished leaving us in pitch black. I soon went back and forth between open and closed eyes passing through my inner and outer journey until the visions looked the same whether my eyes were open or closed.

Don Guillermo, the older mentor to my guides and renowned tobacco shaman from Tarapoto drank with us and started singing before going off into incoherent babbling when the brew hit him hard. José kept talking to him, but Guillermo was somewhere else and did not respond. Finally helpers had to take him away because he was disrupting the circle. They apologized to us for his disruptions and told us that he was not a regular Ayahuasca drinker.

When I returned to my tambo sweaty and stinking after the session at 1:00 in the morning I took a Guayusa plant bath and air dried in the buff which was my regular practice after every jungle ceremony to record my initial impressions on my cassette recorder while they were still fresh. I had an intense night and my first comment was that an atomic bomb had hit.

As I pointed out there was not much rational about the experience, so my recordings come out disjointed and out of order the way dreams do, but the impressions were fresh. They had no consistent chronology, so everything that follows whether dreams or visons is edited to bring some degree of lucidity to incoherent experiences. In terms of clarity in perception, the stars in the night sky shone crystal clear and stellar like beautiful sparkling gems as I recorded while the raucous symphony of jungle night denizens serenaded me.

When the ceremony began with my nine companions I felt submerged in a deep plunge into icky muck with bugs crawling all over me, but I had no fear and felt blessed. When I went to put on my hat I saw something moving around in it, so I shook it and a spider fell out.

I felt exceptionally shitty when I drank and soon flew way out into incomprehensible realms of color, geometries, and fast moving inexplicable states of consciousness while Guillermo struggled with his own challenges, then I was snapped back to the moment hard. I opened my eyes and saw a deep electric blue glowing ball entity on my friend Penrose's leg which I thought might be there to help her beat her cancer.

I looked around and felt tremendous pressure and spider-like webs everywhere. A Tinkerbell looking winged fairy being and a whole gathering of similar fairy beings and other creatures, some like dragonflies studied me while being present with me. I looked at Penrose again and saw the blue glowing ball entity perched on her knee. When I questioned what it wanted it dimmed and grew brighter, then the Tinkerbell nymphs and fairies all gathered, and at that moment I vomited. I turned around to launch it outside the railing of the maloca and purged so hard that tons of shit came up out of my lungs. I coughed and got wracked over and over again with dry heaves while sweat poured from my face, then I started farting powerfully while every orifice in my body purged something. My mouth, nose, and ears all erupted like I was being wrung out and sweat poured from every pore. It was the most powerful purge I ever had on Ayahuasca to date and I surrendered to it, letting go, losing all track of time and space.

At some point José came over and fanned my back with feathers or a *chacapa* which made things start to clear, bringing me back from wherever the purge had brought me. I finally sat back with my face soaked, and sweat and snot running from my nose.

Prior to the purge my visions were intense and colorful and the energetic pressure had been building. I had the realization and belief that all the fairy spirits that came were stalking the sickness in me. They had all snuck up on it and when they got my attention, they pounced unexpected as if out of nowhere. I continued returning from wherever I had been and not only was my headache gone, but I felt better, energized, and cleansed!

At that point some of my companions took a booster dose, but I was so tapped out at that I didn't need any more. I continued having amazing visions and did some inner work thinking about Penny, her kids, her ex-husband, and the repercussions I might experience dealing with all that, which came as a warning. I saw Penrose coming back from the latrine and realized that I hadn't even known she had gone. My experience leading up to the purge had been powerful, colorful, and unbearably intense.

Utterly exhausted after recording, I crawled into bed and eventually fell asleep waking to daylight with a mild headache. I felt both spaced out and clear at the same time, but much improved, and my sinuses had cleared. After a morning plant bath with fresh Guayusa I started my first pitcher of Chuchuwasi, which I was counting on to fortify my spirit, physically strengthen me, and increase my endurance.

As I sorted through the remnants in the aftermath of the night before I realized that in terms of awareness and life, things that didn't seem to have any importance needed to be paid attention to, and seemingly irrelevant things had greater importance. Even when they didn't seem to have much significance in the moments that they happen they can have great impact later. I was never one for subtle things, so this dawning awareness was something new. In the moments when things like this came to me in visionary states they are so dense and overwhelming that they cannot be integrated then, so the impact comes later when my intellectual mind catches up to the massive download that my heart and intuition have experienced. My visions of Santa Teresa from the year before had hit hard like that and continued unfolding as a gift that keeps on giving.

I reflected back to my beyond lucid dream connected vision from my first dieta. When José played his mandolin-like *charango* I saw flowers and butterflies, then without warning, I beheld the sweet, beautiful girl of my dreams revealing herself to me in my visions in the most exquisite way imaginable. At first I resisted her urgings, but she gently persisted until I let her in and embraced her. When I did, Santa Teresa De Avila spoke in my mind in what I can only describe as telepathy, yet her communication encompassed far more. I felt her presence inside of me as an integral, intimate part of me as our spirits joined as one. As she informed me of who she was, her words or thoughts came to me in Spanish and to my further awe and amazement; *I understood every word she said.*

All of the pieces that had been hints from my dream coalesced in my mind, making total sense. Teresa had come to me in the first short dream, then I awoke to look up at the moon, another symbol of feminine energy. When I went back to sleep she came to me again, picking up in the new dream where she had left off in the first one, leading me to the gradual revelation of her presence merging with me in all her glory. Not only did she merge, she possessed me, and in that sublime and ecstatic rapture, I possessed her with equal fervor, embracing the sweet essence of her femininity with undying love. No matter how much of myself I gave away, I couldn't give enough to equal her love. Never before had I felt such overpowering love entwine and become such an intimate part of me. Teresa's loving presence overwhelmed me on all levels, profoundly merging our spirits to my core. Physically, the power of her love insinuated itself into me so deep, intimate, and all encompassing, that it became erotic to the point of embarrassment and I felt so united with her in every cell of my being that I could not hide my feelings.

After an interminable moment of rising discomfort at my eroticism, she reassured me that there was nothing wrong with my feelings. They were the natural physical manifestation and genuine expression of my deepest love, and the biological expression of a love so pure and powerful was nothing to be ashamed of and certainly nothing to hide and suppress. It was in fact cause for celebration.

My legs and my body twitched, spasmed, rocked, and convulsed like an epileptic for quite some time, only this felt like pure bliss, and in the throes of my ecstasy I understood and experienced first hand the true meaning of rapture and never wanted it to end. In the midst of my experience I came to terms with my sense of connecting and feeling married to Mother Earth, realizing that Santa Teresa was an aspect of the Cosmic Mother, the feminine side of the One. I understood this conceptually and wordlessly on all levels and my irrepressible longing for it continues to haunt me in my dreams.

As part of the dieta, aside from spending time simply being and not doing, reading can be a great influence, especially if it is relevant to the experience. In this my second trip to the jungle I decided to read ***The Three Halves of Ino Moxo: Teachings of the Wizard of the Upper Amazon*** by César Calvo translated from Spanish to English by my friend Ken Symington for the second time in the jungle where it happened while doing the dieta.

One of the things that struck me when I read it this second time was the legend of the Chullachaki. The Quechua word chulla means one-footed, single, odd, unpaired, or asymmetric, and chaki means foot. A Chullachaki is a mythical forest creature of the Peruvian and Brazilian jungles described as short and ugly with one leg shorter than the other and one foot either larger than the other, pointed backward or in the form of a hoof. He is said to persuade his victims to follow him deep into the jungle where even experienced trackers cannot find their way back. Some say he appears in the shape of a short man dressed in rags, waving his closed fists in the air looking for a fight. In this case indigenous people believe a man has to accept his challenge and beat him until he uncovers all the richness he has hidden in the jungle. Whoever declines this challenge is cursed with the inability to hunt and with foul luck. Family and friends turn into enemies, wives leave with other men, and other misfortunes befall them.

They say a Chullachaki has the ability to turn into any animal of the jungle and is a forest spirit who guards the land and animals, and punishes a man if he breaks a taboo or acts unwisely in the forest. According to legend, a Chullachaki is a member of an older species that lived in the jungle long before humans. Most of the time they are uninterested in humans and inhabit forest spots far from human habitation where they have their own gardens and fields to tend. If a human dwells too close to those gardens, they might attack and put a spell on the unlucky human. Sometimes Chullachakis are thought to steal human children and raise them as their own, or lure humans into a trap for mating purposes to become one of them.

With these thoughts in mind intermingled with my tender memories of Santa Teresa I set off on my own to visit my old tambo where I had my Santa Teresa experiences that had flowed so beautifully into my visions. On the way I startled myself when out of nowhere I saw a limping man with a tattered shirt and broken teeth and imagined crossed eyes and a club foot, but in retrospect it was my overactive imagination as I later discovered that the man who was the caretaker of the land wore tattered clothes, had bad teeth, and limped.

When I made it to my old tambo I discovered that it had caved in and was gone in a year's time, reinforcing the notion that nothing is permanent, especially in the jungle and that nothing is as it seems in this world. Tiny tree frogs and cicadas sound like birds, some plants look like animals, and some animals look like plants. While on an intense plant dieta where the boundaries between the worlds of sleeping, waking, dreaming, and visions dissolve, all bets are off. Now that I was immersed in the jungle, comparing this second year to my first, I found that I was more flexible in any conceptions of reality I may have held, and most certainly learning more in ways I never could have imagined.

EIGHT

Dancing With Death Between The Agony And The Ecstasy

Between night time ceremonies, the restricted diet, the humid heat of the day, and the combinations of ingested plants, the stresses your mind, body, and spirit go through on a dieta make your personal energies fluctuate. As the days progress you get physically weaker and your awareness heightens to the point of flashes of telepathy while the blurring dreams, visions, and waking consciousness make normal sleep impossible. You can lie awake at all hours in the pitch black of the night regaled by the cacophony of the nocturnal jungle or be fast asleep amidst active day time creatures announcing their presence in the heat of the day.

Your passages through fluctuating levels of consciousness are dictated by the demands of your shifting energies and those are influenced by your inner and outer conditions. There is no pattern to any of it so you might be awake all night and sleep all day, while another day can find you moving through the opposite cycle.

When I share my jungle experiences people get starry-eyed and express a desire for them until I explain that far from Club Med pampered tropical ecotours, shamanic dietas are not for the faint of heart. They are ordeals that bear out the ancient wisdom of the jungle which says that the psychological, physiological, spiritual, and emotional discomforts you live through are the price you pay to prove yourself worthy of the gifts that the plants and other jungle spirits have to give you.

I awoke again some time on Tuesday five days after leaving San Diego to my three day headache which came back with a vengeance. I ate a meal of boca chica, a boney local fish which is a staple of the dieta, boiled quinoa, and plátanos and took three aspirins out of frustration which diminished the headache, but it still lingered. To add to my joy, when I took a shit at my friendly latrine I got overrun by literal ants in my pants swarming all over and biting me.

Welcome to the jungle.

A little later I got an acupressure treatment from a friend which diminished the headache more and I was brought more food, but I had a hard time eating it. I forced down less than half a plátano and half the quinoa, took one more aspirin, and laid down to read some writings from Santa Teresa that talked about a third level when you get sucked up into God, then I set the book aside and closed my eyes in hopes of falling sleep to escape my misery.

Sometime later, I awoke from a volley of intense dreams, relieved to discover that my headache had gone. I grabbed my cassette player and recorded my most recent vivid dream and worked my way backward through an illogical emotion filled narrative.

I went through what I could only describe as a Death and Rebirth Portal and came out the other side in a dream that I could visualize, but could not explain in words, except to say that I dissipated into The Void in super fine pinpoints of energy, which I believe I embraced as a result of my frequent 5MEO experiences, then everything coalesced.

I was in Paradise with a dawning realization of being incredibly joyful coming into conscious awareness in the jungle where I was acutely aware of being part of all the thriving life, meaning all of the trees, insects, and animals that I was immersed in while passing through terrifying collapsing darkness and alternately exploding into joyful expansive light, traveling through the Universe that I am.

I often had a feeling over the preceding weeks and months that I was figuring things out in that semi-dreaming state that came together just before I woke up; something that continues on occasion to this day. I didn't know what it was consciously, but it felt like something connecting within all the sounds of jungle life. Millions of scattered points of energy all came together in a oneness and intensifying before popping out the other side where I was answered by all the sounds of the jungle. This verbal description of a non-verbal experience falls short of articulating the depth of the actual experience and the feelings were amazing passing through terror into joy, not being into being, and hearing everything and knowing on a conscious level that paradise exists. All of it came to me in an intense, inexplicable manner.

In another dream series I was trying to assist one of the shaman's helpers to be a singer and the group was supporting it. He was very talented and could sing and dance. I tried to sponsor him because there was no one else to do that, then I was on a variety show which I had been on before a number of times, either as a writer or a musician. This time I was part of a weird contest of men trying to put on women's makeup, but not in any cross-dressing way, more as a way to disguise myself. I started out doing a perfect job with blush and makeup and the spectators were all oohing and aahing. I got carried away and messed it up, so I wiped it all off and kept trying to do it again but I couldn't get it right, then I realized that my loose leaf notebooks that had to do with work and some equipment were missing and I couldn't find them.

I looked everywhere and got mad, then somebody showed me some other notebooks, but they weren't mine, so I got madder and was leaving when an old woman tried to hit on me, but I avoided her. After that I was going down a street with one of the guys who worked for me along with some other people. I rented a Harley and we were going to go riding. I went to a house where a lady who had been my father's secret lover lived, a place I had gone to as a child.

I hurt my back and thought I was dying and everyone around me acted scared. I believed I was on the edge of death and I could kind of move, but I couldn't, so I called 911. Nobody understood my intolerable pain and nobody could do anything about it, then a truck came with a construction crew who were all in the house where I tried to move, but I could barely walk. I left and started walking, but I was stumbling until a big ambulance came and lifted me into it with a hoist. I screamed and wailed in incredible pain that felt mournful and intense.

They managed to get me into the truck and drove me to the hospital where the attendants had music playing. I wanted to change the music, but I couldn't move. Though I started out getting driven to a hospital I ended up on a beach walk hoping I could move some, but I was still in pain.

I went down to the shore where I wanted to jump around in the water and waves, but the lower back pain hindered me, then I was in a house with people who were upstairs in a young girl's bedroom. It all seemed to be related to family on my mother's side and she was asking me to clear away a bunch of vines and ivy by her window and to put up a belt and an article of clothing so somebody else could find the house from off in the distance. I did that and teased her saying we didn't know anybody was going to visit my house. Are you going to do this for me there and put some of your clothes up on my window?

I said I was only teasing her, then there was a big wall. I heard noises from a party so I climbed up and saw a black girl I worked with and some other black girls talking shit to each other, having fun, and inviting me to come over.

At some point me and others went to a gym where I was supposed to be working out. I was trying to tell a guy who was also trying to work out and taking direction from me, wanting to do crunches while my brother was being a wise guy doing push ups that I couldn't do because of my back problem.

My lower back pain came and went through different segments of the dream as I moved rapidly through scene after scene. The second set of dream segments appeared to be subconscious concerns about my identity and purpose, and whether I would ever have any success accomplishing anything artistically or professionally. I can see now that the women's makeup contest represented my inner struggles to accept my long repressed feminine side. I was a manager over a large group of technicians in my day job, but also an accomplished writer, drummer, and vocalist spending a lifetime trying to get recognition and hoping to someday support myself that way as opposed to working simply to support myself. I think the recurring back pain and presence of death in the last segments reflected my fear of failure and dying before accomplishing anything of real substance.

After waking and puzzling through my confusing mix of dreams that took me through highs and lows, Maestro Guillermo came that afternoon and sang a Chuchuwasi and a Bobinsana icaro for me and gave me lots of information in Spanish, but I didn't understand it all. Regardless, I embraced it for the blessing that it was and felt deep appreciation for the time he spent with me. I found it interesting that he sang icaros for the two plants I had worked with, Bobinsana from the year before and Chuchuwasi that I was presently working with.

After he left they brought me a bowl of runny oatmeal and 3 plátanos. I went to shit in my hole in the ground latrine in the nude to avoid literal ants in my pants which was a good decision. We were scheduled to have a second meeting that night without a ceremony. I felt weak, but overall I felt good. No headache, runny nose, or any other sickness.

After we checked in, Don Guillermo spoke about the plants and I was happy we had a translator present. I didn't like the idea of missing any part of the esoteric knowledge he carried. Guillermo was a living library bursting with rare first hand knowledge that is not in books, but passed down through generations. Some of the plants have Spanish names, some Quechua, some Shipibo, and mixtures of languages and dialects carried forward from the distant past, so some translations are phonetic and may vary.

Here are Guillermo's translated words.

"I spent twelve years learning about the different plants and testing their effects. My parents taught me about them. My father was a vegetalista. I did a one month Ushpawasha *dieta* and two months without salt. These plants teach you their song and speech. Ushpawasha is a very big black spirit and if you take it and lay down you will see big black spirits surrounding you which are the doctors of this medicine that heal and cure you.

My father and my grandfather in turn were vegetalistas and my grandfather taught my father who in turn taught me treatments for pains in the lungs and strong pain in the body and joints. They used to do diets with different plants for many days and sometimes for several months. Once they did the diets and were healed they did Guayusa for months, taking plant baths and blowing it over them, sometimes for a month or more and the pains would go away, then they would get out of bed and feel strong and vital again.

With the Sanango they gave them a potion to drink. People who had been disabled or handicapped and could not walk for five years or more were treated with plants and baths for two, three, or four months could get up and walk again after five years of disability. There is one plant called Wachusa used for treating women that have been operated on in their uterus or vagina. Sometimes they get the tea and massages rubbed all over their bodies rubbing the plant into their skin for eight or nine days which cures them. My wife specialized in this.

They used the fat milk of the Oje tree boiled for people with anemia and malaria and yellow fever that makes them sweat heavily which purifies them. They also have the milk sap Yantama to give to women who have just given birth. They boil the tea and let them drink often to remove post delivery pain and discomfort in their bodies which makes them feel much better with vitality and health in the post natal time.

The milk or sap of the red tree is very good for black and yellow hepatitis. Black goes for twenty four hours and yellow takes forty eight hours. One hopeless case came with bad hepatitis pissing nothing but blood and was treated with Oje until he pissed clear. Black hepatitis gives you a very high fever and you usually get it by drinking stagnant water in the back jungle that is not flowing.

For vomiting and diarrhea they give people a tea made out of cinnamon and oregano and sometimes they add penicillin. They use Yaguarpanga which is a plant that makes you vomit, often used to treat addicts like those addicted to crack Cocaine or cannabis. After Yaguarpanga eight consecutive night time Ayahuasca sessions are recommended, then they are given Ushpawasha. Eight doses of Ayahuasca are followed by eight days of Ushpawasha and they are healed after sixteen days.

A man from Tingo María was in bed for five years and could not get out of bed. After he was treated with Ushpawasha he was able to get out of bed. A man from Lima had an operation on a leg, but a sore remained after the operations that would not close and heal for three years, so he planned to use Sangre de Drago. You cut the tree trunk and it oozes out a red sap. You apply it and cover the sore for a day, then you expose it to air, wrap that with corn leaves, and make like a bread from the Sangre De Drago rosin, boil that, and put it on the wound for another day, then the patient has to keep the wound from getting wet.

For poisonous snake bites they take the juice of five or six lemons and mix it with tobacco and a few drops of kerosene. This combination is heated and given to drink several times. If the poison has come up the leg and formed nodules, those wounds are rubbed with lemon and the following day they are given a hot tea with Arnica and plantain broth to drink and applied to any part of the skin that has gangrene."

When asked about the spirits of the plants Guillermo said:

"The spirit of the plant they call the mother of the plant appears to you in the shape and form of a spirit and blows over you, and touches your feet to heal you. When you take the plant and follow the diet you will sometimes hear the song of that particular spirit and the spirits will continue to come back to you as you continue taking the plant."

When asked about how the Ushpawasha helps memory, he said, "If you diet well and follow the correct procedure you remember things and see the spirits of the plants and remember things."

Ushpawasha Sanango was a specialty of Guillermo's and a plant I had a strong desire to work with. My wish would come true the next year in my third and one of the best ever plant dietas that I would do. As a formal introduction, here is some information I found about it, some from my own notes and some from other sources.

Ushpawasha Sanango, classified as Tabernaemontana Undulata is a plant that works on the memory of the heart. Traditionally used to heal traumas, help in mourning processes, it will also remind you of things forgotten, repressed, and needing integration, especially childhood memories. It will also teach you how to let emotions fill your heart and talk from your deepest truth. It can make you cry or laugh. A strong healing plant, it will work on feminine organs, immune system, and joints.

As I returned to the jungle in the years to come, I would work with Ushpawasha and many other plants, which I will elaborate on at a later time.

NINE

To Hell And Back Again

Prior to Wednesday night's session they upped my doses of Chuchuwasi considerably and I slept hard and deep for a couple of hours which made me a little late for the ceremony. Soon after arriving I took a full dose and though I didn't think things could get any more difficult, I was slammed the hardest I had ever been to date.

Shortly after choking down my dose I lost all sense of my physical body and the present moment and was soon travelling through bizarre worlds and dimensions to dark and hellish places where I spent an eternity in what I can only describe as torture. I didn't want to be there and I didn't want to experience it. I wanted to deny and escape it, but I couldn't, so I passed through it. My traumatic passage defies description so what I share here is encapsulated and beyond any real coherence.

I plunged deep into other dimensions and beings, but found unexpected help at one point after passing through some of the worst hells when I opened my eyes and found myself in a cave with Inca Warriors. One of them stood beside me and two or three others were present. The unspoken understanding was that I was on a vision quest and they were all supporting me, telling me, "You are a warrior!"

With that support and confirmation I flew off again to more "places" and experienced pure terror on many levels as well as awe and beauty in the strangest ways. I purged hard, I think twice, and thought I made it over the railing, but I missed and it ended up all over the floor. I sweated through my pants and soaked the 3 inch foam I sat on as well as copious running snot and heat, all of which came in waves.

Maestro Guillermo's singing felt exceptionally powerful and his icaros took me the furthest. During that passage I lost the songs, my physical presence, and everything else, and felt deep gratitude that the shamans were there to watch over me. As the Ayahuasca came on my body became progressively inert and fuzzy until I felt pinned down hard by a massive amount of weight to the point where it took me out of my body and passed me through a maddening flurry of bewildering landscapes.

Somewhere in the midst of the awe, terror, and madness, José played his flute. My heart opened up and Penny and her kids came to me powerfully, especially her older daughter. I loved these kids deeply and they meant so much to me. With that thought I realized that my hellish terror filled experiences were strengthening me and going to hell could be the best thing that ever happened to me. In terms of transformation, this night's visons were deeper and darker than the first night and my first night held some of the darkest I had ever experienced.

Immersed in darkness I learned volumes about myself, life, and the world, then Yoda told a story about the life of a tree that put things in perspective for me. I puked hard when I heard it, and with that I decided to take on Penny's ex and his family because I saw that the kids were the ones who suffered the most from all the antagonism. Before the ceremony was over I hacked, coughed, and snotted profusely while my insides went chaotic and I purged powerfully from both ends until I was emptied.

I was not cognizant of it at the time but the overwhelming darkness that engulfed me so forcefully was a premonition of acting out my misguided belief in the myth of riding in on a white horse and saving the day, something I had been conditioned to do from a young age. I thought I was protecting and saving everybody, and I did to a large degree, but my agenda was flawed and I paid for it. At that point I had no clue of the massive life's lesson that would unfold for me as a result of my flawed convictions.

I never dream after an Ayahuasca ceremony, but in the aftermath of this one I had a series of painful, hellish, chaotic dreams, but felt fortified by the thought that the terror and horror would strengthen me in my helplessness. The darkness I experienced terrified me, but there were also moments of extreme awesome beauty, painful in its own unique intensity.

My friend Penrose and I had a gay friend who was manic depressive and troubled who went to visit her and in his attempts to clean her house he broke things and threw out things he shouldn't have, then a few months later he committed suicide.

I awoke the following morning from bizarre dreams about him.

He was following me in a car and stopped late, crashing into me. He was asking for help, then he jumped on me and tried to kiss me. I opened my mouth when he moved to put a lip lock on me and bit into his lips.

After that he was still pushing to do something. I was supposed to go to a music awards show and I had some time to get there, so after he tried to kiss me I said, "Look, leave me alone and get the fuck out of here!" He kept following me while I was telling him to leave me alone.

He got into my car and started putting custom metal gas and brake pedals that looked like feet onto my rubber pedals. I told him to get out and drove by a hospital where I stopped and saw him in there telling them it was an emergency and that someone was dying and that someone was me.

I left and had an hour to make the awards ceremony which I missed, then I was at a school doing yard work. An older lady like one of my writing mentors was trying to get branches cleared away so I took them away for her. She was grateful after I put them in the trash, then she invited me into the house and started doing strange things like shaking her ass at me and sticking it out on some stairs, then she told me about a breast operation she was getting. Somebody else was there and she forced my hand up under her blouse to get me to feel her breasts, then she sat on my lap, so I got out of there.

I was outside at a school again standing next to a mosquito net without any clothes on, something I often did in my waking moments in the jungle. Some people came looking for me and I said I would be there in a minute because I needed to put some clothes on, so I did. They brought me the place mat and all the stuff I missed from the awards banquet I missed.

The night before somebody wanted to sell a van for a really good deal and my friend wanted to buy it and it turned out that he knew the guy who was selling the van.

All of these disturbing dreams were bizarre, disjointed, and episodic and maybe not worth retelling, but they have their own unique personal meaning stirred up in piecemeal sediment from the depths of my subconscious. Though nonsensical, later examination revealed my deepest emotional insecurities wrapped up in the bizarre cryptic conceptual, emotional language of my right brain connection to the elusive mysteries of my subconscious.

I started Thursday with my head full of this clutter, trying to make sense out of the weird emotional conceptual language of my dreaming mind. Guillermo came for a visit and confirmed that the hell experiences were great learning, then he told me about Sachamama the great underwater serpent life giver, and he confirmed how hot and sweaty I got and how it was an important part of the cleansing.

I understood that to be a warrior I had to pass though the hells and thought of Carlos Castaneda's teaching that a warrior had to follow a path with heart. To pass through those hells and your worst inner fears and survive them is what makes you a warrior and makes you stronger, which is what the Inca Warriors told me telepathically in the cave in my vision when they said, "This was a very big warrior's rite of passage."

I felt beat up and abused which increased my determination to follow the path in spite of feeling physically and emotionally drained with a mild headache. I had not eaten for a day or so and the Chuchuwasi was making me nauseous. They only brought rice and two plátanos for breakfast, but that combined with the Chuchuwasi made me feel energized and stronger.

My previous night's journey and the chaos it tapped into made me realize that Ayahuasca and the other teacher plants amplified my deepest fears and whatever else might be rattling around in my subconscious and forced me to experience them. I've felt this at my deepest levels, which is how I felt the energies of these plant allies and on this day I was about to get introduced to them on a plant walk to get a detailed "preview of coming attractions" to plants I would be working with in the years to come.

In the green of the jungle the plants and landscape start to look the same. Many of the insects and animals look like plants and many of the plants look like insects and animals. This magical and intentional camouflaging is amplified by the crossing of perception and boundaries that come from the continuum of visionary journeys that blur dreaming, waking, and agitated subconscious material like my questionable perception of a Chullachaki with a real person.

The keen wisdom filled eyes of Don Guillermo knew these plants and the surrounding jungle intimately and pointed out nuances in how certain plants grew. He showed us where they grew, the structure and color of their leaves, what other plants they grew with and their relationship to them, and whether they were vines, bushes, or trees, as well as the uses and what parts of them are effective along with their preparation.

Some of these plants have Spanish names, some Quechua, some Shipibo, and some have unique names of mysterious origin as well as corrupted translations like Sangre de Grado which was originally Sangre de Drago, Spanish for dragon's blood. The Indians struggled with the pronunciation, changing it to the former and bringing it into common usage.

Some of the plants we were shown have already been mentioned, so what follows is a loose narrative in the context of our plant walk that was orally translated, so like before some names were recorded phonetically, but I made my best effort to be as precise as I could and added a few details from my own research.

Guillermo talked a lot about Ushpawasha, his specialty and one of my all time favorites. He educated us about its use as a plant bath and as a drink. He also showed us Cat's Claw known as Uña de Gato, because of its claw-shaped thorns, formally known as Uncaria tomentosa, a woody vine. The powdered bark is used as an anti-inflammatory for tumors, an immune system fortifier, for prostate inflammation, the kidneys, and as a cancer cure, and it is now sold as a dietary supplement. Energetically it regenerates you and you get sick less. I have used it since and can attest to its miraculous healing qualities.

Renaco is a rubber tree growing throughout the Amazon which brings down aerial roots from its long branches that descend to the ground and take root, giving rise to new trunks. Renaco trees originate from a single trunk with the oldest and largest tree at the center surrounded by a maze of tangled aerial roots. Used for snake bites, it is scraped into the bite. The sap is used as a vaginal wash for women who have recently given birth to regenerate damaged tissues and restore flexibility. It is also a teacher plant used in dietas and to heal in massage by rubbing the tea into the joints, necks, and backs of the person being worked on. It also teaches how to heal the body by touching. Mixed with alcohol it is applied where there is joint pain and prepared as a tea with alcohol.

Often mistaken as a tree, Renaquilla, another of my favorites, is a large vine-like plant that wraps itself around a host tree until it becomes one with its host. Its unique healing modalities work with the same binding energy to join, bond, and strengthen broken issues across the physical, emotional and spiritual spheres of life. Considered a feminine plant, the Shipibo love Renaquilla's unifying nature which is reputed to bring back harmony with the natural world and our relationship to life. Her powerful teachings help resolve disunity between couples and family members by unifying and connecting through forgiveness. Renaquilla is believed to have the ability to reprogram neural networks by coding them with improved cellular health that results in expanded awareness and a shift in consciousness.

Trumpetero Sacha in Quechua means wood. It is cut, boiled, and bathed in to help get energy to walk. Another plant used for plant baths is Ajo Sacha, a teacher plant used in dietas that smells like garlic. It is also used for rheumatism and is said to be good for the immune system like garlic. Ajo in Spanish means garlic, so the translation is garlic wood or garlic of the forest.

A palm with spines called Huicungo or Supaicasha is known as Thorn of the Devil. A tea from this tree is used in a dieta by sorcerers to see devils and learn witchcraft and black magic. It is reputed to teach you how to use its spines as energetic darts to hurl when you want to damage an enemy physically, energetically, and psychically by lodging in their body and making them ill, and in theory it can kill them. If that happens the victim has to go to another healer who has knowledge of this and they extract it by sucking and spitting out the toxicity.

There is a dark side to Ayahuasca which is neutral in and of itself, but with intention it is used by black sorcerers to inflict harm. There are many stories in the jungle of people who pay these dark sorcerers to get rid of somebody. If you train as an Ayahuasquero you have to learn the ways of the light and the dark to be able to defend against dark magic like this. At some point you have a choice between becoming a healer or a dark sorcerer or brujo, but once you choose the dark and do evil you can never go back.

Ayahuasqueros believe that the origin of all evil is envy and that all darkness comes from envy. Any harm or damage you receive from anybody else is due to envy and you constantly have to protect yourself and learn the defenses against the darkness of envy. Many of the locals are envious of the healers that brought us to the jungle because we bring in money and other benefits like gifts that they covet. Concentrated blowing of air, Florida water known as Agua de Florida, and tobacco smoke are all used to clear the air and form a protective shield.

One of the reasons allies and protective energies are called in when creating a safe container for an Ayahuasca ceremony is to keep these dark energies at bay because the ceremony is believed to act as an energy generator that can draw them to it. It is also why it is important for everyone to stay in the circle in a ceremony instead of wandering off creating an energy leak and diminishing the combined collective energy created by the circle.

I was told what sounded like Boeychanga is a type of metal. The underside of the leaf is full of tiny irritating spines. Healers blow tobacco smoke on the underside of the leaf to "tame" the plant, then they rub the leaf over the part of the body that has pains where it irritates the skin and heals the pain.

There is also a variety of Copal. If you cut the tree it oozes resin used for incense, but you have to be careful as there are many members of the Burseraceae, a family of about 540 species of flowering plants. Also known as torchwood, frankincense, and myrrh, or simply the incense tree family, this includes both trees and shrubs characterized by nonallergenic resin and smooth, flaking, aromatic bark.

Estoraque is a tree with oval leaves covered with whitish fluff and white flowers. It smells peculiar and is made into a tea for men that gives them potency, helps erections, and is considered an aphrodisiac.

Esamburo is a tree that in certain seasons of the year attracts a large, luscious fat worm they call gusano that feeds off it. Locals fry and eat the worm which is tasty and rich in oils.

The fruit of the tall Ubo tree is edible and its reddish bark cuttings are put on cuts, wounds, and bruises, and a tea made from the bark is made for women to use as a douche. It's also used in large amounts to bathe people who are inflamed all over the body to bring down inflammation.

Yaguar means blood in Quechua and panga means unleash. Yaguarpanga which I mentioned earlier has a bloody red sap and climbs as a vine with Cat's Claw and is a powerful purgative. This small plant grows close to the ground and has heart shaped leaves with red veins on the underside. A few leaves are crushed and the juice is mixed with a half a glass of water. Once you drink this you vomit continuously for about five hours and have to keep drinking water over and over again to refill your stomach to give it something to vomit out. After a Yaguarpanga session you can participate in many Ayahuasca sessions with little or no purging.

A rare and obscure plant known to a few is Joster Sacha. Sacha means water in Quechua. This is a creeper vine made into a tea that sits overnight in the dew and used for kidney problems.

Sangre De Grado mentioned earlier has heart shaped leaves with reddish stems. If you cut the bark a red sap oozes out that is useful for cuts and skin openings. It gets soapy when you rub it and it forms a latex skin over the wound which is antiseptic. It is also used for coughs or bronchitis with a glass of boiled banana water mixed with a few drops, and a few drops diluted in water are used to treat ulcers and hemorrhaging blood in women.

Clavohuasca, another of my favorites is fragrant and used for waist and lower back pain. They make an alcohol tincture with that they drink for healing.

Elephant Ear is put around the body and irritates the skin, but if you put it in the fire and half cook and bake it, then put it around and wrap the part of the body, it is reputed to protect and cure sorcery when somebody has sent a dart known as a virote into you.

Copaiba is a huge beautiful tree. Its wood is used for the planks of the tambos and for treating hemorrhoids by taking the sap and applying it. A few drops of it in hot water is used by women for a douche. It's also used as an anti-tumor by putting a few drops of the sap in banana water to drink.

Red and white Lupuna are very powerful tree spirits. The White Lupuna Spirit is a very benevolent old man with a white beard full of wisdom while the spirit of the Red Lupuna is an irascible angry red-headed, red-bearded short dwarf who comes after you if you bother it.

José told us that sometimes when dieting with the plants the spirit or mother of the plant will appear to you in different forms and teach you icaros.

When we finished I felt physically weaker, but energized and very aware. It took all of my focus and energy to participate in the plant walk, but it was a rare experience that I did not want to miss. When it was over I eased my way back to my tambo and took some much need down time to recharge myself so I could face whatever was coming with as much energy and attention that I could muster.

TEN

On The Wings Of The Condor

I woke up in the middle of the night from a vivid dream that gave me some insights into my life's situation. The coming Friday morning was the start of a writers conference run by my former unethical publicist who not only burned me, but her son who worked for a political opponent of my brother's had tried to smear my brother's character when he ran for city council.

> *I was at the conference and this woman wanted me to be there supporting it. When I told her I couldn't do that she whined that I didn't know what was going on with her life and she had all these problems. I said it was no excuse for what she did to me and walked away. I couldn't understand why I wasn't in the jungle where I was supposed to be and couldn't figure it out.*
>
> *I also dreamed about a younger guy who was one of my best techs and a major ass kisser. Once he moved on he ignored me and his friend, my other top technician told me that's how he was, a major ass kisser who used people and discarded them. My former publicist was the same way in how she used people I knew to get her conference going.*
>
> *At the end of the conference there was a big bowl of candy I wasn't supposed to eat so I took a handful and my best writing mentor showed up to support me. My publicist's son implied that I was in trouble for growing illegal cannabis. I told him I went to Peru and got cured of my problems and there was nothing he could do.*

In the waking aftermath of the emotion tinged imagery of this dream I concluded that in my dark dreams I was re-experiencing my shadow which strengthened me by being "put in my face" by Chuchuwasi and Ayahuasca. I thought that sooner or later unethical people end up exposing themselves when others see who they really are by their actions. To me it was shamanic mirroring that demonstrated how vindictive acts will bounce back toward the perpetrators and the more they try, the more they damage themselves in a karmic way. I felt the truth in this and understood that it only scratched the surface of what was inside of me that attracted them to me as a victim in the first place.

Waking suddenly from a vivid dream to find yourself alone in the dark of the jungle in the middle of the night is stimulating, so sleep doesn't always return easily. You can lie awake for hours in the darkness serenaded by the cacophonic symphony of the jungle night wondering at it all.

In those contemplative times my mind often spins and these words spun out to capture the essence of that moment in the seemingly eternal primal jungle night.

Starlit Sky
Firefly
Cosmic Beauty to my eye
Through the trees
Without a breeze
This gift of life
Is mine to please
I'm thankful for this magic time
To share this life oh love of mine
I'm thankful for this magic place
My life, my love, it's in my face

I passed into unconsciousness again at some point and woke up later that morning around 7:30 sorting through a jumble of more bizarre chaotic dreams.

I was going to a barbeque with Penny in a big house full of people. We went into a store on the way where a young girl gave me a hard time about not being pierced, I wasn't experienced enough in my life, I was not far out enough, and more. I told her I was more far out than she could begin to imagine.

We went into the store for food and I went for Cracker Jacks. I was going to eat them until I remembered I was breaking the dieta. I went to put them back and went back and forth and ended up not taking them, so I took something else not as bad and not as sweet, then I remembered dreaming of sweets on my previous dieta.

The young girl got in the car with Penny and I with me sitting between the two of them, talking to the girl while holding hands with Penny who didn't care for the younger girl, so we dropped her off and went to the house full of people. All of my neighbors and friends showed up. There were more people than I expected and they didn't seem to be meshing with the people who lived there. I kept looking for Penny who had hot dogs. I thought we didn't have enough food so I wanted to buy more. I kept looking for and following Penny who seemed unhappy. I found the people I had to entertain and there was a big black guy there who I knew. We were talking when I saw Penny's kids hanging around the house.

There was a brother of this family that we were visiting, but I didn't know who they were and it seemed like the kids were into him more than me because he had more money. He was smoking cannabis and wanted me to get him some because his mother had cancer and wanted the cannabis for medical purposes. We were trying it out with some pipes. I went into the garage alone and tried another little pipe, then someone came in who caught me smoking it and they were not happy about it.

I was by the ocean and we needed water and we were hungry. There was no food and we were trying to figure out how to catch something to eat. We saw fish and seals and I thought about clubbing a seal, but didn't feel good about doing that so I went into the water to grab some fish. I grabbed one and wondered how long it had been dead because it was decomposing so that was off, then we were swept into a military operation heading off to war. I put my belongings in a car with some other people and got ready to go until Yoda said "I heard you got caught doing something. Mrs. Apinaré was very upset and said if you ever do that again you'll never come back," then he gave me a hard time saying, "I told you not to do anything around here with these people."

I said, "Yeah, you're right I got caught, but the reason I was doing it is because I was trying to help cure the cancer."

He was understanding about it and was smoking a cigarette. He blew it in my face and said "I'm sorry," because it was unintentional, then Mrs. Apinaré stood up.

I had never heard or known anyone by the name of Apinaré, which came out of nowhere, and no matter its origins or significance, I find it fascinating how it played out in the weave of my rising subconscious.

In between these dreams I drank two glasses of Chuchuwasi, fell asleep, and continued dreaming.

I jumped out of an airplane and parachuted into the jungle. I kept looking up and felt like I was connected to the jungle and the maloca that I thought of and referred to as a space ship which was like the plane. My duffel bag and other belongings hung from its roof. At the end of the dream I gathered all my belongings and prepared to leave while pulling it all together toward the end of the jump. I thought my chute wouldn't open, but I landed safely. While flying in the dream, I had a number of dreams where I was in the dream and knew I was in the jungle, but I didn't make the connection and I didn't become lucid.

A little monkey came and went down a hill, then came up to me. I was playing with him and I gave him some leftover food and talked about taking him home, but I couldn't because I knew he couldn't be in captivity.

Someone who worked for me was giving someone else trouble, but they were only teasing. They were supposed to be going for their karate brown belt test and I was at a house with more people who were all supposed to be taking their brown belt test.

Friday would be my 3rd ceremony, that I thought of as mid-session which was also when the writers conference started in San Diego. It felt "cosmically right" to me to be in the jungle in a powerful spiritual space that I thought counterbalanced the darkness that the conference held.

I had been sleeping hard and felt like I was recharged and looking forward to powerful visions in the upcoming session and I was wondering when Guillermo would come with his cure for my chronic heat rash. When I asked if he had anything that could clear it up, he said there was a plant called gusano that he mixed with tobacco.

When I completed that thought I heard his voice and he walked up with Carlos, a dark-haired younger apprentice. The same telepathy happened with another friend. I thought about him and he appeared right after I completed the thought. This happened to me frequently during my dietas.

Guillermo and Carlos made a nasty smelling paste of tobacco and gusano and spread it out in a handkerchief, then applied it all over the rash on my ass, wrapped it, and told me to keep it there indefinitely. After they left I relaxed for the rest of the afternoon to conserve my energy for what would surely be an eventful night.

I was not disappointed.

At 2:00 on Saturday morning I was back from my mid-session air drying from my plant bath, dictating the night's adventures. On this night they gave us a new brew that felt more powerful and different in the experience. It felt like I flew harder after drinking a lot less to the point that I ended up lost for some time.

Maestro Guillermo planned to do individual healings and I wanted to record mine, but I was so out of it I forgot, even after an offer of help, which meant to me that it wasn't meant to be recorded.

In the beginning different beings surrounded me, joining together floating in front of me serpentine and web-like. After a moment of doubt as to whether I would journey any further, I took off and went through a multitude of worlds, places and dimensions at an insanely high speed that were all beautiful, intense, detailed, and beyond any verbal description. I had a strong sense that I was travelling back and forth through time.

A sudden unexpected massive purge erupted causing me to puke all over myself along with a lot of shit that came up from my lungs. I continued purging while passing through shifting dimensions and lost all sense of physical reality. I had no idea where I was, then I came back from that powerful experience and saw the vomit all over myself. I tried to find my water to drink, which took a long time because I struggled to find it. When I did I finally drank and rinsed puke off of me.

Guillermo sang powerful, intense, focused songs making my whole body twitch and tremble. I sat cross-legged and my legs started going up and down on their own accord, whoop, whoop, whoop, first like the flapping of butterfly wings, then like massive bird wings that I believed to be the wings of a condor. My whole body spasmed and jerked with bird-like movements and in my visions I flew through a high mountain range both visualizing and feeling first like a butterfly, then a condor at the center of creation flying through valleys and soaring upwards looking at the stars. It was all so spectacularly beautiful that any attempt at expression falls woefully short at articulating the experience.

After that transformation I went to some dark places that were not as intense as prior nights making me feel like I was being shown a little mercy. In these dark places I was "shown" that the visions and dark energies were tied in with Penny's ex-husband and the people around him, except her kids which I interpreted as a warning of what to watch out for.

After my flight through the darkness I went to Penny and her kids and felt joy and beauty in an exquisite experience of deep love and connection. At that point Penny may have taken some LSD or mushrooms on that same night, something we had discussed, then I was alone with her.

Guillermo came singing to me and blowing tobacco and cinnamon into the top of my head and all over my body. He had me take my socks off and went right to my stomach which I hoped might be to cure my lipomas. He blew on my stomach then sucked at it and spit out phlegm or energy then he talked and sang into my stomach. He blew into my hands a number of times, then into my feet and on my legs and spent a lot of time on my stomach. He seemed oblivious to my stink and the smell of puke all over me and continued blowing tobacco into my stomach and the rest of me so I closed my eyes and went with the whole experience.

After he finished I started coming down as he made the rounds of the whole circle. One of the guys was yelling and growling like an animal, which he said later was his jaguar totem. The lady beside me twitched, spasmed and banged the floor while I did my best to stay quiet. My legs continued flapping like massive wings for the longest time as if carrying me along through portals and dimensions of what I thought of as shamanic soul travel. Though physically and mentally challenging, each progressive journey seemed to get better each time.

I took a partial plant bath when I got back to my tambo so as not to disturb the tobacco plant mixture poultice on my ass. I hoped that my rash and fatty bumps would be gone forever with a little passage of time, but I was willing to accept that they might not. Part of my learning there was to discover what expectations were realistic and which ones were not.

ELEVEN

The Numinous Apinaré

Saturday was a resting day before two sessions in a row on Sunday and Monday nights, giving us Tuesday to recover before breaking the diet and leaving on Wednesday morning. At this point I determined that the jungle was where I truly went to school, worshipped, learned, and found guidance. I felt blessed to have found the shamans and the people working with them, and lucky to become deeply connected with them. Part of me felt sorry for all the people who would never have the experiences I was having, but I also knew that it was not for everybody. Relative few were willing to pay the physical, mental, and emotional price they exacted.

That morning Guillermo came and brought me my Chuchuwasi and checked the poultice on my rash. I wondered about his icaros and how my flapping legs became the flight of a butterfly that transformed into a Condor, but I didn't say anything. He put his arms out wide, gave me a big smile and flapped his arms like wings as if he was flying which confirmed for me that he and his songs had a part in taking me there. When I flapped my own arms and asked him about my flight his smile widened and he said, "El Condor!"

Prior to going to the jungle I sometimes had strong feelings of being on the verge of figuring something out just before waking, but I couldn't figure out what it was when I did wake. When I had that same experience in the jungle it felt like I had come there straight from the same experience at home, like an instant portal that I left back then brought directly to the jungle, bypassing everything that happened in between. Even though I wrote it down it still seemed inexplicable as did much of what I experienced in the jungle.

On the physical plane it was a challenge keeping the poultice on every time I had to shit while keeping the bugs from literally crawling up my ass, but I was determined to follow through with every aspect of the program.

I drank more Chuchuwasi before going to bed and awoke in the middle of the night hovering somewhere between waking and sleeping from a vision of myself inside a dark cocoon becoming an emerging chrysalis with emerging wings, then a loud voice startled me fully awake out of nowhere that said, "Apinaré!"

I remembered the prior dream in the big house full of people and the puzzling appearance of Mrs. Apinaré who was upset and admonished me for procuring cannabis to help someone with cancer. I had no knowledge of ever hearing the word Apinaré, which added to the forcefulness of how it startled me awake, combined with the fact that I experienced clairaudience, what I jokingly call hallucihearing, literally loud and clear. The energy behind that utterance and its repetitive occurrence that began in my dream demanded my attention.

I looked up Apinaré later and it loosely translates from Spanish meaning to cram, pack, crowd, or jam together. In the dream, the setting had been a big house full of people which could be a factor. In another respect it could refer to everything happening in my highly active brain, a large family of plant and other spirits connected to me through the dieta, or all of it for that matter.

I laid there for awhile unable to sleep and felt a strong urge to get up so I went to the riverbank and looked up to see a bright star among all the rest, right in the middle of the open space above the river clearing that reminded me of a breast. I watched it feeling awe in its stark glittering beauty up in the sky and a shooting star blazed across the sky beside it which struck me as a profound, magical moment, even if it could have been a coincidence. After awhile I crawled back under my mosquito net and drifted off into more strange dreams.

I was in a bar with my brother getting ready to go to a concert. These guys came in and I was talking to them. I knew them but not very well, but they knew each other. I was between them and said, "I'll get out of your way," and I backed off. They laughed and I was laughing with them until my friend's wife ran in, in a little bit of a panic. She asked me if I knew how to fix the water in José's house because it was leaking.

I went outside where she was trying to do some watering by a water tank and water came out of everywhere. I ran around looking and found the spot where it was leaking and asked her to turn on the water. I found the fitting where it came out and struggled to plug it in for the longest time, then someone came to check on me.

The house was in a different place. I tried to get a light bulb into the fitting and realized it wasn't working, then I was finally getting it in and giving up on it at the same time. At that moment everything around me brightened and all my senses felt enhanced making me feel much more fully aware. I was looking for breakfast and other things, then I was with some people going down to a building like the ones in the jungle. I was sitting there and a lady came and sat on my shoulder for awhile and didn't seem to realize it, then I stood.

She apologized and I said, "Don't worry that happens to me all the time." Another lady Cathy who I knew from my visits to the Maya ruins of Palenque was there and had her possessions spread around. I looked up and saw she had tiny gloves nailed to the wall in a little bag. When I looked at them they fell, then some guys got into a heated discussion about how they taught. They were both sure their way was right, but I wasn't so sure if either one of them was. I listened for awhile then walked back to my place where there were other people. I hear a third guy join in the argument with the first two, then they walked past me dressed like shamans. One had a colorful sash and one had a necklace. They were saying, "Don't touch this because it is too powerful." Somebody touched it and something happened. I also saw feathers, weavings, and similar items. The shamans said that they were all their power objects and nobody else should be touching them.

I left that and went into a room where my brother was and said, "People should be allowed to say what they think, say what they feel, and should be allowed to have their own thing."

My brother was lying in bed and the light was on. He had the covers over his head and we got into an argument about what I said. I couldn't understand why he was arguing with me because what I said is that everybody can have their own opinion.

José was the shaman I worked with from the very beginning and the archetype of the house I saw as a big symbol. I think plugging the water leaks at his house represented loss of psychic energy, and once the water stopped being lost the expanded perceptions heralded a higher awareness from the recovered energy.

It's also interesting that this troubleshooting and repairing dream sparked to life when I got out of the way of the two groups of people at the beginning of the dream. It felt like I had two disparate groups of people, or subpersonalities and my act of stepping out from between allowed them to integrate, rewarding me with a higher awareness. The situation with my brother brilliantly reflected my deeper feelings as he openly ridiculed my spiritual beliefs on occasion.

As a visual, conceptual, emotional narrative, it is a great metaphor for healing trauma and the fact that the shamans at the end showed up with their power objects to let me sense their power.

Guillermo came by later and took the poultice off. The rash was gone, but a bigger area was red and inflamed, so he put a fresh poultice on.

Our last two sessions, two nights in a row were coming. They fed us two bowls of chicken vegetable soup and two plátanos, I think with the intention of fortifying us for the energy we needed to endure the last two ceremonies.

I took stock of myself. Seven days to home and I was happy that I had no canker sores like the bad ones from last year, but my ass was red, swollen, and burning. Guillermo said that when that inflammation clears up, the rash would be gone. In my mind I thought that Apinaré was somehow connected with the Chuchuwasi.

One of my ongoing unstated intentions was to get a greater understanding of sacred geometry, but I never verbalized it. On this adventure I met Scott Olsen a professor of comparative religion who gave his doctoral thesis on sacred geometry and published an award winning book titled *The Golden Section: Nature's Greatest Secret*.

Scott told me that Sacred Geometry consists of the construction of the Antahkarana, the rainbow bridge and path back to the father that encompasses all consciousness entering into the presence of the eternal now. It is the most central study in the sacred institutions of the mysteries from time immemorial and the ancients possessed the key.

Pythagoras and Plato learned it from the ancient Egyptian which brought Plato recognition as the world's interpreter, even though he had to veil the message to give everyone the opportunity to construct the bridge and consciously navigate the crossing. Scott also pointed out that the maloca that we did ceremonies in was a perfect dodecahedron, a Platonic solid of twelve pentagons with twelve flat faces that looks like a soccer ball with edges. This information made me think about my Apinaré star experience and the possibility of something out there talking to me. Everything made sense and felt connected in its own strange way, but I held some skepticism as it could also be the shaman's one third unknown territory and I could be reading things into observations that were either synchronicities or coincidences.

At that point I thought of Apinaré as my shining star and the path of the shining star that was coming to me over the last few days and when I questioned it a shooting star flew close to it, as if confirming my feeling of conviction.

Prior to that night's session Guillermo told us that fate led him into being a plant man. His grandfather was a vegetalista healer, his father was a doctor, and Guillermo felt it was in his blood. The first plant he worked with was San Pedro and after that he started taking Ayahuasca.

In this, our fourth session Guillermo's icaros sent me deep into the darkness of my heart swallowed by all the cataclysmic fear, cowardice, and shame that I held inside. I went in kicking, screaming, and whining, and kept going for quite some time, struggling to figure out why until something clicked inside me, prompting me to say to myself, "Quit being a candy ass and start owning up."

Once I did I was taken on wings soaring into the darkness. Each time I soared I went into a mass of pain and suffering, but each time I soared in a predatory manner into the depths of my heart of darkness, I let go and came back up soaring high with brighter visions before swooping down again into the darkness for more shit. I felt more cleansing and let go over and over and over again. In the midst of it I puked my guts out and hacked and spit up tons of phlegm and I more or less prayed to Santa Teresa to guide and protect me while looking for answers.

Guillermo shapeshifted into different beings and at the point where I felt the most lost is when I found my strength and power. In those moments he became a giant praying mantis looking insect that danced around ringing bells and empowering me to fly into the darkness. He came and stood over me, taking me into a giant cavernous alien city inside of him. He kept changing colors which were overwhelmingly beautiful, yet there was a grotesque aspect to it all, and in my confusing mix of perceptions I saw a number of different giant insect beings, spider creatures, wasp things, grasshopper, and ant types that lived in a multitude of different worlds and dimensions.

After all the deep cleansing I felt like I had soared through millions of years of negative trauma within that dark inner space. In this moment of new found clarity and brighter visions Yoda shocked me by talking about how to find your shining star and how the path to it is through the heart, which is how I thought of Apinaré as my shining star and guide.

He talked about how a numinous experience like this is how the divine truly tattoos your heart, your soul, your being, and your essence. Numinous is defined as an experience of awe and wonder in the presence of an almighty and transcendent God and an awareness of human nothingness when faced with a holy and powerful being. Numinous comes from the Latin numin- meaning "divine power." It also comes from numen, a word that describes the spirit or divine power characteristic of a thing or place.

As Yoda spoke I was struck by something like a bolt of lightning that blew me away on every conceivable and imaginable level, scattering me in all directions. He spoke of Yeats and a moment in his life when he was fifty or fifty-five when it struck him that he was blessed and understood how he could bless other people, which empowered me. I thought that these visions were where the real battles were fought in what I characterized as spirit wars and I was being blessed by the shining star and passing on the blessing to others.

This articulation falls woefully short in conveying the spiritual emotional experience and the way I got answers to my questions. Even though I had tons of resistance, I became helpless when I was drawn into the terrifying darkness that swallowed me, more proof of forces far bigger than me.

When Yoda finished he translated what José said when he talked about seeing the star close to your heart, saying it was *your* star that is your heart's secret that is in your heart between you and the star.

The dreams I had been through and everything in the dieta preceding this night of revelation had built up to this powerful epiphany as if it was all coming together and quickening. All that was spoken felt perfect and applied to me making me feel like it was not for anybody else there but me, and I thought part of this gift came from the fact that I stuck solidly to the diet and directions, while others did not follow through, took less than prescribed, and cheated in other ways. I had pushed myself to the limits and this epiphany-blessing was my payoff.

I felt like all the pieces of my life's puzzle gelled and would keep going forward on an infinite path of integration.

TWELVE

The Dark And Light Condor Blessing Of A Spirit Father

After my last session I expected to firebomb into the dark gathering more shit bombs and dropping all of them. In our last session I discovered that the condor, the sacred bird of the Andes is revered even more than its counterpart the American Eagle. In Andean cosmology condor eats carrion and converts it into something beautiful, and it represents love, symbolized by the color rose.

When I had been summoned by the Apinaré star it came first in a dream in the form of an older woman as an auditory call that woke me and wouldn't leave me alone until I went out and looked up. A shooting star punctuated the whole chain of events like the proverbial dot on an exclamation point, and if all that was not enough, the numinous words about the shining star from José and Yoda sealed the deal. This powerful calling whether real or imagined opened the door and the session on this second to last night brought it all together.

When I finally passed into unconsciousness in the predawn hours Guillermo came to me with icaros in my sleep and I went through a lot more material while sleeping and in my dreams. I wanted to wake up and look up at my Apinaré star again, but I couldn't find the energy to fully awaken.

I was speaking at a grammar school and had problems with the class who were not getting what I said. I was also writing about speaking at the school as if I was living and writing it at the same time, so I invited a biker with a guitar to play and sing to the class but he smashed the guitar in front of everybody to teach some kind of lesson.

Class got out and we walked out and met my brother, some other people, and a writer friend who in real life was the news anchor from a local San Diego station who said, "Am I going to see you tomorrow night?"

I said, "Sure."

Next I was at a writer's conference walking in with a new book I had written. A lot of my long standing writing friends were there having a good time talking with each other.

Monday was my last day drinking Chuchuwasi and my final night drinking Ayahuasca. My intention was to heal other people I felt close to. I didn't know if *I* could do that, but I wanted to ask for others to be healed because I now felt blessed by the numinous.

During the course of my dieta I had many visual, audio, and smell manifestations when I was alone walking through the jungle, among them 5MEODMT, wood smells, and other inexplicable tastes. Whether real or imagined I distinctly heard a voice from Apinaré. I characterized these things as hallucihearing and hallucismelling, but they felt more real than normal waking consciousness.

I read in **Ino Moxo** that in visionary states we become multifaceted crystals with openings to multiple dimensions. At one point in my previous night's visions when José sang an icaro my reality became a giant multifaceted crystal with hundreds of windows that looked out into a different dimension and we were all in the midst of it. My thinking was that alternate selves traveled in each dimension that were all me and I was becoming consciously aware of all these disparate parts of myself that were being spoken to in these visionary icaro moments, and they were responding. I thought the key to it all was to try and put my full awareness in each self experiencing that particular thing at that distinctive moment, a nearly impossible task.

Guillermo came and told me about the plants and that I was a condor the night before as well as the prior night and my legs were flapping wings that swooped down and let go. He said I did lots of work and that I went very far and got lots of help from spirit helpers. When I told him his icaros and energies followed me into my dreams he lit up like a Christmas tree. After he left I drank two glasses of Chuchuwasi, laid down, and went out hard, having a short dream.

I was being told a story and living it at the same time with Spanish elements. I was with a guild moving around and being invisible with pots of money and resources as a Spaniard, but I was being humble and raggedy looking, then I left dressed up in great finery. The words in my head were, "You are looking like a grand Englishmen," then my name was called out and I woke up.

What woke me was my friend Penrose who was down swimming in the river calling out to check on me.

Tuesday Morning well after sunrise I stumbled back to my tambo from our final session thoroughly beaten and exhausted. The names Arimparé and Apinaré pulsed through me like a double beat. I believe Arimparé was Apinaré spoken in my muddled state. I couldn't function and do my normal recording due to my fatigue and confusion and I desperately needed sleep and down time.

I awoke a little while later looking forward to breaking the dieta with a meal and passing through the "gateway back to the world" with a pinch of salt followed by a normal, healthy meal. In this literally spaced out time where I regained some coherence while recovering from one of the most brutal and rewarding visionary journeys of my life, I struggled to make sense of the previous night's experience and record what had transpired.

It thundered when I prepared to go to our last session adding to my feelings of being a warrior heading into a pitched battle and it started raining hard with continued thunder when we met. We moved around, sitting in different places for each session, and for this last one I sat near the front, close to Guillermo. Two of the women in our group did not drink any Ayahuasca for this last session.

I choked down a dose that put me in the zone, but I wasn't flying. A little over an hour later Guillermo did a healing by blowing tobacco over the top of my head, stomach, arms, and hands. He spent a fair amount of time singing into my head, stomach, and the rest of my body, periodically sucking at different spots, then he blew tobacco smoke, and tobacco crumbs into my hair.

One of the ladies asked José if he would sing into her rose quartz to charge it with healing power, so I asked too and he did the same with two quartzes I had. In those early days I always travelled in my journeys with a quartz in one hand and a chipped stone spearhead in the other that had been gifted to me by Lorenzo of Psychedelic Salon fame who had gotten it from his grandfather who found it plowing a field. After Guillermo did the healing on me, a second dose was offered and after about ten minutes of consideration I was the only one to take it.

I soon felt it come on and got hit the hardest I had ever been hit up to this point and it sent me to a vast assortment of places. My body twitched and spasmed and my crossed legs flapped hard like wings and I went incredibly far out to the point of once again getting totally lost. At the point when I was flapping intensely I looked up and saw a giant black Condor which I was convinced was both a gift from Guillermo and Guillermo himself. He was massive and on the underside of his spread wings I saw a multitude of beautiful sparkling gems and jewels, and I was caught up in all of it. He was so massive, imposing, powerful, and beautiful, that he seemed like a big spaceship, but it was definitely a Condor and I was ecstatic.

Yoda came over and put his hand on my leg as I was apparently getting very loud and his touch brought me back. Other than those intense moments I don't remember a lot, but they told me I purged six or seven times hard while hacking and snotting while Guillermo sang. At one point in all the insanity he let me lay my head on his lap and he was like a great father patting my head while I was helpless in his lap. Later the others told me he was "fathering" me all night which was a novel experience for me.

Guillermo took care of me and did more healing on the back of my hands, down my arms, and blew into my hands while I laid down in his lap and held his hand. He kept me close and stayed with me more than anybody else. I was the only one who took a second dose and it knocked the shit out of me in more ways than one. At one point I felt like I was literally at death's doorstep beating my "wings" hard while coughing and hacking, and I feared lying down, puking, and suffocating from inhaling my vomit.

At the lowest point where I was lost and the most helpless I felt abandoned in the jungle and Penny's kids came to me which helped me start coming back. I found myself in Guillermo's lap again, then Penny came to me on an incredibly beautiful white winged horse and baby winged colts all white, sending me off again, flying through multiple geometric dimensions and other inscrutable realities and experiences.

At some point the ceremony ended and they lit candles, but I have no recollection of that and don't remember much else of what happened. I swooned and swayed from side to side and had visions of a wedding I wanted to do in Florida with Penny and I thought I got the right Apinaré spelling, but I was physically all over the place.

People left the maloca but I was incapacitated. Everyone had gone except my friend Penrose who decided to spend the night there as it was raining and the trails were muddy. I couldn't walk and I kept peeing and peeing, so I stayed too.

My ass burned from the poultice being on there for all those days, so I apologized to Penrose who was totally cool, then I took my clothes off and laid down. My hips were reddened and almost bruised from the bandages. I laid there for awhile looking around to see my belongings spread out all over half the maloca. My recorder was in one place, my cushion in another, my clothes someplace else, and my water in another spot. It took me a long time to concentrate, so I poured water on myself which shocked the hell out of me and gave me enough focus to get everything together.

I made a pile of cushions and curled up on them and stretched out on the floor of the maloca wet and shivering, laughing at myself and my condition, then I put one cushion between my legs and one on my chest and hugged them as if hugging Penny and thought of her with a little winged unicorn with a butterfly that I left her on the pillow and I thought about dreaming each other. I was still flying hard and there was no way I could sleep.

I got it into my head that I needed to reach out to everybody I knew to give them healing, loving energy, so I thought of my close friends and family who I thought needed the most healing first and hugged people and put my heart into their pain and sickness visualizing going through it, becoming it, and blowing it out. In those sporadic moments I believed I could heal everybody doing that. I also had some skepticism, but I did it anyway.

I went from those closest to extended family and friends projecting love energy to them all and spent hours doing this. I felt like a giant condor of love flying, circling, and swooping down into their hearts to purge them of their pain and suffering the way I had experienced it. It became more difficult to do because there were so many, so I started doing whole families until I was exhausted and wanted more than anything to go home. The whole time I spent there twitching, coughing and shivering I felt Guillermo's spirit coming to me over and over again in an uncanny, almost palpable way to check on and comfort me.

I started circling wide and kept bringing them in closer and closer saving Penny and her kids for last, spending extra time with them. I heard and felt Apinaré calling me so I walked out into the mud with bare feet to look up, but I couldn't see anything, so I went back in and laid down again, but couldn't sleep. I opened my eyes and saw that it was beginning to get light. I sat up and saw Penrose was awake. We talked for awhile and decided to head back to our tambos, so we gathered our things and trekked back through the muddy trails.

I drifted off to sleep around eight am and woke up a little later from an alarm a friend had left me. I had a headache and felt weak, but I managed to get it together and Penrose and I went down to eat a group breakfast of an onion and garlicky salad with tomatoes and a wonderful chicken soup with noodles, potatoes and carrots, and some bread. I ate two bowls of soup.

On our walk there I told Penrose I felt embarrassed about how far out I had gone and she told me I shouldn't because what I did took a lot of courage. I apologized to everyone for spewing my energy all over the place the night before and they all looked at me with a deep respect because I had gone harder and further than all of them. The respect they gave me felt gratifying and all my time walking through that emerald forest sparkling clean from the recent rains I heard the icaros continuously in my head.

Back at my tambo I packed to leave the following day leaving out my bare necessities so the porters could take the rest of my gear, then I took my first full on plant bath in five days. I had been unable to do that due to the poultice I had on and it felt great, then I went down to empty my bucket and slipped and fell on my tailbone on a rock and almost passed out from the pain, but miraculously did no damage!

In the end I was enormously thankful for all the pain, misery and suffering I had been through and the amazing lessons I learned and when everything was said and done I felt deeply emotional and vulnerable.

In my last night sleeping in the jungle I awoke in the middle of the night from a vivid dream.

I was running up a hill at San Diego's Pacific Beach with my friends. I saw a black guy and we ran around a corner, then I was on roller skates which turned into a sports competition. They wanted us to play a certain way but there was a trap. I went down to an apartment building where I saw some guys sneaking from one building to another to escape.

I went with the guy who brought me through the apartment complex and up under another apartment building that was like a big porch to a homeless community. They took me through it to where they were going to go and two guys came out the front and went into another building. Something didn't seem right. I started through another door and realized it was a set up, so I grabbed one guy and started calling out, then I grabbed another guy who had hooks on his hand that he was trying to rake me to pieces with. I held him by the arm and called for help.

Next I was on a baseball team with some cops and we wanted to get new uniforms. There were three or four sets of uniforms in different colors which is what the treachery was about and I got called out about it, then I was in New York with some people and a talk show host friend of mine came to get us, then I had to go back to meet another friend. We were supposed to meet someplace else, but came back to Central Park and I was looking for Penny and her kids. I was with her daughter and I saw Penny off in the distance sitting on a bench. She hadn't seen me for a long time and I wanted to get to her, then another talk show host friend of mine was there with a pile of clothes. I had something for Penny that ended up in the pile. I was trying to get it back and ended up arguing with a group of people because I couldn't find it. The talk show host was talking nonstop. I was walking away with Penny's daughter and the first talk show host walked by me again.

Penny was sad because I had not gotten back to her, so I went to find her and she was gone, but all these other people were there. I walked around through them and couldn't find Penny. I went back with her daughter to the pile of clothes and argued with people again trying to get that stuff back, then I was in a car. Penny was mad at me, so I said "Fuck it!", got upset and walked away. Penny ran up to me and caught me by the arm and slowed me down, then she understood and it was ok.

Both talk show hosts in the dream I knew from television shows I had been on and I think my subconscious concerns and its symbolism revolved around my burgeoning writer's life and my new situation with Penny and her kids. As things unfolded in that relationship over time I puzzled over how she claimed to support what I was doing but showed no real support for it or how she tried to ruin events with irrational behaviors at critical times.

This second dieta created a major transformation at the core of my being where my inner reality shaped my world view based on how I filtered my perceptions and decided what was worth my attention. This radical shift had a profound influence on my outer world and what I focused on there, but the raw material for the terrain I had to navigate came from events occurring outside of me that I could not change, only how I reacted to them.

In the aftermath of the 911 terrorist attacks, the United States had a series of anthrax attacks over the course of several weeks beginning on September 18, 2001. Letters containing anthrax spores were mailed to several news media offices and to a couple of Democratic Senators, killing five people and infecting seventeen others.

We had been cut off and out of touch with any world events and off the grid during the course of our dieta as these events unfolded. A few minutes before our final session, one of the shaman's helpers heard about this on the radio. After passing this along in the translation process, what came to us was that there was an anthrax plague in the United States. Needless to say, this information coming moments before drinking added to the chaotic apocalyptic visions that became the hallmark of my dark night's journey, and when we left the jungle, we expected to be confronted by this worse secondary disaster.

On a more positive note, once we left the jungle we spent an extra day in Pucallpa to help ease the integration process and were invited to visit Usko-Ayar, the painting school of legendary Ayahuasca painter Pablo Amaringo. I had met Pablo the previous year and had deep respect for him, his work and for how he had dedicated himself to teaching young people how to paint free of charge.

Pablo offered to show us his latest work in progress and to my shock and amazement, I recognized the deep electric blue glowing ball entities from my first session and the gathering of fairy like beings and other winged dragonfly-like creatures that came and healed me, bringing the most powerful purge that I had ever had on Ayahuasca.

Seeing this unexpected external validation of the inner reality I had experienced expressed in the work of Maestro Pablo and being shown it by him right after my recent experience blew my mind. When I pointed to the beings I recognized on his unfinished work our eyes met in what I can only describe as a near electric acknowledgement and deeper connection from him. He understood that I "got it" and had spent time with the same beings in the same realm he had.

I returned home to the United States on October 27th 2001 with my inner and outer realities changed in ways that guaranteed that my world and my place in it would never be the same and there was no going back to the old ways.

Ever.

THIRTEEN

Caught Between The Worlds

In spite of the madness and tragedy of 2001 and the subsequent blow to **Land Without Evil's** hard won rising sales, 2002 became one of life's peaks for me. I had my own adopted family who I loved deeply, I owned two houses, and had a great job as a manager overseeing twenty-five technicians in eighteen buildings taking care of all the computer equipment in the largest employee owned technology company in the country. All of the hassles of purchasing a home for my new family, moving in and remodeling were done and I looked forward to settling into a new family life.

My buddy Hawk had enrolled in a two year shamanic study program that met every two months to travel to the Amazon to study Ayahuasca shamanism, to the Andes to study Andean Huachuma shamanism, Mexico to study Huichol Peyote shamanism, and locations throughout the United States to study American Indian shamanism. Hawk was in the first two year program and the second one was scheduled to begin in May of 2003.

Some of my friends said it would be a waste of time and money because I already knew plenty, but I thought I had a lot more to learn, and this opportunity exceeded anything I could get from any formal institutions. The prospect of experiencing Huichol and Andean shamanism along with more in-depth study of American Indian shamanism became a powerful draw for me, especially after doing Ayahuasca ceremonies with the people leading the two year study.

I wanted to do the program with all my heart and struggled to figure out how to do it while keeping up with my work responsibilities.

My boss Rob, who was one of my best friends, supported me in this, but I had doubts about my ability to navigate the extended time off needed to complete the study. In the interim I attended more ceremonies with the teachers while trying to find a way to participate in what I saw as a rare opportunity to learn things on levels beyond anything most never get to experience.

I remained dedicated to my original group and did three ceremonies a year on Easter weekend and three around Thanksgiving along with five in the jungle for a total of eleven. I added nine more with the new teachers bringing the total number of ceremonies to twenty a year.

When I wasn't participating in Ayahuasca ceremonies I did LSD, mushrooms, DMT, MDMA, and a number of research chemicals like 2CT7, 2CB, and many others from the Sasha Shulgin library. I also smoked 5MEODMT frequently and guided hundreds of people through that experience as well as first journeys with LSD, mushrooms, MDMA, and other substances.

My rekindled passion for altered states drove me to push the boundaries, exploring any limits to perception I could find. Aside from the variety of experiences I discovered many novel substances, but the wildest, most exotic inner and outer landscapes originated from the timeless primordial depths of the Peruvian Amazon. I returned there in October of 2002 for my third shamanic plant dieta, drawn like the proverbial moth to the flame to embrace the mysteries it held.

I flew out of Carlsbad California on Friday morning October 11th 2002 thinking about my primary intention which was to try and heal people at a distance, particularly my mother who had been diagnosed with colon cancer and other friends and family who also suffered from cancer. I noticed crows when I brought Penny's son to school and again at the airport. Once on board the plane I took out the book I brought to read titled, **Circle of Shaman: Healing Through Ecstasy, Rhythm, and Myth,** and opened it right to a chapter about using the raven for healing at a distance.

I watched three movies on the flight from LAX to Lima on LED screens in the back of the chairs which was the first time seeing screens like that on planes. Fourteen people converged in Lima consisting of five women and nine men evenly split with seven Canadians and seven Americans. The Canadians were from the town of Nelson in British Columbia. Most of them were older than me, but some of the women were my age. I roomed with and became fast friends with Terence, one of them on the way there. I also met a chiropractor about ten years older than me who had an office in Escondido California close to where I lived, who I am calling Dog for reasons that will become apparent later.

We slept for four hours in Miraflores in Lima and had a buffet breakfast at the hotel before flying to Pucallpa where José and Ronaldo met us. Tito La Rosa, an Andean sound healer and Grammy winning musician who specialized in pre-Columbian instruments would be joining us in the jungle.

With little sleep I felt beat and had a persistent headache from caffeine withdrawal from giving up coffee which plagued me when I went to sleep in the hotel in Pucallpa that night. We headed out to the jungle the next morning, first in cars down muddy dusty dirt roads to the village, then in long canoes upriver to the shaman's camp. I felt fortunate to land the very last tambo at the end of the row that lined the river with nothing but jungle on the other side of it. This isolated magical spot on a small promontory close to the continuous white noise of rapids became my home away from home this year and for the next nine years of dietas.

It had been raining so the river was high allowing us to take canoes right up to the camp instead of trudging through the jungle. I looked forward to the dieta while battling major internal resistance to it like I did the last two times I came. Once I was there my situation had its own self-contained motivation similar to skydiving where you have the choice of that one step, then you are committed with no turning back.

We had a group meal Sunday night where we planned our first session for Monday night and four more sessions every other night after that. The plan for me was to work with the rare Ushpawasha Sanango, Guillermo's specialty. Ronaldo told me it was a small tree a few meters tall that was ash colored under the leaf that grew in a dangerous snake infested hilly region near Chazuta. The bark and the root had to be used, so the tree had to be killed which is a big part of why it was so rare. Yoda and I would be the only ones working with it. I felt lucky because this was my third dieta and I was becoming seasoned enough for this rare privilege. Ronaldo told me that Ushpawasha opens your heart and helps you to remember.

That night I discovered a fist-sized tarantula perched at the opening of his burrow beside my tambo doorway and loved having him as a roommate. I slept the longest I had in weeks and awoke from vivid nonsensical dreams feeling very good. I felt obligated to record them as part of my psychological adventure and to track how the dreams and visions from my subconscious played off of each other, particularly with the rare gift of Ushpawasha I was about to receive.

I went into a restaurant with somebody. I was wearing a trench coat carrying a long knife. Two guys came and grabbed me and the person I was with, putting them in a headlock. The reason they were upset is because I had a big knife.

People were upset about the terrorist situation and they threw us out of the restaurant. I couldn't understand why I went into the restaurant with the knife out in the first place as I had no intention of causing trouble or hurting anybody.

I was looking to steal a car to get away, then got in a pickup truck driven by an older lady who was one of my writer friends. She was supposed to stay with me but I took off with the truck and drove to the end of the street without her. The brakes barely worked and the gas pedal seemed stuck. I turned the truck around and went back to get her dodging other trucks and driving on the other side of the street like they do in the movies, and together we went back to a house.

Next I was in school in a class. I left and couldn't find out where my class was and didn't know where I was supposed to be, then I was in a math class and didn't know where I was supposed to sit. The teacher rambled on about some math problems but I had no idea what he was talking about. When the class was over I went from desk to desk trying to find my books and other things and finally found my desk which had a binder on it with the logo of the technology company I worked for. I had to open it to make sure it was mine.

When I figured out that it was mine a girl showed up and gave me a hard time as if I was stealing her things. I tried to tell her that I wasn't going through her stuff and that it was mine. I saw a heavy set younger guy who worked for me in real life who had on a beret and was hanging around with some gang members, but I wasn't worried because the guy who worked for me was a good guy and he was having fun.

I went into a room and found three guys floating a few feet off the ground. At first I thought they were on invisible strings, then I floated up like them and said, "See, I can do this too!" I asked them how long they had been able to float and spent some time floating around the room with them on the verge of becoming lucid, but I didn't.

Next I was lying down somewhere with a beautiful woman. Both of us were nude, but it wasn't sexual. She needed comfort somehow. Penny and another unknown guy were present. I was worried about her being jealous as things had not been sexual, then the beautiful woman said she was leaving, so I got together with

Penny who was understanding about all of it. What I thought were submarines came in large groups that floated by looking like upside down boats. We followed them after they passed and they made noise that made an angry complaining man come out of his house.

As disjointed as my dream sequences unfolded, they had an underlying narrative spoken in the cryptic alien emotional conceptual symbolism of right brain languaging. Though nonsensical, these dreams had been vivid and emotion packed almost to the point of me becoming lucid. The first part with the knives and confrontation in the restaurant followed by looking to steal a car to escape tapped in to my fear based aggression from earlier in my life woven in with my newer concerns of terrorism.

The problem with operating the car and truck involving my writer friends followed by my classic being lost, trying to find my way around school, finding my books, and the confusion of that reflected long standing fears about the direction of my life.

After that passage I found freedom, almost to lucidity, ending with me in an intimate non-sexual situation comforting a beautiful woman at the risk of making Penny jealous because I was helping people which reflected recent concerns.

They brought me my first pitcher of Ushpawasha that morning and told me it was bitter and I responded saying, "*Everything* that I drink here is bitter."

They told me to drink three glasses a day, so I downed the first glass which *was* bitter and left a long lasting aftertaste, but it didn't seem as bitter as Chuchuwasi. I soon felt altered and mildly stimulated like I had taken a light dose of amphetamine and I became lightheaded with a gentle overall sense of pleasant buzzing.

They brought rice and plátanos for breakfast a little while later. After that José came for a short visit and enjoyed the sound of the rapids with me and told me how the sound of rushing water was healing.

The **Circle of Shaman** book I was reading talked about the psychological breakdown that happens prior to growth when you outgrow the form you hold as a container for what you have learned, forcing it to break outside its restrictions. To grow outside the structure you inhabit based on truths and untruths you have to break it and go through heartache and chaos that brings new understanding and a new way of being. When you are in the midst of it you don't know it and don't realize it which adds to the difficulty.

This experience is referred to as getting swallowed by the jaguar when your shadow rises up and consumes you. I had gone through it a few years earlier and nearly killed myself after taking a concoction of water, honey, chocolate, and nine grams of dried Psilocybe Cubensis mushrooms with thirteen Hawaiian Baby Woodrose seeds when I was depressed.

When you live in and touch the past you relive those traumas over and over again. When you go forward you have nothing to go to because you don't have any experience to base it on. You have to go past the emptiness and wait for a new motive or new way of being to come from your heart in order to act correctly.

The Ushpawasha acted fast and I felt good buzzing along with no edge and a heightened awareness. When I went to eat my plátanos and rice my appetite had diminished, so instead of forcing myself I threw out half of it. I drank my second glass of Ushpawasha and continued buzzing. Lying down I fell fast asleep slipping into a wild panic state. I couldn't wake up for quite some time and struggled, stuck in a hypnagogic no man's land between waking and dreaming. An ongoing theme appeared to be resurfacing in these dreams.

I drove down a highway and couldn't see where I was going because my eyes were closed and I couldn't open them. The car moved fast and Penny was telling me to take a certain exit. I somehow made it even though I couldn't see.

We drove down the street to her apartment. She drove and I tried to get her to move over because I couldn't get into the driver's seat to get to the gas pedal and brakes. I tried to steer but couldn't see again.

I kept hearing voices and couldn't wake up. I thought of this as a metaphor for our lives together represented by the car and for how fast it all happened. I thought the brakes, the gas, and the loss of my ability to see and drive, and the confusion over who was driving were valid subconscious concerns in light of how integrated our lives became, so the inability to open my eyes and see held a powerful premonition of great significance.

I kept trying to wake up and thought I was walking around a neighbor's house. I couldn't see or walk, but I was trying to move around. A lot of people were going in the water and I tried to move around there then I was at the Santa Barbara Writers conference where I saw a friend who had lost a lot of weight and gained it back again which was upsetting. I was late for the conference and kept trying to find my workshop but couldn't find it on the schedule and I couldn't see what time it was which was the same scenario of my lost in school dreams.

Some of the people I was in the jungle with were having a workshop at the conference and asked me if they could pick plants at the hotel to make flower bouquets. I said no because I thought the hotel would think they were damaging their flowers and see it as vandalism.

Recurring themes were being in a car, not being able to see, going fast, not being able to drive, not being able to get to the gas or brakes, fear of crashing, and being in a place of learning whether as a student or a teacher not knowing where my classroom was or how to find it.

When I pushed to wake up I almost made it and clearly heard a strong male voice, but I didn't know what it said. When I did lie down I didn't feel tired and was surprised at how quickly I fell asleep experiencing mild visionary patterns.

I was supposed to drink three glasses of Ushpawasha and had drank two, so I downed the third one after waking up. It felt like hours had passed trapped in my struggling hypnagogic state of semi-dreaming. My feeling after this first pitcher was that Ushpawasha was powerful and brought up recurring patterns that I thought of as buried fears, something I wanted to explore on deeper levels.

A dinner of runny quinoa and a plátano came around 4:00 that afternoon prior to the upcoming night's session which I thought would provide good substance for the purges I anticipated. Yoda came by and when I told him about my dreams he told me everyone was dreaming vividly. We thought it was the collective energy of the group. I felt stimulated every time I drank the Ushpawasha which kept my mind spinning while making me sleep most of the day after sleeping most of the night.

I had my quartz and the chipped stone spearhead gifted to me by Lorenzo to keep in each hand in the coming Monday night's journey. The brew came from wild plants as opposed to cultivated ones and I was prepared to go to hell because the more I went to hell the more heavenly visions I would get to balance it out.

Darkness was the price I had to pay to get the reward of the light.

FOURTEEN

Moving From Light Through Dark Desperate Panic

I came back from our first session around 1:00 in the morning and took my plant bath to wash off a night of profuse sweating and record my experience feeling cool and refreshed singing icaros with wrong mangled words, but the melodies kept playing in my head. We had a great session enhanced by the presence of Tito La Rosa who had arrived that day. We had a total of eighteen people in the group and my new Canadian friends were all a great caring and loving addition to the mix.

My visions came on fast and chaotic and things changed so rapidly I couldn't make sense out of anything. I was up, down, and all over the place overwhelmed by what felt like a multitude of spirits streaking through different dimensions. At first I felt things bubbling below the surface, then I had a sudden purge that sent me down into the darkness of Penny's ex-husband's family shit that I was dealing with in my daily life.

I had the sense when I went into the darkness that everyone in the circle came with and supported me in those murky depths bringing a beautiful light shower that I can only describe as wide, sparkling, and expansive. Compared to the last time I went hard into the same darkness, this time felt like I went in and out with surgical precision. It felt physically uncomfortable. One second I felt like I had to shit and in the next I had to piss. These alternating sensations kept changing rapid-fire making me incoherent, not knowing which end was up or what was going on with my body.

Everything felt incredibly powerful as José, Ronaldo, Tito and Yoda went around to each of us singing, playing music, and doing healings, creating a beautiful experience all around. Tito danced and played pre-Columbian flutes and panpipes which made phenomenal sounds, many of which I had never heard before. I also experienced amplified audio experiences where tiny sounds from across the room sounded loud, startling me as if they were right beside me.

In the midst of passing through a mass of chaos Tito started playing *The Prophecy of the Eagle and the Condor.* As soon as he started playing I snapped back into the moment and became lucid and grounded, staying that way for the rest of the night. In my lucid moments Yoda told us one of his stories that carried extra impact in such a wide open receptive state.

"You walk into a tall building and discover that it is full of diverse stores that sell you habits. You can purchase all the habits you want so you pick up habits until you get to the point where you have collected more than you can carry in a shopping cart that is full before you know it to the point where you need another cart.

You soon fill it up and move along with two full carts until you can't carry any more. You want to find your way out and realize that you are deep into the building and can't find your way out. You look and look until you finally see a sign that says EXIT by an elevator that says it goes to the 37th floor and you wonder how you will get out.

You are lost and there is no place else to go so you get on the elevator and take everything up to the 37th floor where you find a computerized ATM machine that says if you want to exit you have to press a button. You're lost and need to get out, and there is nothing else to do except press the button. You press it and it spits out a contract that says you can only keep one third of all the habits you collected. You read the fine print, sign the contract, press the button, and feed the contract back in. The machine scans it and you get back into the elevator and go down to the first floor where you go out into the street with a third of the habits you had and go home happy. You sleep peacefully for the first time in a long time because you now only have a third of your original habits."

A little later Yoda gave us a gem of a one-liner that said, "You need to burn the mask that you put on in order to get affection."

Another message that came throughout the night said that unconditional love rules all which is what is needed to go forward in all things, especially when dealing with adversaries. My easier journey into the darkness showed me this as I never became overwhelmed and kept more objectivity throughout the whole experience.

After my plant bath and journal recording I fell fast asleep, sleeping deep and dreamless and awoke feeling ravenous. Breakfast finally came and after that Rolando spent some time with me drawing pictures and diagrams, teaching me about Ushpawasha and how it opened your heart and helped you to remember.

I had a premonition that all the chaos and darkness I was going through personally was a preview of what was coming for humanity as a whole and I felt blessed to go through it first so that I would be past it when it hit everybody else collectively, bringing me compassion which I felt would be guided by spirit.

I saw myself as a holographic microcosm, honored to be among the first to embrace and pass through the pain that came with the chaos of death and rebirth that the human race was hurtling toward. I accepted myself as water that is both the drop and the ocean riding the peak of a fast breaking wave. I thought of my Mother as my guiding inspiration for unconditional love. I was starving when dinner came consisting of rice and a plátano with no chicken or fish which was the second day in a row with no protein. I had a dull headache and thought it was my body trying to adjust to the diet and my different set of circumstances.

The night came with thunder. Tito stayed in my tambo from last year and I was two tambos further down at the end. He started playing a flute amidst the sound of thunder which felt magical. My dull headache continued and I felt spun up, antsy, and wound up like I was approaching a breakdown; maybe my time for a personal pre-collective moment of chaos. I thought I needed to make a big effort to go deep for longer. One of our coming ceremonies would be on a full moon and I considered that night as the one to do a second dose of Ayahuasca. I thought back to my last session the previous year and felt trepidation about a repeat performance, but I knew that passing through fear was the price I had to pay to go into the darkness and the secret rewards it held.

Before going to bed I went to the latrine and thought I had better check before sitting down and found a big centipede waiting for me on the seat. After that adventure I kept feeling steadily worse. My head hurt, my stomach became upset, and I felt on edge, jumping at small noises and feeling oversensitive. My burgeoning headache and equally uncomfortable stomach upset grew to unbearable proportions, driving me to take three aspirins and crawl into bed under my mosquito net hoping to escape from my misery into sleep. I felt so horrible I prayed for relief, then I relaxed some and slipped into a tossing, turning, twisted, and sweating uncomfortable sleep, awakening in the pitch black of the night shaken from a terrifying nightmare.

I was at a military base and sent an email about getting a year off to go somewhere. It came back because I had sent it to a wrong address and I knew I was in trouble for sending it to the wrong place, so some guys came to kill me. They caught me and I was resigned to dying, but managed to escape through some doors.

They tried to recapture me and I saw a group of people out in a parking lot. I tried to get them to help me but nobody would. I screamed and cursed them out, making a scene while my enemies continued pursuing me. I ran and a mysterious guy figured things out and got in a car with me. Somewhere in the time between when they found me in the building and captured me they shot me and I was now gut shot. They kept coming and continued chasing me in the car, then cops came after me too. We went around corners and smashed into things, zig-zagging while they were shooting. I didn't have anything to shoot back with, so I spit and threw stuff at them in desperation.

The chase continued with crashing cars and throwing things at them until we ended up in a small parking lot where I jumped out of the car. Two or three people chased me all over the lot. A big rock, can, or bullet hit me in the stomach, causing great pain. I dodged between two of my pursuers and ran by a storefront, then turned around and saw an older lady holding me at gunpoint with a .357.

She sneezed and pulled the trigger but I grabbed the gun and pointed it toward her causing her to shoot herself. A real cop arrived and I had the gun and was going to shoot her again, but the cop talked me out of it so I handed him the gun and woke up.

I was afraid to wake up more fearing that my headache would come back, but I had to piss so I gently got up, relieved myself and crawled back into bed thinking about my car thief friends that I grew up with in Dorchester when they were chased by a motorcycle cop and threw a full beer can at him, knocking out his teeth. When the cops caught up with my friends they beat the shit out of them with fists, feet, and billy clubs. I also remembered when I began working with and paying attention to my dreams, with few exceptions, they had all been violent. In one of them I had an intense shootout with my father and in many of them the gun didn't work right, I had the wrong bullets, or I couldn't find any. I also remembered dreams where I blew myself up and died in other ways.

I thought about how I felt sick, spun up, and antsy like I was approaching some kind of a breakdown prior to my nightmare, then I remembered my leg bouncing out of control on its own volition when I ate earlier and how I had to stop it and how I was in a bad mood with the growing headache prior to my added stomach upset.

I didn't know if the dark experiences and physical discomfort would continue but I was resigned to accept and get through them hoping it might be the proverbial peeling back of the onion. I also thought of the repeated themes running through my dreams; being lost and unable to find my way to classes in school, then lost in the same way at the writers conference, then violent chase dreams with guns that often didn't work.

Yes, Ushpawasha helped me to remember, but in ways I never could have imagined. I hoped that returning to and navigating my fears would bring me peace. One of the interesting things about this last desperate nightmare is that I did get help, first by the mysterious stranger who showed up in the car, then by the cop I surrendered to after shooting the older lady.

I remembered reading a book on lucid dreaming that said in a chase dream you should turn around and confront or embrace your pursuers which was something I did when I could, but in this case things happened too fast and too intense to get a chance to think. Both my dreams and many of my visions came too fast for me to think, so all I could do was react and in the midst of my internal conflict I felt that parts of me were catching up with me and parts of me were running.

Now that this episode completed itself I felt better and hoped that a cycle had passed that would not repeat itself. Though I felt fearful and woke up sweaty and uncomfortable from nightmares, I felt stronger and had more of an attitude toward it and considered taking two doses in the coming night's ceremony. I was prepared to go deep into Hell if I needed to clear out whatever shit I was holding on to. With those thoughts I fell back asleep and felt better waking up that Wednesday morning, hopefully on the upswing after more dreams.

I was with Penny's family in a house. First we tried to go shopping. She wanted me to buy a Halloween costume, but I needed a car battery and we fought over it. She got mad, I got out of the car, and she drove away, then I was back at the house.

My nephew showed up and we were having a good time visiting with Penny's family, including her parents, then out of the corner of my eye I saw my former unethical publicist there with someone she was using for her own gains and it seemed like they deserved to be used by her. I wondered how she had gotten there, then she was gone.

Next I entered into two swimming meets at different schools. One was a relay race and the other was an out and out race. I won the relay race and had to travel some distance to the other school where I entered the second swimming race against some high school kids. I won and got a big trophy and everyone was proud of me. My former fiancé and a younger teenage girl who was like a little sister to Penny showed up and hugged me. My mother was there and I kept saying, "Jeez, I never even trained for this. Not bad for a fifty year old man. Gee Mom, I hope you're not mad at me for picking on the little kids."

I came out of it hoping I was done with the sickness and headache. I felt groggy but otherwise clear, like I had gone through some kind of cleansing and purging that started with dreadful jittery anticipation and increasing discomfort to the point of extreme sickness. I hoped I had hit a pocket of darkness that needed clearing and that it could be validated by the literal award winning dream that followed my horrendous nightmare and I was curious to see what would come next.

Breakfast came of quinoa and a plátano with no chicken or fish and at this point I had gone three days with no protein. I spent the afternoon listening to the magical sounds of Tito playing his flutes coming to me through the jungle in the soft rain amidst the sweet songs of crickets and other trilling insects and animals.

FIFTEEN

The Prophecy Of The Eagle And The Condor

I sat air drying in the buff in the predawn hours of Thursday morning recording my experiences from our second ceremony on Wednesday night, stating once again that I had the most incredible journey of my whole life. Just when I thought it couldn't get any better, it did. It was deep, intense, and it took me through a plethora of wild places.

I gagged down a healthy dose and my visions quickly flourished into the most amazing, brightest, fluorescent neon colors I had ever seen, and yes, words fall pitifully short describing them, but to the best of my ability I flew endlessly through fantastic spaces where spirits and beings came to me seemingly from everywhere.

José, Tito, and Ronaldo moved around the maloca and when they moved into certain spaces I saw spirits moving with them in what I could only describe as magical energy domes created by the music that carried us all along. José sang and chanted while I and others drummed along with him summoning a dizzying mixture of spirits. I felt overwhelmed to the point where I didn't think I could take anymore and they kept coming with escalating intensity until I went into a dark space to battle with Penny's ex-husband.

I had fallen into a similar space the previous year and felt hopeless until condor came to me and provided a turning point that brought me back. The result of that put us into a new second house for Penny and her kids. In this inner battle her ex had dark allies that came like big vultures that I fought on my own without any sense of hopelessness or helplessness and I didn't feel like I needed any help in the thick of it.

I dove deep into combat fighting with my eyes closed, then I felt

Tito, Ronaldo and José standing over me blowing tobacco smoke while singing and chanting and I sensed an army of spirits behind them. It was an incredible loving event. I didn't expect help and didn't feel like I needed it, but their presence made me feel strong, triumphant, and empowered. At one point I got a whiff of Agua de Florida which sent me into a deep satisfying purge.

I saw a multitude of spirits and sprite-like wood nymphs and I felt they came so strong and powerfully to me because of the amazing loving group I was with, especially my new friends from Canada. The manifesting spirits and energies went on for a long time and I never wanted it to end.

Later in the session Tito moved around the circle playing and dancing. One of our group had become sick with fever and they spent a lot of time around him while the rest of us sang, danced, clapped, and stomped our feet, directing our energy toward our sick friend.

The energy of the group rose while Tito spun around wildly dancing and hopping on one foot, jumping over a candle, and playing his heart out while most of the group stood up and danced. I rose and danced, putting my arms out, waving them like Condor wings, honoring the Condor with my dance. We went through that magical moment for a seemingly interminable time. The only word that comes close to describing the experience is ineffable.

Yoda told stories and one particular pearl of wisdom stood out when he spoke about the past saying, "You shouldn't let the past bother you too much because the past has a big weakness which is envy because the past is trying to be here and now, but it can't because the past is no more, which makes it powerless. There is only now."

This dieta in 2002 came before cell phones and he told another story in this context.

Imagine that you are going to call a friend. You dial the number and an authoritative voice that you don't recognize picks up the phone and says, "Hello, this is not an answering machine. This is a questioning machine and there are two questions. The first question is, who are you, really?

The second question is what is it that you really want out of life?"

Then it says, "You have three minutes to answer and don't babble."

After his story they did individual healings and when my turn came they blessed me with Agua de Florida and shook rattles around me.

Tito played to me and spun a wind wand or a bullroarer around me which seemed to open up other dimensions that made me feel cleansed, fortified, and strengthened.

My hands cramped up on me which concerned me because it had happened the previous year later into the dieta. This was the second ceremony only a few days in with three ceremonies and another week to go. My concern heightened because my father died from Lou Gehrig's disease known as Amyotrophic lateral sclerosis or ALS, an incurable nervous system disease that weakens muscles, impacts physical function, and leads to death. I felt relief when Yoda said it probably came from drinking too much Ayahuasca.

When the ceremony ended Tito could not find his way back to his tambo, so I felt honored to guide him back on the way to my own tambo at the end of the trail.

One of his renowned songs was **The Prophecy of the Eagle and the Condor** which he won a Grammy award for with a recording of it with native American flautist Mary Youngblood.

The Eagle and the Condor prophecy speaks of a long ago time when human societies split into two different paths, that of the Eagle, and that of the Condor. The path of the Condor is the path of heart, intuition, and the feminine. The path of the Eagle is the path of the mind, the industrial, and the masculine.

The prophecy says that the 1490s would begin a 500-year period during which the Eagle people would become so powerful that they would nearly drive the Condor people out of existence. This can be seen in the voyage of Columbus, the subsequent conquering of the Americas, and the killing and oppressing of indigenous people in the five hundred years that followed, up to and including the present.

The prophecy says that during the next five hundred year period, beginning in 1990, the potential would arise for the Eagle and the Condor to come together, fly in the same sky and create a new level of consciousness for humanity. The prophecy only speaks of the potential and it is up to humanity to activate it and ensure that a new consciousness can arise.

My new Canadian brothers and sisters came to the jungle deeply steeped in native American lore and practices and sang native American songs and danced. Jim and Carol, the main husband and wife of the group had participated for four years running in the native American Sun Dance which originated deep in the past. In this ceremony participants request power or insight from the supernatural. The dance requires up to a year's preparation by those pledging to dance and a dance structure is built with a central pole that symbolizes the axis mundi, a connection to the divine, embodied by the sun.

Those who pledged to endure the Sun Dance do it to seek spiritual power and insight. Supplicants begin dancing at an appointed hour and continue intermittently for four days and nights. Self-mortification is done through piercing by inserting two or more skewers made of chokecherry wood through a small fold of the supplicant's skin on their chest or upper back. Long rawhide thongs tie a heavy object like a buffalo skull to the skewers. The dancer drags the object along the ground looking up at the sun until they succumb to exhaustion or their skin tears free. The thongs are tied to the center pole and the supplicant either hangs from or pulls on them until free.

I have done a lot of challenging things to advance my spirituality but I don't think I could go as far as my friends did which gave me even more respect for them.

All of this played into my thinking of the eagle as the sacred bird of North America and the condor as the Sacred Bird of South America. I felt a strong sense that I was becoming an integral part of this prophecy based on the timing of it, the profound experiences I was going through, and the deep seated native American spirituality of my new Canadian brothers and sisters. This had even greater significance for me in the way that the spirit of the condor came to me and became my ally as a gift from Guillermo.

SIXTEEN

The Condor's Kiss

I felt clear for the first time in months on Thursday morning and the icing on the cake was chicken and a plátano after four days of no protein which invigorated me. I went swimming in the river and drank my second glass of that day's Ushpawasha. After lying down I felt like I had just dozed off when I awoke to my second meal of the day, but I had been sleeping most of the day.

That evening in a break between ceremonies Tito gave us a concert in the maloca and showed us all of his flutes and panpipes, one of which was fashioned out of Condor feather quills. He played and sang a Condor song, blessing us with Condor feathers while blowing and fanning sweet scented Palo Santo smoke on us. He also played the flute into our heads and into our chests to our hearts. When he came to me flapping his Condor feathers, caressing my face with them, and beating them against my chest and head I trembled and broke out in tears. The power of this beautiful experience convinced me that Condor was my spirit totem. I had always thought of wolf as my main totem and knew it would always be with me, but now Condor took the stage, front and center.

Back at my tambo I drank my third and last glass of Ushpawasha for the day and went to sleep hearing nearly audible voices in my head, and awoke feeling weak on Friday morning from more chaotic dreams.

I was looking for classes at a college with my sister in law and felt conflicted because I wanted to take classes, but part of me didn't want to. A cop showed up with a dog that playfully bit my hands which became a little bloody from puncture holes from his teeth. I tried to make a big scene and exaggerate it so I could sue the cop, but it wasn't the cop's dog.

My brother showed up and I saw a broken camera that someone had kicked and stomped on. My brother said he was looking for his camera, and I said, "Oh man, I hope that wasn't it." I picked it up and said, "Is this it?"

He said, "Yeah, thanks." He was bummed out because it was broken and I felt bad for him.

Next I was downtown San Diego heading toward Point Loma on a bicycle and people recognized me as a writer. I rode my bike behind a group of them and an attractive woman with dark hair told me that she liked my older author photos from the 1994 back cover of **The Small Dark Room of the Soul**, *my first published book better than the author photo on* **Land Without Evil.**

I agreed, particularly since the older picture was of a younger me.

People on their bikes stopped in front of me, slowing me down and I became impatient. I kept riding along but the pedals on the bike skipped and there were other small malfunctions. I kept going and met up with some family members and we headed back toward downtown San Diego, something that we had done as a family in real life a number of times. We all moved along, then a guy pulled up in an old car with steam coming out of the radiator and he needed help. I tried to help and his car turned into a panel truck housing a machine shop and we got things fixed.

In the next segment I was in a weird coffee shop with a strange gay guy dressed in a black trench coat with long black spiky hair. He said he was a publicist who would help me out with my book. He pulled out a big artist's posterboard case that carried painting canvases and said that he checked up on me and they knew about me, but they didn't think much of me, but he had booked me into some coffee shops to do readings. One of them was in New Orleans, one was in Boston, and the rest in three or four other places, then he took what he had and ripped them into pieces and tried to stuff them up my ass!

I pushed him away, took all the pieces and held them in a metal shower room drain. They smelled bad and I tried to figure out what he was doing. Was he messing with me? Was it a test? Was he trying to see how bad I wanted it? I had all the pieces and realized that it was a drain I held, so I put it back in the floor and kept the pieces of paper.

My dream shifted and I was late getting to the Southern California Writers Conference. I had a room at the hotel and my name was on the podium where I was supposed to speak. I had a good speech planned but I wasn't prepared and didn't know what to say, then I knew what it would be and realized that I didn't have my name tag. I went down the hall and couldn't find it until I saw a sign that pointed to the registration table where I found it. The name tag was oversized, like three feet by three feet, and it said something like, "Matt Pallamary, late again as usual." It looked so big that I couldn't wear it on my front so I pinned it on my back like a sandwich board, went out and found the conference director and told him what happened.

He said, "Nobody was at registration?"

I told him I found my badge and he said, "That's good."

One of the guys who worked for me and sold me cannabis wanted something. First he wanted one, then two, then four, six, and more, so I asked him to wait for me at the coffee shop. It turned into a karate studio with some guys who wanted to fight. I was willing to fight and they all thought they were badasses, but I wasn't afraid of them. I told them I didn't have my sparring gear with me. The guy who ran the place said it was a tournament and I had won first place beating this guy, but I had no memory of doing that. When they were going to close I saw that he and his wife lived in something like a closet on the side of the studio.

My employee was waiting for me at the coffee shop and the weird publicist was still there asking me to wait. I got fed up and walked out to find my employee still waiting and I apologized to him. Together we walked down the street past a bunch of punk rock gay people who were razzing us because they thought we were military. My employee and I figured out that the bike I had been riding earlier was also not working and the broken car I thought I fixed was not working either. He had a car and started driving away so I ran after him chasing him up and down streets.

I couldn't figure out why I was chasing him and finally stopped him. I got in the car and asked why he had taken off and was he pissed at me. He said yes and acted weird and pissed off because I made him wait for so long at the coffee shop. The car was an old white Ford that was supposed to be my car. My employee was going to let me drive so I got in the driver's seat and I was still lost.

I asked which way to go and he told me to go down a side street. We got lost and went down another street that turned into a dead end with some rocks. Every place he told me to go was wrong and I became frustrated with him. He kept saying he wanted more of something from me and I said, "You ain't getting nothing from me because you are jerking me around giving me the wrong directions."

We stayed lost trying to figure out how to find the way, then I realized that I had on my Air Force field jacket. The sleeve was greasy from trying to fix the car and my hands were dirty from the shower drain I had been holding, so I felt frustrated on all fronts.

I woke up on Friday morning to the sound of rushing water from the fast rising river that had swelled from night rains and I felt depressed but looking forward to the third mid-session that coming night in spite of the fact that I felt depleted. It would be the last ceremony with Tito.

I thought about my long convoluted dream and named it the frustration dream because everything I tried to achieve was thwarted. I thought about how I tried to publish **Land Without Evil** with a clear intent and a good heart and got screwed over, first by my unethical publicist, then by the 911 tragedy. All of those disappointments appeared to be summed up in the successive failures of this dream.

I hoped that re-experiencing the emotions of my litany of failures would serve as an active processing exercise that would clear out the negativity that I still held in my subconscious and I hoped to correct how I was not right with it all.

Ushpawasha helps you to remember. No argument there!

The dark nightmare I had of getting shot I thought of as a dream of fears. I hoped that I would continue to be touched by spirit to work through these dark energies during the course of this dieta. In the end I resolved to forge ahead and keep going with the pursuit of my goals in spite of all my failures.

Breakfast came of quinoa and a single plátano. Since Sunday I only had one piece of chicken over the course of five days. My friend Jim from Canada of the Sun Ceremony fame came for a visit and read me some writings from Hafez a 14th century Persian poet which lifted my spirits and I felt more energized after drinking my first glass of Ushpawasha for the day.

SEVENTEEN

Stories In The Dark

I came back from our third session and the last ceremony with Ronaldo and Tito feeling clear, exhausted, and highly aware. I sat in the darkness of its aftermath in the pre-dawn recording my impressions. Yoda suggested the possibility of a smaller dose, but to gauge ourselves on what we thought was best. I asked him and José if they would pick for me and José gave me a solid full dose which gave me a completely different journey from the previous ceremony.

The medicine came on slow while the icaros and music moved ahead and I thought nothing would happen until spirits came to me. One in particular came right up to my face and looked me in the eye. I looked into its face which I can only describe as looking into infinity while Ronaldo sang icaros, then I saw the outline of a body that looked totally black. I saw infinity inside of Ronaldo the same way I saw it in the spirit that came up to my face. He struck me as being egoless, standing as a portal between infinity, the cosmos, and the here and now, bringing energy through as if he were there and not there at the same time as if I perceived *his* bilocation.

I saw other vague things, but the session seemed to be progressing lightly and nobody purged for a long time adding to my sense of a slow start. I thought that things wouldn't go any further and had weird thoughts when the dose hit me full force, sending me flying into diverse places where I saw and experienced innumerable things.

I was the first to have a hard purge which didn't last long, but went deep, bringing up a mass of phlegm from my lungs. After that I sat back and flew through colors, places, patterns, and dimensions to the point where my physical discomfort became unbearable. I wanted to purge again, but couldn't. I was held in that torturous place for what felt like an eternity and had no choice but to endure the agony and thought of it as a teaching. The rapid landscape continued unfolding and I became acutely aware of myself as a flying spirit. Condor came and flew with me making my crossed leg wings flap. I spent a lot of time trying to heal my sister in law's sister of cancer and a lady friend whose boyfriend had recently died of cancer who asked me to try and heal her from dying. I also spent quality time with my mother.

Penny and her kids came to me in a sweet loving way. I swooped down, gathered them into my heart, and held them close with loving energy, inspired by the flutes I heard which brought me visions of butterflies, something I associated with Penny and her kids.

Tito played throughout the ceremony and someone sang a beautiful song in Spanish that I partially understood about an earthen jug and how our remains were buried in it, and of how quickly the time passed with so many things we wanted to do or things that we did.

I also was gratified to enjoy beautiful icaros sung by Carlos, the young apprentice who had assisted Guillermo with my healing the year before. He had come a long way from his first ceremony that I had been part of two years prior. It had been the first time he drank Ayahuasca and he lost control to the point of being taken out of the circle and now he was singing icaros. As my passage levelled out Yoda told more stories, one by an unknown Russian poet which went like this.

"The sun burst into a million shards and a million shards of sunlight fell upon the earth. Night came and people fought over and killed each other for them. I went out and took the shards while the others fought over them and stole and hid them within my heart and I am never cold."

In another story Yoda said to imagine your consciousness floating out in the cosmos when you come upon a department store. You walk in and buy a body which you take over. You are happy with your purchase and you go home and have that body for a number of years until you discover over time that it is defective, so you get the phone number for the place that makes bodies and call them to get the service department. The phone rings and they pick it up, but it is not the service department, it is the creation department and they don't do service. You ask. "Who else can I talk to?"

The creation department says, "We can send you to the whining department but that will be a waste of time. They have an answering machine that you can whine into for as long as you want but it automatically erases your message so it won't get you anywhere. You call around trying to find out who else you can talk to and eventually end up at the office of the president where the line is picked up by a nice lady who sits opposite the president. You say, "I would like to speak to the president because I have a complaint."

She says, "The president hasn't been here for thousands of years."

You don't know what else to do and you shuffle around some more and try to get to different places. Each time you try, you get frustrated because each place sends you someplace else and you eventually find out that the president hasn't been there since the fish stopped singing in the waters and people stopped talking to the animals, so you have a defective body. You also learn that the defects were built in on purpose which frustrates you even more.

You finally say, "The hell with it. I'm going to fix it myself," and you get sent to the spare parts department. When you get there they say, "We don't make spare parts. That is a very special custom designed unit you have and you can't get spare parts for it."

Frustrated with no place left to go for help you decide to go home and deal with it, so you do that, brush it off, wash it, clean it up, and realize that it really wasn't working so bad after all.

Yoda also regaled us with another short verse.

"The garden of my life, I owe you nothing, and you owe me nothing, but the thorns that you prick and pierce me with are for the roses that I have stolen from you."

After dutifully making my journal recordings I crawled into bed under my mosquito net and was on the threshold of falling asleep in the predawn darkness when a huge tree fell close to my tambo. The sounds seemed to come from everywhere, like a herd of stampeding elephants, startling me to sit up straight, screaming with a pounding heart. Once I calmed back down, I managed to fall asleep, waking up on Saturday morning feeling worn out and physically dragging, but very good energetically and I could not wait to eat.

Ronaldo said there were big forces at work in the jungle where we were working and that the transformation of traveling through and enduring the heavens and hells that we were undergoing was on the leading edge of advance work for the rest of humanity. Our changes, growth, comprehension, expanded consciousness, and understanding meant that we were transforming and evolving to lead the way for the rest of humanity which indicated that there would be heavier things to deal with in the future.

We will have already been through it on a personal level before the rest of the collective which verified my earlier thoughts, feelings, and strong sense of becoming an integral part of the prophecy of the eagle and the condor and the profound experiences I was going through that connected with the native American spirituality of my new Canadian brothers and sisters. This effectively doubled down on the great significance all of this held for me that was confirmed in the way that the spirit of the condor became my ally as a gift from Guillermo.

I felt more and more certain of this with the passage of time in the same way that shamans of old hunted animals in their visions before following through in the physical world, as if the actual hunt had already occurred and the physical act simply followed through what already happened in the visionary state. This added confirmation of my secret inner thoughts would allow me to help guide people toward a new and greater awareness and higher consciousness worldwide, but it would take a lot of pain to get there.

A meal finally came of rice, a plátano and boca chica the local fish with tiny bones which was only the second time in an entire week that we got any protein. After eating I took a dunk in the river fighting off biting horseflies, then I filled up my bucket with water, took a guayusa plant bath, and stretched out in my hammock after drinking my first glass of Ushpawasha for the day.

EIGHTEEN

A Premonition Before Meeting My Many Selves

I felt good on Saturday night and looked forward to what might come to me in my dreams. Our last session would be Tuesday night on a full moon. We had three more days on the dieta and two more ceremonies. I went to sleep after dark and awoke in the middle of the night from another puzzling dream.

My mother and grandmother joked about using shampoo like they have in hotels and who was using it. My mother was a little upset because of an article about my father in my company newsletter was all lies. In real life he had a knack of getting himself in the news with articles about himself that were all lies which used to upset her. In the dream I saw a picture of him with a full beard, something he never had, and he was working with the CIA backed technology company that I presently worked for in real life. I didn't know what the article said, but the point of contention was that it was all lies.

Next I went to work which was not at work, but work nonetheless. Someone brought me a stack of papers. My buddy and boss Rob was there and the paperwork consisted of reports about our employees who were embezzling the company by falsifying hours they had not worked. I went through them and Rob asked me what was happening. I said that I had a lot of stuff that needed to be checked out and that I would take care of it. When I set the papers down they got knocked over and turned into a bunch of spoons and other utensils. I picked them up, put them back in their place, and another manager got in trouble for the situation. Upper management came down on him hard. He begged them saying, "Please don't, I'm ruined."

I didn't worry because I didn't think we were in the same kind of trouble but I was a little shocked that this other manager was in so much trouble. I listened to him being reprimanded for mismanagement while I looked through the items in question, then upper management started firing people. I walked down into a place somewhere in the company where military guys worked for a subdivision. They too were shocked and upset with management that their boss was getting fired. I walked around with them as a manager wearing a tie while they all wore military style coveralls that implied that they were blue collar workers.

They had a small army navy surplus store with camping gear. In the next moment the disgruntled workers rebelled and took things into their own hands. Alarms and klaxons went off and they all scrambled, then a hydraulic floor rose up like an aircraft carrier to airplanes where they all went to battle stations. One of their heads opened up revealing him to be a robot. Planes took off and guns started firing and I ran through a complex kind of a place. People were getting blown away and I was getting shot at. I ran down hallways avoiding getting shot and ran around corners trying to hide in stairwells while people continued dying. The chaos continued and robot powered planes floated by like balloons shooting while I kept running, hiding, and trying to escape.

I awoke from this long convoluted dream feeling apprehensive while struggling with what I thought of as a fear of responsibility dream. Looking back on it twenty years later, I saw that in spite of if its confusing nature, it was prophetic, warning me about what was coming regarding my job.

One overriding intention of my entire journey was to integrate all the parts of myself and be more whole without self-defeating attitudes. In my contemplative moments in this dream's aftermath I thought that the players in the dream were disparate subpersonalities of me. I thought back to the previous dream with the biting dog representing my fear of not having enough nipping at me. I blamed the cop for my troubles of not feeling deserving of any success which tied in to my father's part in its beginning. He had abandoned us in real life and done prison time for embezzlement. After falling back asleep I awoke later that morning from one of the most fantastic vivid catalyzing dreams ever.

It started at a house that I owned. Two friends came to take me and I became lucid and knew I was dreaming. It felt more real than where I knew I was physically in the jungle. They took me out to the driveway where there was the front half of an old fancy blue Ferrari sports car.

I faded into another car and tried to drive through traffic beside two big trucks and had problems working the gas and the brake. My legs were twisted but I managed to get them working. The brakes felt weak but I stopped before crashing into a big panel truck in front of me. When the two trucks drove off they glanced off of each other. One swerved to the left in front of me and the other swerved right in front of me. I pressed the gas pedal harder and my feet twisted up again but I moved forward faster, though not as fast as I would have liked.

That part faded into a big party with different people at a triangular house near a big body of water surrounded by a second floor deck. I faded in and out but the times when I was fully present I was amazed at how real it felt because part of me knew it was still in a dream and I was trying to tell people that.

Some older women escorted me and talked with me and younger women were around a circular area on a porch above the water. Somebody looked at me, then got up on the railing and dove down into the water to join others already there.

I faded again and was brought out into a yard by a couple of older women near a fence, then we went up into a room filled with people I knew. Yoda was there with some Agua de Florida. When I picked it up he said, "That's mine!" I saw black matchbooks and cards with writing on them and remembered that if you read something in a dream and look at it again to see it changed then you know you are dreaming. I looked at one which had writing symbols on it, then I picked up another one which had different symbols confirming my hypothesis.

I was blown away at the strength and reality of this lucid dream as I still had the bilocation experience of being aware of myself asleep in the jungle while still in the dream. I was with a young dark haired woman who was my date who I was getting to know. I thought it was the same dark haired woman from the bicycle dream I had previously. She was friendly and loving and I was attracted to her, then I was taken back to a porch area. I turned around and saw one of the ladies dressed in a silk butterfly costume beautifully painted up like a butterfly with a silk cap, antennas coming out the top, and big elegant silky wings.

A suspicious looking younger man across from me had a backpack and a jacket with a bunch of pockets. My young foreign dark haired date stayed with me along with a few other people. The younger and older ladies and my date surrounding me made the young man seem jealous. He took the backpack and threw it over a chain link fence into another yard where there was a dog, then he climbed back over to get it.

I faded out and came to again feeling tangled up in the fence with the backpack. I had a hard time trying to get back up. Something held me to the fence that I couldn't figure out. I looked over the fence and it looked like a graveyard. I heard voices but everything was fuzzy. I couldn't see very well and I had lost much of my lucidity. A wizened old woman came to me wearing a red shawl and said to me, "They are all waiting for you now. Come."

She took my arm and guided me across the yard, down some steps, and around a corner. Thinking it a dream I floated up a little, then back down as she took me to them and said, "Just be careful what you say and only speak the ghost talk or you will scare them."

I felt concerned because I didn't know what I should say because I didn't want to spook anybody. She brought me around to the front of the place I had been to a large group of people who felt like a mixed tribe. Four or five wise looking older men with withered faces stood to my left, a lot of other people stood across from me and five or six young girls were beside me as was the attractive dark-haired girl, and more people stood behind me. Some looked foreign, some dark-skinned, swarthy Mediterranean old men types, young Nordic looking girls, and older women. In some respects it felt like a rave with so many different costumes, colors, and characters. There were about thirty people total.

I sat down and they all paid attention to me. I started to speak and two or three of them ran away into an old big building in the background that looked like a school or church. I said, "All I really want to say and do is to work together."

They all got on their knees and bowed to me over and over again. I felt a soft woman's leg up against my head which felt very good and the dark-haired girl said to me, "But I don't want to do that."

I asked her to explain saying, "How can we get anywhere if twelve of us want to do one thing and six of us want to do something else? We're not going to be together," then the dream faded out.

I didn't want to awaken from this last part which felt exceptionally lucid and far more than real. I had a strong sense that I had met all the different aspects of myself who were all the different people I had been in different lifetimes. The fact that they all bowed to me so many times reinforced the feeling that I was in charge of them all at the moment because I was the one alive and aware in the present day.

I felt a little fearful of some of them and felt love from others as well as jealousy toward me because of the attention I got from the women. Some of them were talking and questioning, struggling to figure out who I really was, and from time to time the older woman guided me to all the different places.

Throughout it all I experienced bilocation, fully aware of myself asleep in the jungle while fully aware in the dream, only the physical reality of the dream felt more real than the reality of sleeping in the jungle. I tried to tell people in the dream how I was experiencing bilocation from both worlds and how their reality felt more real than my physical world.

The only other time I remember ever having such a vivid lucid dream experiencing bilocation was my life changing Santa Teresa dream from two years ago.

I felt like I had met and accepted most of my diverse selves and hoped that the three who fled would return. I hoped to integrate them all and spend more time with them by overcoming their skittishness and the mix of conflicting emotions they held.

It was now Sunday morning which meant our fourth ceremony would be that night. I felt weak, but hoped that my dreams would play into my visions the way they had in the past and I would get to visit with my extended inner tribe that I had been with in the dream.

In all my time alone with all my ruminations I became aware of how self-abusive I was and how horribly I talked to and treated myself in the deeply ingrained tradition of abusing yourself to improve yourself by the no pain, no gain model. I realized that these instances of abuse were directed at whatever subpersonality might be involved at the moment it happened. How could I ever love myself if I was constantly abusive to the subpersonalities I created? This revelation made me pay more attention to my inner dialogue, shocking me when I became aware of how often and how unconscious this abusive autopilot habit was.

Yoda came by that afternoon and left me one of his handouts.

Some Wet Places

We always tend to relive our history, in effect repeat the patterns or imprints we have learned, especially as infants so the key is to learn to get off the wheel and stop living in the past, manipulated by old energies and events that have nothing to do with the present. There are many symbols to represent this rat race; the wheel of fortune in the tarot, Ixion's Wheel in Hell in the Greek myth, the oriental idea of reincarnation, and many others.

In other words we are stuck in a swamp when we enter these swamp lands of the psyche and who of us hasn't? We enter the realm of the shadow with attendant fears, anxieties, grief, doubts, and

loneliness. Jung suggested that when we are there we ask ourselves.
" What task are we avoiding by entering these dismal places?"
In every case the task is some variant of the following.
A.)   We seek to gain permission for something.
B.)   We need to leave a dependency; a relationship, job, lifestyle.
C.)   We need to find courage to stand vulnerably and responsibly
  before the Universe.

We therefore have by an act of the imagination to reinvent ourselves in the present and abandon historical imprints. In every case we are challenged to grow up to become more conscious. It is not easy or pleasant, but it is the only way to go.

The mind as distinguished from the self is always playing tricks on us and two of its favorite tricks are denial and transference. All addictions are anxiety management techniques. There are two great unifying mythic patterns.
1.)   Death and Rebirth.
2.)   The Hero's Journey - Leave home, suffer and become conscious, and reach a new home.

When we visit a foreign country, an actual geography, or in places in the mind, notice that we seek to make ourselves comfortable by groping for words or customs familiar to us in order to reduce our anxiety instead of accepting the strangeness of it all for what it is.

Dinner came that afternoon before the fourth night's session which was rice and a plátano. Ronaldo and Tito were gone leaving José and Yoda to lead the ceremony.

NINETEEN

The Heart Of The Mother

I returned to my tambo in the early Monday morning hours from a long, hard journey and sat down after my plant bath feeling inadequate trying to find words to articulate my intense emotion charged experiences.

My Sunday night full moon session began with a full dose that took awhile to come on. One of my intentions for that night was to try and do a healing for a lady friend stricken with an aggressive cancer the same way I tried to heal my other friends and family.

Before trying to do any healing I waited to see if I would purge because I didn't want to try anything until I was in a more settled place. I thought I had to pass through the purge which acted as the portal to the visionary state on the other side of consciousness beyond my nausea and it felt like it took an extra long time until I finally did purge.

In that state I got an urgent message to break away from an unstable woman I had been helping as a writer who was an energy drain, and potentially dangerous. Once I accepted that I flew hard and fast through colors, geometries, dimensions, and other worlds. A little later Howie, one of my Canadian friends who sat beside me in that ceremony went outside and danced in the moonlight. I felt drawn to follow him in my bare feet to dance in the mud. Soon the rest of the group came out and joined us, each doing their own unique version of personal moon dances.

Tito had told us that this was the biggest full moon of the year and Saturn and Jupiter were in alignment creating a six pointed Star of David in the sky. This moon looked particularly bright and beautiful here in the clear jungle sky and held extra feminine magic seen through the eyes of my Ayahuasca influenced perception. José and Yoda joined us and José played the flute while everyone danced. At one point each person went to the middle of the circle and did a dance solo.

After dancing we went back into the maloca where the music and icaros continued, launching me into another unexpected journey deep into what I believed to be the literal heart of Mother Ayahuasca, one of the most beautiful things I have ever experienced. It swirled with preternaturally shifting bright purples, reds, and blues that looked like verdant hills, valleys, and textures, all exceeding any description of its beauty, deeply impressing me on every level of my being with its intelligence and the power of its presence.

This awesome in every sense of the word experience and its lasting impression tattooed itself into the depths of my being as one of the highlights of my very existence and its memory continues to haunt me in the best way in all the years since.

Physically I was in agony while my spirit soared through that inner landscape in heavenly ecstasy to the point where I couldn't take any more. It kept coming and in the end the rewards were well worth it. The overall love within the group increased with each passing day and each person brought their own unique gifts to the circle.

They gave us one piece of chicken and one boca chica fish for the whole week. Monday morning and Tuesday night would be our last ceremony and Wednesday morning would bring our first meal to break the dieta. Wednesday we would have a group dinner with plans to leave camp on Thursday morning. Friday we planned to visit Pablo Amaringo and the Shipibo village of San Francisco. We were scheduled to fly out on Saturday morning to Lima and visit the Indian Market in Miraflores before going on to Los Angeles on a 1:00 am red eye flight.

After our epic full moon session I climbed into bed and slept dreamlessly until I woke up later Monday morning happy to get a big piece of chicken and a plátano for breakfast. They upped my doses of Ushpawasha to four glasses from three and I was invited to join a group at a small waterfall where eight of us took mud baths. My Canadian friends took pictures of me covered from head to toe in mud with a huge leaf covering my lower parts and I went back to my tambo feeling squeaky clean and refreshed.

Later that evening I had a pleasant synchronicity reading **Earth to Tao** by José Stephens when I opened the book up to a chapter about using external tools from the environment and the planet for healing and how they can assist with balancing. The first thing mentioned was mud of various mineral contents smeared all over the body, something I had just done that afternoon! It also mentioned plants taken internally and applied externally to the body, which is what I had been doing for the whole dieta as well as the sound of running water, something that came to me constantly during all my time there in the jungle at *my* tambo.

My little jaunt to the waterfall and mud bath took most of my energy, so I took one more dip in the river, drank another glass of Ushpawasha, and napped heavily through the afternoon without dreams. A dinner of watery oatmeal and a plátano came later that afternoon.

After a few days of no rain, thunder and lightning came followed by heavy rain. I drank my fourth glass of Ushpawasha before bed and woke up in the middle of the night from another incomprehensible convoluted dream where I felt like I was observing it more than being in it.

I was involved in a contest that had a drawing where they kept calling out numbers and letters like in bingo. I tried to write them down for different people but couldn't keep track of them all. It felt like I had an order in for something that I couldn't seem to get. It was in a box that I knew was there, but I couldn't get the number right.

Next I was in a store with friends that seemed to be dated in the sixties or fifties and it was closing down and having a sale on appointment books and notebooks. I got a good deal on three or four things along with some old pictures. One of them was a Wizard of Oz picture up on a shelf with the tin man in it.

We left, went to a park and drove around. We were supposed to go to a movie but I was walking around. A woman stopped me from behind with a hand on my shoulder and we walked into a group of people who were with Rod Stewart. They were all going into someplace so we got in behind them and drove around looking for a movie. We couldn't find it so we went looking again in a 1957 Chevy. The movie was supposed to be in an old building that was being renovated into a juvenile delinquent hall. We ended up at the end of the street at an old run down house with a barren patchy lawn and circled it in the car, ending up back out front again. We drove around the side and some old black ladies came out. One of them had a gun.

Some friends wanted to play music and one of them handed me a cool guitar like a Rickenbacker with no strings on it that I really liked, then I showed them my drum set with one of the cymbals tilted off at a bad angle. They wanted to play and plugged in a guitar and a bass, but it was two in the morning and I said, "We can't play, it's too loud," but they kept trying to play. I told them it was my mother's house and they could come back the next day to play, but they didn't want to do that.

Somebody turned on a television and it was Happy Days, a show about high school life in the fifties, so we watched it. Richie Cunningham, the main character had a 1957 Chevy and he was meeting his girlfriend who climbed into the back seat, then climbed into the front seat to be beside him. They recklessly drove down the street goofing around, almost hitting cars, then they changed seats while still driving. She drove and they almost hit something.

Next I was out on the street with a bunch of guys in a paintball fight that I found myself in the middle of. I wasn't scared, but they surrounded me and took my ammo, then we got chased by the cops. I ran but was tired and my body and legs could barely move. After awhile a benevolent biker character named Mel pulled up looking for love and an aggressive threatening guy from another gang pulled up. We told him to get lost or we would whoop his ass, so he left and I woke up.

After waking I tried to make sense out of the dream and the recurring themes and characterized it as a dream of missed opportunities. Seeing the tin man picture made me think of the quest for my heart essence by opening my heart and trying to find it, the work I was doing in the jungle with Ayahuasca, Ushpawasha, and the dieta.

I missed the raffle and couldn't get the numbers right when I knew the prizes in the box were for me. I couldn't play the guitar because it had no strings, which is the heart and essence of the music. Later I couldn't play music at all, couldn't make it to the movie, and couldn't respond in the middle of the paintball game when I was surrounded because my ammo was taken.

An astrologer told me that if I let my inner feminine emerge it would represent my inner shaman manifesting itself and I thought that the nonstop male aggression of the dream and the uneasiness of a woman driving out of control represented my inner struggle to give up control to the masculine feminine shifting over.

I thought that the girl in the last part of the dream climbing into the front seat from the back and driving recklessly represented me allowing my feminine side to take over from my life time dominant masculine side which had been in charge, protecting me my whole life.

Women had been the ones talking to and coming to me in the dreams all along, especially in the lucid dream of my many selves.

In my struggle to decipher the cryptic emotional language of my subconscious, I looked for meaning and coherence in these disjointed episodic narratives that revealed my deepest emotional insecurities. I admired what presented itself as incomprehensible logic because of the creativity that went into what it created. Like a mad genius, my subconscious incorporated elements and symbolism from my waking state along with past, present, and possibly future experiences, spinning dreams with recurring themes in interactive situations as if "consciously" repeating the message that I didn't seem to be getting.

Fear and insecurity ruled many of them woven in with concerns about my identity and purpose, fear of dying, failure, frustration, and all of the disappointments summed up in a narrative filled with thwarted attempts at everything I tried in a dream of missed opportunities.

On a positive note, interacting with these dreams involved disparate groups of "people", or subpersonalities and reacting to them in the right way rewarded me with a higher awareness evident in the magic of lucid dreaming states which always featured women who acted as guides.

TWENTY

Lucid Dreaming

I fell back asleep and woke up from another extraordinary dream.

It started at a big house that I owned with Penny. My brother and mother were there along with others I knew. Though I owned the house I didn't know it and kept saying I didn't recognize it. It seemed to be inside a big amusement park, but it was unfinished. Instead of a roof it had plastic and the ceilings and beds looked weird, but I had a vague memory of it. There were little courtyards, nice places, and unfinished not so nice places and a big party in progress. Everybody was tripping on psychedelics and I felt bad because I had invited them all, but they were making a lot of noise and I was afraid they would wake my mother.

I saw a guy named Trevor in the back chained up like a dog. He had shoulder length wild curly matted hair and he flopped around in water babbling incoherently like an animal, a truly mad man. Somebody let him off the chain, put him someplace else, and gave him something to eat. He ate slobbering and getting it all over himself, then he climbed up into a cupboard and made a lot of noise. I asked him if he could keep quiet because I didn't want to wake my mother, but he was out of his mind and kept going while looking at me without seeing me.

In the next moment I was out in front of the house with a girl who was like a younger sister to a lady writer friend who was also there. She had dark hair and asked me, "Do you want to go on a plane flight or are you too busy?

I said "Okay, why not?"

The two ladies left and returned saying "Here's a treat for you."

They gave me a brown paper bag which was warm. It said, "For a special man," and it was worth ten or ten thousand dollars, so I took it and went up some steps back into the house and ate a big wonderful warm blueberry muffin.

One of the guys doing the dieta said I was really stinky and smelling and I said, "You are too!" I kept looking for a shower, but I couldn't find one. I went back to another room and my brother was there lying in a bed in a little pond. He kept apologizing to someone named Amelia saying, "I'm sorry I did this." Some friends of his were there with some kids who were fishing.

I went back out to a courtyard where I recognized people. One of them named Paul said "Hi." I walked out and another big guy came in. I Said "Hi" to him and he was happy to see me. I said "It's really good to see you," and walked out to a group of people and it seemed like Disneyland, then I saw a guy with a nametag and I became lucid.

I walked along smoking cannabis that I didn't want to be smoking because I had put such hard work into cleaning myself out on the dieta. I saw the director of the Southern California Writers Conference and walked with him, saying, "God I don't know where to go or what to do." The crowd went in a general direction and I said, "Should we follow the crowd?" He said, "Yes, of course."

I followed them toward a ride that was like a big launching pad and flew hard up into the air which scared me, high above a big city. I was quite lucid and flew up, down, and through the girders of big skyscrapers being built and flew so high I became terrified. I kept telling myself I was in control but not as much control as I would have liked.

I flew over Boston and Dorchester down into my old neighborhood. Because of my struggle to control I missed my street and flew up and down again one street over to the right spot, then tried to work my way around a corner to see the house I had lived in, then I flew high again over a giant hole that was like a crater where it looked like rebuilding construction was in progress.

I flew fast over a giant cityscape and higher to another city that looked like Times Square in New York or someplace in London and flew over traffic swooping down until I started coming down and couldn't stop. I heard, "No more flights for another two hours and tickets aren't available for another two hours and I went down into a hole at an intersection near a park.

I went right to the edge of the hole and down into it deep, catching myself on sides that were like curbstone railings. I put my hands out to pull myself up, but thorns hurt my hands, cutting into them and holding me there. I kept struggling to pull myself up and became entwined in the roots of a tree. I grabbed at a vine root and kept pulling myself up, finally escaping after hurting my hands. People came and couldn't see me, but I could see them. They kept waving a sign at me. I thought it said, CLEVELAND and I tried to figure out where I was, but the sign said CHILDREN, then I woke up.

In all the times I flew in my dreams I never flew that high, that hard, or that intensely. This experience imprinted me deeply. In my first life changing lucid dream of Santa Teresa in my first year in the jungle, I became lucid, and for the first time I focused on staying lucid without taking control of the dream and directing the action to discover how it unfolded in that heightened state of awareness without my intervention.

Like my prior lucid dream I experienced bilocation again and was fully aware of myself sleeping in the jungle while my lucid dream reality unfolded on its own, and I was fully aware within the magical dream. Though fully aware in both places at once my lucid dream reality felt more real than my physical reality and the reward had been the visitation of Santa Teresa.

The impact of this flying dream felt like an expansion of that special awareness that made such magic possible. I thought of it as the next level of the power of surrendering and accepting what unfolds while in a heightened state of supernatural awareness, something I was trying to cultivate.

I drifted back to sleep and had another short erratic dream.

I was in an apartment with a screaming black woman who was having a baby. I never saw her, but I ran up to a second floor below where she was. I had an Apple computer I was searching the web with trying to find hospitals, but I couldn't find any. A really dark black guy came out who I thought might be the husband. He was upset and kept repeating, "You're not going to find it that way. You're not going to find it that way." He looked distracted and trying to find something himself.

I exploded at him, yelling "Get the fuck out of my face, mother fucker!"

He left and I felt bad, then I changed to a phone book trying to look up child birth and hospitals and couldn't get anywhere. The black guy came back out and I apologized to him, saying, "I'm sorry, brother, I really didn't mean that."

He was sweet about it and gave me a gracious hug. I continued looking in the phone book and couldn't find anything while the lady screamed. I woke up thinking I should have looked up doctors.

I awoke early Tuesday morning feeling weak and exhausted thinking about the final ceremony coming that night. I gagged thinking about choking down another dose of Ayahuasca. My last pitcher of Ushpawasha came that morning which was much stronger than before and had five glasses as opposed to the three I had been getting.

I thought that the gift of the warm blueberry muffin that my writer friend and her younger sidekick gave me in my dream was the gift of lucidity that followed. They said, "Here's a treat for you," along with a note that said, "For a special man," and it had value.

I sensed that maintaining a heightened sense of awareness in dreams like these required a certain amount of psychic energy that only lasts for so long, like a battery. There was a razor's edge of difference at the balance point between control and acceptance in that state of letting go and surrendering while maintaining focus and concentration.

I thought the dream of the screaming black pregnant woman represented the birth and acceptance of a new integrated, more complete self that was coming because I saw that pattern in the last two nights of dreaming. Every time I solved the puzzle of a confusing dream I was rewarded by a wonderful lucid dream. All of this came from the women in those dreams as a gift from the feminine in the same way that Santa Teresa had been a gift and visitation from the divine feminine side that was emerging.

I thought that the last three people in my dream, Trevor, the madman, the screaming black pregnant woman and her partner were the last three abandoned entities that came back after taking off from the big gathering dream. I understood distancing myself and abandoning my inner madman and I grew up with a lot of racial violence which would explain birthing and accepting the male and female black aspects of myself. I felt that all the dream characters were me and I was finding all the aspects of myself.

I remembered Yoda telling me that when you are in the midst of transformation you don't know or see it, but you see the results in the coming days, weeks, and months that follow when the shift and the change become apparent.

I had thrown a chicken bone in my latrine and came back later to find it had been brought up out of the hole by ants that swarmed all over it, the seat, and ground all around it, so I smoked them out. By the time I was done I didn't have to go to the bathroom anymore. After that breakfast came, quinoa and a plátano. I noticed that drinking more, stronger Ushpawasha brought up more phlegm out of my lungs, clearing them.

I thought about the end of my lucid flying dream which ended with people waving a sign that said CHILDREN, and the next sequence of the screaming birth dream. I thought that to be reborn and transformed was to be a child again. I wanted to start living a new life which is what I was attempting by working toward integrating my selves to become a whole person. These convictions grew with each passing moment.

I took another mud bath and followed it with a plant bath and drank my third glass of Ushpawasha, then worked at finishing off four and a half glasses of the stronger infusion. I gave thanks before drinking the last glass and heavy rains came the moment I finished, followed by a strong refreshing wind, making me think that the jungle spirits could be acknowledging and blessing me.

I had one last full dose of Ayahuasca to gag down between me and finishing the dieta in my last ceremony that coming night, and no more bitter plant drinks.

I returned from our final ceremony in the predawn hours, took my plant bath, and recorded that we had a good session which was mellow compared to the prior ones.

After singing icaros into each person with flutes and other instruments, José sang into me last with an Ushpawasha infused icaro, singing his soul into me in what they called an arcana protection spell for defense from spiritual evil and danger in my heart, soul, and being. They said José could sing his soul into stones in the same way, making them power objects, so I had him sing into my quartz crystals and stone spearhead Lorenzo gifted me with that I held onto in every journey.

I had a rough start with a strong purge, but not as rough as the other nights and I went down into dark subterranean mud filled visions without any bright colors or any of the prior intensity. Where the other sessions felt stronger, this one felt spread out, broader, and slower as opposed to being focused and intense. I flew through those spaces with condor and my knees bounced up and down accordingly. I spent my time trying to make one last pass through those energetic realms in hopes of healing all those close to me by taking them into my heart, including Trevor my subconscious mad man.

This final journey felt like a gentle landing and winding down of the whole dieta. In retrospect my first ceremony was easy, then the next three grew more intense with each passing night, reaching their peak within the heart of the mother. This last one came full circle, showing me mercy. In this last session Yoda gave a little talk about the heart that he called Anatomy 101 which went like this.

"The heart tends to wander from time to time. It wanders up into your head and interferes with your brain, so you can get into trouble because you keep getting mixed up between your heart and your brain. You need to follow your brain when it's time to think and you can't think your heart. It messes you up and you make the wrong choices, the wrong decisions, and it's confusing, then you take your heart and follow it down into your crotch and put your heart with your genitals. You get into trouble there too because you get confused between the two and the difference between them gets you into a lot of trouble.

You bring your heart back up into your chest where it is in its rightful place, its place of power and that is where you listen to it, when it's in its place of power."

His talk dealt with the three energetic bodies prevalent in shamanism that Gurdjieff referred to as the emotional, physical, and intellectual bodies, or love, power, and wisdom. In Andean cosmology love is the upper world represented as the condor, the jaguar or puma is power, representing the energy of the middle world, and just like in the Christian bible the serpent in the lower world is wisdom.

After recording my journey I went to sleep and woke up around dawn feeling tapped out physically, strong spiritually and cleansed and purified overall.

We had chicken soup for brunch and broke the dieta with salt along with slices of avocado, rice, papaya, and banana dough spice dumplings in vegetable soup with potatoes, carrots, onion, chicken broth, and lemon leaf tea.

This was one of the best meals of my entire life.

I went to sleep that night and awoke in the black of night from an unnerving experience which wasn't a dream. I felt like my soul was in multiple dimensions, as though I lost myself. I was carried through it all by a non-stop protection mariri icaro Carlos had been singing in the ceremonies which felt maddening in its repetition. I awoke hearing it in my head like it stayed with and followed me there from my semi-conscious state.

After hours of tossing and turning wakefulness I drifted off to sleep and had one last jungle dream.

I was under water trapped in a wooden box with an air hose on the verge of panic because the air was running out and I was about to drown. I was frustrated, but finally figured my way out of the box and went somewhere with a female presence that I thought might be Penny. I wanted her to be involved with me getting money into some land or going somewhere and she didn't want to do it. I knew it was a good thing and I tried to talk her into doing it, but she refused.

Next I tried to tune in a television station. All the time I felt a feminine energy that I thought was Penny as a presence, but I didn't see her. I felt her. At first the station came in strong, then the channel filled with static and grew fuzzy. I tuned it in again and again and a reality show came on. I said, "Hey, I've been on this show before."

Next I was in the show in a car with some guys who picked up a cop who beat up people. The guys in the car were going to beat him up. We rode along going to some place like a hotel in a bad location in a suburban neighborhood where an event was happening. We drove in and a friend of mine beckoned me to come. We went into an underground parking lot where they had a dirt bike.

I was now on a bike or a scooter and went over to where the bikes were. It was dirty and muddy and I rode though there and another part of it. Somebody was playing a game of softball or horseshoes and I rode through the middle of their game, but I didn't mean to. I apologized and they were cool about it, then I woke up.

After waking Thursday morning I laid there with my eyes closed and thought about my Canadian friend Terence who would be coming to wake me up then I had that great awareness experience of feeling and sensing him. I sat up and the moment I opened my eyes he came over the hill to wake me.

I lost a pound a day adding up to a total of ten pounds over the course of the dieta along with a ton of emotional baggage that I left behind in the jungle.

TWENTY ONE

Thirteen Condors Converge

The premonition dream I had about mismanagement at work, unjustified firings, and destruction after my third ceremony became reality in early January of 2003 bringing another unexpected shift in life. As unsettling as it was, it was only the beginning of much bigger life transforming cataclysms.

When 2002 ended I owned my amazing three bedroom house on a canyon at the end of a cul-de-sac in San Diego, and half of a duplex in North County. I called the cute duplex the storybook house with the white picket fence that I had bought and moved Penny and her kids into from the one bedroom apartment they shared to comply with the court ordered custody and visitation. I had everything dialed in with an easily affordable fixed mortgage rate. With three of them the kids got their own rooms, while Penny and I split the payment and the utility bills fifty-fifty. We spent half the week at my bigger house close to work and the other half at the duplex when we had the kids, which was an hour drive from work.

My job title was Deputy Manager of Site Support Services and I had twenty five technicians working for me who took care of all of the computers and related infrastructure in eighteen buildings at the largest employee owned technology company in the country. I had worked hard building my organization and always advocated for those working under me. I pushed for pay raises, supported their educational goals, championed other benefits, and I made an extra effort to give some of them raises when I took over as a show of good faith and support.

A few days after the New Year our bigger boss called my buddy and immediate boss Rob and I into his office for a special meeting and told us we had another meeting with human resources next door. When I rose from the chair, I looked him in the eye and, "It's been nice working for you."

When I said it I had no idea what was happening and said it off the cuff in a joking manner. I don't know where it came from, but it came out spontaneously. I saw the way he reacted and sensed I had hit a nerve when I said it. Looking back it's clear to me now that the premonition from my visions had registered something inside of me. I was not consciously aware of it, although some part of me obviously was to the point of speaking it, and even then I did not make the full connection.

I went into the next office where I was grilled and accused of a number of blatant falsehoods by a vindictive human resources representative who could not have been more wrong about what he accused me of and there was not one iota of truth in anything he spewed.

Some months earlier I had to participate in firing one of my technicians because he made a comment about going postal. I knew he was just mouthing off, but they fired him and bent over backwards giving him eight weeks of pay and other considerations.

They fired me outright with no separation of any kind.

My bigger boss that I spooked when I said, "It's been nice working for you got the axe himself soon after. I discovered later that four hundred fifty midlevel managers were axed because they were paring down the books to go public. My boss Rob and I had been among the first. I hope some of the others were dealt with more ethically than the underhanded tactics they used with us.

My brother helped me find a lawyer and we went into arbitration against a half a dozen corporate lawyers and HR reps. I had been emailing my new jungle friends from Canada and they sent me some pictures from our adventure. One of the pathetic things the company did in their frame up to discredit me was to say that I had pictures of nude men on my computer.

The nude man picture was of me covered from head to toe in mud from my mud bath in the jungle with the big leaf covering my happy place.

In the end I got another $15,000 out of them. The lawyer took his $5,000 contingency and I took the rest. With the loss of my job came the loss of my cash flow and I was no longer in a position to pay the mortgages on two houses. I tried renting out my bigger house, but scammers tried to take advantage, so I sold it for twice what I originally paid for it and consolidated everything into the smaller duplex in Carlsbad where the kids needed to be. Now I only paid for half of a stable fixed rate mortgage which cut my monthly house payments by two-thirds.

I worked hard and dedicated myself to my job which I took pride in. Now I was disenchanted with the whole idea of working for anybody after the way they treated me which I took as a clear sign to find another direction. Not only had the company's management and legal team turned on me, but the same people I had given the good faith raises to stabbed me in the back too. One woman from Venezuela accused me of being satanic because I was working with Ayahuasca and writing about shamanism and a short while after I left the company she went as far as to tell people that I was dead!

When everything settled down from all that insanity I worked at writing, editing, and teaching full time. My settlement and consolidation of expenses allowed me to devote myself fully to the two year shamanic study program that I felt driven to complete. I paid the $10,000 registration fee and in late May of 2003 I became part of a two year group of committed kindred spirits all bound together by mutual love and respect.

We first met on May 30, 2003 at a twelve hundred acre ranch in the wilderness at the base of the Sangre de Cristo mountains in New Mexico dedicated to the study of shamanism. The husband and wife team had spent a lifetime studying it as well as psychology, evident by a PhD. They had also spent many years studying with a Huichol elder and were steeped in Peyote lore, practice, and rituals, as well as those of Ayahuasca and San Pedro, a mescaline containing cactus called Huachuma in the Andes. Their magical forested land had a rustic open air wood kitchen and a large yurt for ceremonies. Scattered throughout the property they had a big labyrinth, a shaman's tree full of hung offerings, a sacred burial spot, and a number of beautiful vistas and power spots.

The two year study plan was to meet every two months for a week or so, sometimes longer, depending on the location of the activity. In that focused experiential learning crucible we would visit and spend extended time with the Shipibo Indians embracing their culture and participating in Ayahuasca ceremonies at their village in the Peruvian Amazon. On another journey we would spend time in the Andes working with Huachuma with a master of the ancient traditions as well as the sacred traditional uses of the Coca leaf.

Later in the program we planned to do a pilgrimage to the desert of central Mexico to experience the ancient Huichol peyote hunt and all night ceremony in Wirikuta, the sacred land. The day after that we would go to Real de Catorce and ride horses to the top Mount Quemado to do a ceremony at the temple of the deer spirit.

Many of our meetings would be at the ranch in New Mexico to do ceremonies, wilderness solos, Huachuma walkabouts, and instruction in shamanic practices and traditions, including drumming, feather work, sacred tobacco use, visualizations, perception enhancing exercises, healing, and other shamanic tools. In addition to the cultures we would be learning from, our teachers had knowledge of universal shamanic practices from all over the world. We would learn about elemental spirits, among them plant, and animal spirits, sacred power spots, and other tools needed to follow the power path that leads to the art of mastering energy and becoming a man or a woman of power. In the words of my teachers, a primary goal of shamanism is to be free emotionally, mentally, and physically to use energy at will without being reactive.

For our first wilderness solo we fasted for a couple of days with the exception of a drink made from one eighth of a teaspoon of cayenne, half of a lime, and a tablespoon of maple syrup mixed with a quart of water and we were told to pay close attention to animals, insects, plants, and the weather. We were to work with the four directions, dividing our solo into four distinct periods of time dedicated to each direction, something we continued doing in every ceremony that followed.

Additionally we had to caretake our chosen site and rearrange the rocks there into a medicine circle and mark the cardinal points with bigger stones. In addition to that we were told to pick a pine cone or a small stone to represent each person in the group and make a smaller circle inside the medicine wheel to contemplate the essence and heart connection with each person. The purpose of the wilderness solo was to spend time in non-ordinary reality with no routines to play with time and absorb power from the stars and ask the plants and animals for chi.

An integral part of these teachings was practicing Qi Gong, an ancient system of coordinated body-posture, movement, breathing, and meditation for health and spirituality that has its roots in Chinese medicine, philosophy, and martial arts. Qi Gong is viewed throughout Asia as a practice to cultivate and balance qi, pronounced "chi" which translates as life energy. It is a meditation that coordinates slow-flowing movement, deep rhythmic breathing, and a calm meditative state of mind. Aside from the Chinese tradition we would also be learning ancient Toltec and Maya forms of this practice.

One of the first shamanic practices we were taught and which I have used successfully with traumatized people is to lie face down on the earth and tell it all of our worries, fears, concerns, sadness, and sorrows, then follow up by telling it all of our hopes. As a shamanic prayer we were told to focus on the top right hand portion of our heart, engaging it three times with a mantra.

"I am alive, I am here, what I am grateful for, what I am, and what I want to reinforce; being healthy, inspired, and a magnet for good things."

At the end of this we were directed to stand up and gesture wide to the four directions, reiterating, "I am all this!"

During one of these wilderness solos we were told to bring back a song which we all did, then we were asked to adorn the beams of the yurt with artwork. I never thought of myself as possessing any artistic talent, but among the images I painted I chose a hummingbird and while in the process of painting it I had a revelatory breakthrough with the realization that art, music, and writing were all variations of the same creative process. I was already a writer and musician, and with this eye opening epiphany I saw that I could also excel as an artist if I chose to.

Our teachers apprenticed with a Huichol shaman for many years who told them he would return as a Hummingbird which I had close encounters with every single time I did a wilderness solo. They often hovered right in front of my face, especially when I was doing Qi Gong, and one time one hovered so close to my ear that it felt like its wings actually caressed it.

Following a Huichol tradition, we made prayer arrows using wooden dowels for the shafts, colored yarn, feathers and symbolic items to make a life arrow which would point toward sun rise to show the intentions of where we were going, and a death arrow to point West to represent everything we wanted to leave behind. We each added personal items and I used the book jacket cover from *Land Without Evil*, my historical novel to wrap the shaft of my arrows along with different colored yarn.

One arrow was buried inland and one was buried by the ocean following the Huichol belief of two opposed cosmic forces existing in the world, an igneous one represented by Tayaupá, "Our Father" the Sun, and an aquatic one, represented by Nacawé, the Rain Goddess.

In another magical synchronicity, when we were asked to come up with a name for our group someone suggested the Condors. I kept my mouth shut as I didn't want to bias anything or influence the mojo and they unanimously named us the Condors without any input from me, which thrilled me to no end.

TWENTY TWO

Shamanic Prayer From Beginning To End

While actively pursuing my two year shamanic study program, I continued working with Yoda doing six ceremonies a year outside of Peru and seven sessions each year in the jungle doing dietas which now included two solo sessions added to the five group ceremonies. I also did ceremonies with my new teachers outside of our study group. Overall I ended up doing Ayahuasca ceremonies about thirty times a year for a couple of years running.

In between those events I facilitated San Pedro, mushroom, LSD, MDMA, and Sasha Shulgin research chemical experiences to guide others and share what I was learning. To my disappointment many of the people I taught didn't show the respect these substances required and didn't follow my guidance. In one situation I was blamed for psychological issues that arose in someone who ignored my guidelines.

As my rapid growth and experience grew I sang icaros with the shamans, originally to shift my attention from the nausea that came with drinking Ayahuasca and I taught icaros from the shamans in my first group to the two year Condor group. As a result I took more of a lead spot in ceremonies. During this time I also worked actively with 5MEODMT and had been for five years running, continuing to guide people through that experience.

Two months after our first meeting we returned to the New Mexico wilderness for our second Condor gathering to learn more about shamanism. The power path of mastering energy and cultivating personal power is a path of expanding awareness by altering consciousness and perception through exercises, acts of will, plants, diet, fasting, and other approaches.

One of the things we practiced on frequent hikes was called the walk of attention which is a walk *with* intention of being aware and in the moment with our heart open, connecting to the elemental spirits surrounding us including the land, plants, animals, rocks, trees, and other forms of life seen and unseen. While taking everything in with open-hearted full conscious awareness we became aware of ourselves at the center of it all, recreating the Universe from moment to moment with each shift of perception interacting with all of the overlapping morphogenetic energy fields that we came in contact with.

This concept comes from biologist Rupert Sheldrake's hypothesis of morphic fields and morphic resonance that leads to a vision of a living developing universe with its own inherent memory. Over the course of fifteen years of research on plant development Sheldrake came to the conclusion that to understand the development of plants, their morphogenesis, genes, and gene products were not enough. Morphogenesis depends on organizing fields. How *does* a massive oak grow out of an acorn?

The same arguments apply to the development of animals. Since the 1920s developmental biologists have proposed that biological organization depends on fields, variously called biological fields, developmental fields, positional fields, or morphogenetic fields.

Many organisms live as free cells, including yeasts, bacteria, and amoebas. Some form complex mineral skeletons like diatoms and radiolarians. Making the right proteins at the right times doesn't explain the complex skeletons of these structures without other forces coming into play, including the organizing activity of cell membranes and microtubules.

Morphogenetic fields are not fixed, they evolve. The fields of Afghan hounds and poodles became different from their wolf ancestors. How these fields are inherited has been postulated to be transmitted from past members of the species through a kind of non-local resonance, called morphic resonance.

Fields organizing the activity of the nervous system are also inherited through morphic resonance conveying a collective instinctive memory. Each individual draws on and contributes to the collective memory of the species, meaning new patterns of behavior can spread more rapidly than would otherwise be possible. As an example, if rats of a particular breed learn a new trick in Harvard, then rats of that breed should be able to learn the same trick faster all over the world.

There is evidence from laboratory experiments that this actually happens.

Social groups are also organized by fields, as in schools of fish and flocks of birds. Human societies have memories that are transmitted through the culture of the group and are most communicated through the ritual re-enactment of a founding story or myth like the Jewish Passover celebration, Christian Holy Communion, and the American Thanksgiving dinner where the past becomes present through a kind of resonance with those who performed the same rituals before.

In terms of natural laws it can be said that as nature evolves the laws of nature evolve the way human laws evolve over time, but how would natural laws be remembered or enforced? Many organisms have habits but only humans have laws. The habits of nature depend on nonlocal similarity reinforcement. Through morphic resonance patterns of activity self-organizing systems are influenced by similar patterns in the past, giving each species and self-organizing system a collective memory.

Habits are subject to natural selection and the more they are repeated the more probable they become. Animals inherit successful habits of their species as instincts. We inherit bodily, emotional, mental and cultural habits, including the habits of our languages.

Morphic fields of social groups connect members even when they are miles apart and provide channels of communication through which organisms can stay in touch at a distance, and they provide an explanation for telepathy. There is good evidence that many species of animals are telepathic, and telepathy seems to be a means of animal communication that is normal, not paranormal, and common between people, especially those who know each other well.

The morphic fields of mental activity are not confined to the insides of our heads. They extend beyond our brain through intention and attention. We are already familiar with the idea of fields extending beyond material objects where they are rooted. Magnetic fields extend beyond the surface of magnets. The earth's gravitational field extends beyond the surface of the earth keeping the moon in its orbit, and the fields of a cell phone stretch beyond the phone itself. The fields of our minds extend beyond our brains in this same manner.

During our walks of attention we were directed to narrow the focus of specific perceptions like picking out the sound of one bird and listening to and paying attention to it alone, or the sound of our footsteps, a trickle of sweat, or some other specific bodily sensation. We looked at treetops and focused on the blue in the spaces between the branches as opposed to the branches themselves, making them the prominent feature. These and other exercises in perception and shifting focus amplified the flexibility of reality bringing a textured richness to those moments in subtle ways.

We visited power spots in hills looking out over valleys and other power spots called edge places like mountaintops, cliff edges, the water's edge of ponds, rivers, seashores, and creeks that draw and support life. These edge places are where elemental energies meet, like the earth and the air in the windy mountaintops, or the water, earth, and air at the water's edge. Edge work can be done in these power places because they are where things happen. Life changes and shifts at edge places from beginning to end making them places where you can magnify intention. I experienced my first spiritual awakening with the realization of this very concept I called the Cosmic Flash which I wrote about in **Spirit Matters** and will share here.

On June twenty first, nineteen seventy six, the day of the summer solstice, at the age of twenty one I had a mystical experience that transformed me to my core and changed my life's direction forever. On that day the battle between the energies inside of me that I thought of as good and evil reached fever pitch, flip-flopping back and forth during the course of a day, driven by the fury of my frustrated anger with the help of Hawaiian Baby Woodrose Seeds, a species similar to Morning Glory, classified as Argyreia Nervosa. Woodrose has the distinction of being the most potent of this class of hallucinogens with lysergic acid amide concentrations up to three times that of other Morning Glory species. LSD-25 is d-lysergic acid diethylamide. Baby Woodrose doesn't contain diethylamide, but its lysergic acid amides are psychoactive.

I didn't know any of these details at the time. I only knew that the Woodrose came from a plant and taking it supposedly had similarities to LSD, my favorite substance, so the idea of taking something that occurred naturally in a plant appealed to me, particularly in light of the fact that I had become a vegetarian.

I chewed thirteen Rosewood seeds on an empty stomach on that warm summer day and drove out to a pond to party with my friends. There the Rosewood seeds came on strong, building steam, but never with any edginess like the frenetic energy of LSD. I ended up alone, floating in the middle of the pond on a truck inner tube under warm sunlight. In that magical moment, my flip-flopping rage peaked and my perceptions opened like an unfolding blossom. My whole being expanded, making me highly aware of the magic, complexity, and connectedness of everything both through me and in me. All the while the struggle of light and dark raged inside of me and I had too many contradictions in everything I thought, said, and did.

In a cosmic flash all of the pieces snapped into place. I looked to the shoreline and saw the point where the water met the shore and the earth and water touched, warmed by the sun and cooled by a breeze, meaning all the elements of earth, air, fire and water became present to me at that moment, making it the meeting point and center of the universe. In that same flash I had the realization that *I* constituted the center of the universe. All of this and more flooded me in abstract symbols and archetypal images that communicated information faster, better, and more condensed than any language could.

In the infinite variety of life experiences that we share with others, none of us knows each other's thoughts. We may have psychic, telepathic, and intuitive flashes, but in the end all we really have are our own thoughts that drift and scatter into strange places when we lose consciousness or experience any number of other shifts in our awareness. We receive life through five senses where sensory impressions come to us at our center. We are the focal point where it all comes together, hopefully making sense to us in a meaningful way. If we cease to exist on this earth it is a two way street. Not only do we cease to exist on this earth, but the earth ceases to exist for us and the rules of stimulus and response change.

One of the primary elements in shamanism that carries great significance when you open yourself to Cosmic forces and elemental spirits that can both heal and harm you is to practice protection, the first thing that is done at the opening of Ayahuasca ceremonies in the form of prayers. It is also something that should be practiced in other forms and visualizations when venturing into the psychological wilderness of altered states of consciousness.

Aside from tobacco, sage, Palo Santo, breath, and other energetic clearings, we were taught other methods of shamanic protections and visualizations like creating a Qi filled circle three feet above ground and below, hanging crosses in the six directions, and putting roses up in a field off to the side. We were told that these protections grew in importance as you grow in power.

Prayer is considered the most effective method of communicating with spirit and is most powerful when spoken out loud as the strongest expression of energy. Tobacco smoke, concentrated blowing of air, and Agua de Florida also carry prayers to the field of intent. In shamanism prayer is seen as talking to spirit and it is believed that the more you talk to spirit the more it talks to you, but it is not always a petition. It is opening your heart to God indicating that you see, feel, and notice that divinity as a way to "Say Hello".

This approach and attitude ties in with the shamanic concept of "whistling through the forest" prevalent in the Amazon. This practice of singing and praying when you enter a jungle is done to acknowledge the powerful visible and invisible elemental forces that reside there and recognizing that you are entering *their* home, showing them the respect, humility, and reverence due them and acknowledging that their bigger energies can kill you or heal you. The idea is to honor and flatter them with songs and praise, entreating them to work with, respond to, and help you, which is what defines the act of singing icaros.

The most effective form of prayer is done with an open heart with gratitude, praying directly from the heart. In shamanism the heart in man is the sun of his personal cosmos which is connected to the sun, which is the unconditional giver of life in our solar system, especially on planet earth. This sun in turn is connected to a bigger sun, which is connected to a bigger sun infinitely following a ray of creation all the way back to Source.

Hafez, a 14th-century poet, penned a verse that captures the essence of this belief.

Even After All this time The Sun never says to the Earth, "You owe me." Look What happens with a love like that. It lights the whole sky.

An old adage in shamanism made popular by Carlos Castaneda attributed to Don Juan, the Yaqui shaman, is that, "A warrior must follow a path with heart." If it takes you back to Source, then you have found your way home.

In shamanic thought spoken prayer is the most powerful method of communicating with spirit, making it the strongest expression of energy. Once the prayer is going it can be done with increasing energy focusing in on "I am" statements manifesting as Aum and Amen awakening the sounds of creation.

Yoda had an interesting take on these vocalizing energies when examined in the light of expanding awareness and our alphabet of vowels and consonants. Vowels represent variations of open mouthed vocalizations while consonants are closed off stops whether uttered by the lips, tongue, throat, or a combination, so vowels expand and consonants contract.

The letter **A** is the first vowel and first letter of the alphabet, making it our first expression. If it is spoken in a long breathy manner, like saying the word *heeeeeey* it is a comment of expansive amazement and wonder, coming into a new reality, and it is the sound of creation manifest as the first letter of Aum or Amen signifying the truth of the statement, "I am."

The awe of this realization brings you to **E**, the second vowel and if you extend this out saying *eeeeee*, there's that little bit of fear bringing the contraction and reversal of direction. It's the sound a woman might make when scared of a mouse or something else frightening, and whether by coincidence or not, it defines what we call an E-Ticket ride.

With this expansion, reversal, and contraction of energy we have the pulse of life evident in our breath and heartbeat signifying conscious awareness of self and the third vowel of creation; **I**, also spoken in an extended manner, pointing inward to the point of origin of this expanding conscious awareness.

This realization elicits the next vowel **O**, round and open-mouthed the way we marvel at fireworks and other magical displays and events.

This open embrace of creation and the expansive awareness of being that comes from the expression of the energies we send out and bring back to ourselves become more evident in the reflection and recognition of ourselves that we see in others with the last vowel, **U**, which of course is expressed as the extended word Yooouuu...

TWENTY THREE

Andean Adventures

The third outing of our two year Condor shamanic study group appropriately brought us to the Andes in late August through mid-September 2003 a month before I would return to the Amazon for my fourth dieta with Yoda.

We had amazing adventures high in the Andes working with and learning about local plants and customs. Our primary focus was on Huachuma with the ever present Coca as a close second. I developed a deepening relationship with Coca, another mother plant which would eventually intensify for me in magical unexpected ways.

We flew to Lima where we met two Shipibo shamans and flew on to Cusco, one of the oldest inhabited cities in the Western Hemisphere and the ancient capital of the Inca Empire known for its archaeological remains and Spanish colonial architecture. I had difficulty breathing at 11,152 feet above sea level. It felt like I had a pile of bricks on my chest and I had a mild headache. I could barely sleep that first night in a hotel on the Plaza de Armas in the central square.

Every hotel and most businesses we visited had Coca leaf tea in the lobby which helped oxygenate the blood. When we moved around a lot we chewed Coca leaves with a mineral activator which numbed my mouth and tongue and provided a stronger lift.

Coca is the life blood of the Andes. When the Spanish conquered the Inca, one of the first things they did when enslaving them was to take their Coca leaves away which incapacitated the Inca making them unable to work, forcing the Spanish to let them continue using it.

Those steeped in the traditions of the Coca leaf say, "Coca no es droga!" Coca is not a drug, and the heart attacks, health problems, and heartbreak that comes with addiction is the price that abusers pay for disrespecting the spirit of the plant.

We visited the baroque Santo Domingo Convent in Cusco which was built on top of the Incan Temple of the Sun and still has remains of Inca stonework and we toured local museums. I was told that the Catholic church knocked down the ancient Inca temples built on power spots and built their churches on top of the old foundations to undermine the Inca traditions. Over time earthquakes levelled the newer Catholic structures while the underlying Inca foundations remained intact, proving the enduring superiority of precision Inca stonework.

We also visited the ruins of Sacsayhuaman which locals jokingly called "Sexy Woman", a citadel on the northern outskirts of Cusco, built by the Inca in the 15th century. They built walls constructed of huge stones creating a structure that is considered one of the most amazing buildings in the world. It is believed that more than 20 thousand men extracted the stones from nearby quarries and moved them 20 kilometers to the hill in the city of Cusco.

Sacsayhuaman retains about 40 percent of its old construction, but the site has structures of up to 125 tons. It is a mystery as to how the Incas built Sacsayhuaman with structures of such unlikely weight and size for the time. The fitting of the irregularly shaped stones are so precise that a sheet of paper cannot be slid between any of the massive stones that make up the mortarless structure.

After taking in Cusco we went to the Sacred Valley in the Andean highlands that formed the heart of the Inca Empire along with Cusco, Machu Picchu, Pisac, and Ollantaytambo. We did a Huachuma ceremony in a large room at a classic resort style hotel where I choked down over a glass of thick, bitter Huachuma and had one of my best experiences with great colors, patterns, and inner revelations. I attributed the richness of my experience to the large quantity I ingested and the fact that we were working with it in its native environment. We also visited Pisac's sprawling handicraft market and hilltop Incan citadel where we found stone carvings, embroidery, Inca and pre-Inca artwork, and crafts from tribes spread across the region.

From there we visited Ollantaytambo on the Urubamba River amid snow-capped Andes and explored the massive Inca fortress made up of large stone terraces on a hillside that includes the Sun Temple and the Princess Baths fountain. The village's old town is an amazing

Inca era grid of cobblestoned streets and adobe buildings.

From Ollantaytambo we took a train to Aguas Calientes in the Urubamba River Valley known for its thermal baths and as a gateway to nearby Machu Picchu. The town center is full of eateries and shops, anchored by the central Mercado Artesanal, a craft market. The food and the atmosphere felt magical.

Early the next morning we drank more Huachuma and did a walking tour of Machu Picchu where we did small ceremonies and healings in key places led by the Shipibo shamans. The peak of this experience was visiting Machu Picchu's Temple of the Condor where we did a short ceremony and left Coca leaf offerings which carried great significance for me due to my intense connection with Condor from my dietas, and the fact that we had named our group the Condors.

One of the highlights of my earlier shamanic studies was visiting the Maya ruins of Uxmal, Palenque, and Tulum, under the influence of local Psilocybin mushrooms which I believe allowed me to embrace an enhanced view of the world through the eyes of the advanced culture that created them. Experiencing Machu Picchu under the influence of Coca and Huachuma brought a similar, yet different immersion and added insights into the nuances and intricacies of Inca culture.

We left Aguas Calientes and traveled across the mountains and deserts of Peru visiting lesser known Inca sites and temples where we did small ceremonies and offerings to pay respect to the powers and places. We also bought art from local artists practicing ancient traditions of weaving and ceramics baked in adobe mud kilns.

While passing through the desert we came to a crossroads in the middle of nowhere where locals who seemed to materialize out of nowhere had dug a pit the size and depth of a burial plot and filled it with wood. They burned it down to coals and buried an entire lamb to roast and baked bread on top of that. That simple mouth watering meal of bread and roasted lamb was one of the best things I have ever eaten.

We went back to Cusco and boarded a large bus to take us to a remote spot higher up in the Andes. Part way through the trip we hit a long line of cars, buses, and trucks stuck in a traffic jam at the base of the mountains. A massive mud slide had washed out the road, covering it with massive boulders and thick mud over a foot deep. After a couple of hours of wandering around outside the bus, our driver contacted another bus stuck on the other side of the landslide and made a deal to exchange passengers so each bus could make a U-turn and get their passengers to their destination.

My full pack weighed about sixty pounds, but I was an experienced backpacker, so it wasn't an issue when I had to cross mud half way up to my knees with everyone else on the bus who had to carry their belongings a quarter of a mile to the other bus. In the middle of my laborious slog I took a step and the suction from the mud caused my foot to come out of my boot leaving it stuck in the mud. I had to balance myself precariously on one leg to retrieve my lost boot and get it back on my foot without filling it with mud or toppling over with the full weight of my pack which I somehow managed before happily boarding the second waiting bus. Hours after our scheduled arrival we arrived at a restaurant in a remote spot in the Andes and ate a late dinner, then we camped for the night.

The following morning a cooking crew and porters set up a tent and made us a full breakfast while wranglers brought horses for the day's ride still higher up into the Andes. After eating and packing they broke down the kitchen and packed it and all our gear into trucks and drove around the mountain where they would be awaiting our arrival after we spent the day crossing on horseback. These Peruvian horsemen used rope bridles so our horses did not use bits in their teeth the way American riders do, which struck me as more humane, and their connection to the horses felt more primal and natural.

We started out at 11,000 feet above sea level and spent the day riding up the mountainside, sometimes crossing wide meadows, eating lunch in the breathtaking views in the middle of one. Other times we traversed narrow trails that hugged the side of cliffs at dizzying heights above deep canyons with barely enough room for our sure footed horses to navigate. I had my camera slung over my shoulder and wanted to take pictures at different points of this spectacular death defying passage, but the logistics of manipulating the camera, lens cap and focus on a bumpy horse ride hugging a narrow canyon wall. This felt too risky and I did not dare take my hands off the reins or saddle horn of the bobbing horse.

As if to confirm the wisdom of my choice, on one of these edge trails my buddy Mike's horse ahead of me had a thing for the horse in front of him and kept sticking his nose between that horses' hind quarters until it bucked. Its hoof caught Mike in the shin with an audible snap, ripping though his pants and cutting a gash deep through to the bone. To his credit, Mike was stoic about his injury and we were not in a position to treat it for some time.

At one point we stopped at a meadow higher up on the mountainside. While sitting upright in the saddle I fuzzed out, losing consciousness for a moment, coming to a little shaken and thankful that nothing like that happened on the trail along the edge of the canyon.

Around 18,000 feet we reached a broad meadow closer to the summit where we dismounted to let the wranglers take the horses back down the trail the way we had come. We had to hike the last mile and a half on foot to meet a waiting shuttle bus to take us part way down the other side of the mountain to our waiting cooks and porters who had set up camp beside hot springs where we would be working the next day.

Exhausted from exertion, a long day, and lack of oxygen we made it to the shuttle and to our unpleasant surprise and horror the driver had swabbed its black rubber floor with kerosene making it pristine and shiny. Our forty five minute fume ride to our camp brought me and others pounding headaches and acid stomachs that made us belch continuously for the entire ride and for some time afterward.

We arrived at the site of ancient Inca and more than likely pre-Inca thermal waters in the Pasco region of central Peru that has healing properties in the middle of Huayllay, that reach a temperature of more than 140 degrees Fahrenheit. These hot springs consist of two springs, one geothermal hot, and one cold. Both of them fed into a large swimming pool sized rectangle about four feet deep. The water temperature was regulated by moving rocks in the hot and cold spring streams to control the flow and mixture of water to easily create ideal conditions. Nearby sat a primitive looking helipad laid out with white rocks in a pattern which was used by Peruvian presidents to visit by helicopter so they could spend time in that renowned place of healing mineral waters.

Somehow amidst the distracting misery of our sickness, my friend SJ and I managed to disinfect and bandage up the bone cutting wound to Mike's shin. We both had concerns over the possibility of infection and cleaned and changed the dressing a number of times over the next few days which did the trick.

I stumbled around wrestling with the tag team pain of my own massive headache and perpetually belching acid stomach until I took a number of aspirin and drank a bottle of Pepto-Bismol which took the edge off of my combined discomforts, eventually allowing me to fall into an uneasy sleep.

The next day we awoke to a light breakfast and a massive pot of thick San Pedro cactus cut up like slices of bread which was boiled down and filtered into a strong drink. Huachuma is exceptionally bitter in comparison to Ayahuasca and challenging to choke down to start with, but the high altitude lack of oxygen and sensitive stomach increased the difficulty of drinking it.

Once we got it down we eased into the hot mineral water of the pool and donned water wings which allowed us to float on the surface of the water while a shaman came around and did body work and massage on each of us. It felt like my stuck negative energies drained off into the warm, soothing water. I did a lot of inner work during this strong experience which only hinted at colors and patterns, but I felt those energies leaving me. At one point I had a mild purge into the rocks at the edge of the pool and felt the invisible psychic negativity leaving me bringing greater clarity and a sense of lightness.

TWENTY FOUR

The Elementals Speak

The next day we visited the open fields of the Huayllay Stone Forest in the Pasco region in the middle of Peru's highest plateau to admire its rock formations. The stone forest covering 15,000 acres is dotted with diverse rock forms resembling a bear, cobra, alpaca, fish, toad, condor, snail, turtle, and elephant. In addition there is the thinker, the tunnel, the nuns, the kiss of the bride and groom, the dinosaur, the tourist, the fungus, the face, and figures of the angel, which all stand out for their beauty and uniqueness. After spending a day there we took a bus that dropped us at a ramshackle storefront in the middle of nowhere where we waited for a second bus to pick us up.

Our last stop was the town of Puno, capital of the Puno Region in southeastern Peru on the shore of Lake Titicaca. Puno is a major agricultural and livestock region where llamas and alpacas graze on surrounding plateaus. Much of its economy relies on a black market fueled by cheap goods smuggled in from Bolivia.

We checked into a hotel which had an eclectic vibe like the rest of the town which consisted of a mixture of traditional Inca art, modern day hippie, and a touch of a laid back European vibe. We were happy to sleep in beds, take hot showers, and eat local dishes after all of our camping. Our final destination on this last leg of our journey was a small island on Lake Titicaca populated by Quechua speakers called Amantani.

Lago Titicaca is on the border of Bolivia and Peru and is the highest navigable lake in the world. By volume of water and surface area it is the largest lake in South America with a surface elevation of

12,507 feet. Older cultures lived on it prior to the arrival of the Incas. Archaeologists and divers found the ruins of an underwater temple thought to be between 1,000 and 1,500 years old, most likely built by the Tiwanaku people.

We took a motorized boat with an enclosed cabin and rear deck that held about a dozen people. Forty five minutes into our trip we stopped at one of sixty man made floating islands clustered in the western corner of the lake near Puno. The Uru people make these islands from layers of cut totora, a thick, buoyant reed that grows in the shallows of the lake and keep them viable by continuously adding reeds to the island's surface.

According to legend the Uru came from the Amazon and migrated to that part of Lake Titicaca in the pre-Columbian era where they were oppressed by the local population. Unable to secure land of their own they built reed islands which could be moved to different parts of the lake for greater safety from hostile neighbors on land.

Golden in color, many of the islands measure about 50 by 50 feet and the largest are half the size of a football field. Each island has thatched houses that belong to members of extended families.

After a mini tour of the island, its crafts, fish farm, and other ingenious customs and practices we took a ride on a large woven reed boat before setting off again to Amantani.

About 4,000 people live in 10 communities on the circular 6 square mile island of Amantani which is topped with two mountain peaks, called Pachatata for Father Earth and Pachamama for Mother Earth. Amantani is considered to be a mystical power place because of the ancient temples on each peak. The islanders who belong to the ancient Aymara culture say that they are more than 4000 years old.

Both temples have very different energies. At Pachatata many people experience clarity, centeredness, inner strength, and a connection with their higher selves. At Pachamama some experience a deeper sense of beauty, love, nourishment, and connection with the earth. These complementary characteristics define masculine and feminine energies. These ancient Inca and Tiwanaku temple ruins on the top of both peaks that sanctified them were the destination of our pilgrimage.

Some locals met us at the boat dock and guided us up through terraced hills planted with wheat, potatoes, and vegetables. Long low stone fences divided the fields and cattle and sheep grazed on the hillsides. There are no cars or hotels on Amantani and machines are not allowed, so all agriculture is done by hand. A few small stores sell basic goods and there is a health clinic and six schools. Electricity produced by a generator provides limited power for a few hours each day. Some families took us into their homes, fed us, and arranged a tour guide for us.

The following morning we drank a healthy dose of Huachuma and started up the trail on a wind free, crystal clear cloudless day toward the peaks on a path up through stone arches reputed to act as initiatory gateways. After a scenic hike we came to a plateau at a crossroad. One path went to the lower temple of Pachatata and the other to the higher temple of Pachamama.

We went first to the distinctive square masculine temple of Pachatata and wanted to do a short ceremony there, but our priest guide said that the temple was only open once a year for ceremony on a special day. He appreciated the respect we had for it and was sympathetic to the fact that we had travelled so far to pay our respects, so he went off alone and offered a prayer to ask for special permission and was granted it. With this added blessing he let us in and joined us for a brief, heartfelt ceremony within the temple walls, then we set out for the circular feminine Pachamama temple higher up on the more open, wider peak.

They let us look inside the ancient round structure of the Pachamama temple but we could not go in. We felt lucky to have been given access to the Pachatata temple, so we accepted this restriction and set ourselves up outside the temple gate to offer prayers to the feminine under a pristine cloudless blue sky without any sign of wind all day. While hiking the day had grown warmer, so I took off my fleece jacket and flannel shirt and piled them a few feet from where I sat across from my teacher.

He started off soft and slow praying to the feminine and his prayers grew more fervent while rising in volume, passion, and intensity. I was touched by the depth of his sincerity and at one point felt a little embarrassed for him at such an outward display of emotion and vulnerability, as I had never experienced anything like that with anyone before.

When he reached a crescendo a small dust devil appeared over my shirt and jacket and intensified as if driven by the energy of his emotionally charged prayers until it lifted my shirt and jacket about a dozen feet into the air. I'm not sure how long they floated there as the whole mind blowing experience felt timeless, but that extended magical moment felt like it was a direct message for me.

As his prayers diminished the dust devil gently lowered my shirt and jacket back to the ground and disappeared, leaving me stunned and what I can only describe as activated. This had been one of those knock on spirit's door moments where spirit knocks back and shakes your world similar to the way my lucid dream of Santa Teresa did in the jungle, which had been my first life changing contact with what I now call the Cosmic Feminine. Not only had it impressed me on multiple levels, its manifestation solidified my understanding of the nature of working with elemental spirits. We had been told that power and energy moves in vortexes and that spirit moves in journey work in the same spiraling manner. I can't think of a more direct way to witness and experience an elemental show of power than this.

I joked with my teacher on the way back down the path and called him Moses and questioned whether we would be seeing a parting of the waters. That night after being fed by our hosts we were invited to a fiesta at a hall in town where they put on a traditional dance show for us, then they dressed us in their traditional clothes to join the dance with them.

The island's generator went off for the night and I had about a half a dozen kids escorting me back to where I was staying. I was at a loss for the language, so I trooped along with them marching behind me in the dark while I made animal sounds of a dog, cat, cow, rooster, and seal, although I figured they didn't know what a seal was. Every time I made a sound they had a giggle fest and were soon imitating me until we had an ongoing dialogue of animal sounds between us all.

TWENTY FIVE

Cross Cultural Shamanism

While bridging my Condor group and Yoda's group I shared information and practices I was learning between them. One of the valuable things I learned from my two year study has infused my shamanic studies and my writing which was not only an ancient cross cultural belief, but central to Gurdjieff's teachings which had already made a lasting impression on me. This knowledge is also integral to Joesph Campbell's hero's journey, something I was intimately familiar with and its central place in the art of storytelling, and it all tied in with the statement that everything is energy.

One of the primary goals of shamanism is to master energies starting with personal subjectivity where our perception of reality is created, outward to all its manifestations in the "objective" world that surrounds us. The essence of this is what I call shamanic mirroring.

In this observational practice the people in our lives mirror our subpersonalities, providing us with reflections of our inner world. The outer world is a reflection of the inner, much of which is shadow, both good and bad. Some of the reflections are beautiful and many are undesirable and denied. This circular diagram from Robert McKee's **Story** provides an excellent map of the zones and levels of personal conflict we can experience. Any zone can interact with any other zone providing ample opportunity to discover the complexity of our inner and outer relationships.

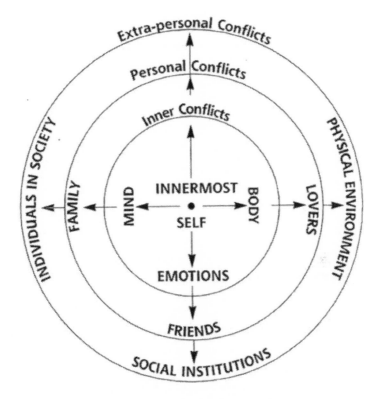

This can also be envisioned as the "center of the universe" where our world view is formed as it maps the interplay of energetic interactions that start in the middle and work their way out. At the center we find the innermost self which is composed of mind, body, and emotions. Everyone knows what it is like to have conflict between these three forces. Typically, one of them leads while the other two are relegated to shadow until a strong stimulus causes them to pop out, sometimes when least expected.

When confronted with something we might react in the following order; first with our intellect (mind), because that is what we have grown to depend on, then by acting (body), then we may feel good or bad about what we did (emotion). Anyone can act in any combination of ways, but usually lead with their most habitual response at the expense of the other two.

One of the goals of integrating the shadow in the process of individuation, and one of the rewards of personal power a shaman gets from getting dismembered or swallowed by the jaguar is to cultivate the ability to react with all three simultaneously in a balanced way.

These three primary energies have been characterized throughout myth and history in many ways. The thinking mind is referred to as knowledge and wisdom, the moving body is referred to as energy and power, while emotion is referred to as love. On one end of the spectrum the modern divide and conquer scientific mind set has given mind the most attention. Energetically it is the most stable. On the other end emotion is the quickest, most mercurial, and hardest to control. The body usually serves the other two, though it holds deep wisdom of its own that is often ignored.

The Inca view of reality is a shamanic one that has three worlds; the upper world, represented by the Condor which is rose colored and thought of as love. The middle world is represented by the jaguar or puma and is electric blue signifying power, and the lower world is represented by the serpent which is gold, signifying wisdom. When the three are combined in harmony they create a beautiful electric violet hue.

I discovered how these three energies have been depicted in stories, particularly when we take into account secondary characters who mirror the inner life of the protagonist. One of the most striking examples of this is in **The Wizard of Oz** where Dorothy embarks on her hero's quest to find her way home. Her three primary allies are the tin man, who wants a heart (love - emotion), the cowardly lion, who wants courage (power - body), and the scarecrow, who wants a brain (wisdom - mind).

Shamans navigate multifaceted realities because they realize that their power lies in how they filter, see, and react to the realms they come in contact with by manipulating their perception with the knowledge that all they encounter comes through their subjective experience where everything is connected to everything else. Plants, animals, man, and elemental spirits all interact with each other in visible and invisible ways. Shamans more than anyone else know that even though the center of the universe is right between their eyes, their real home is where the heart is.

This ancient belief is symbolized by the **chakana,** or **Inca Cross**, a stepped cross made up of an asymmetrical cross indicating the cardinal points of the compass and a superimposed square to represent the other two levels of existence.

The three levels of existence are *Hana Pacha,* the upper world inhabited by the superior gods, *Kay Pacha*, the world of everyday existence, and *Ukhu* or *Urin Pacha,* the underworld inhabited by spirits of the dead, ancestors, their overlords and other deities with close contact to the Earth plane. The hole through the center of the cross is the Axis; the cosmic vault that shamans transit through to the other levels. It also represents Cusco, the center of the Incan empire and the Southern Cross constellation.

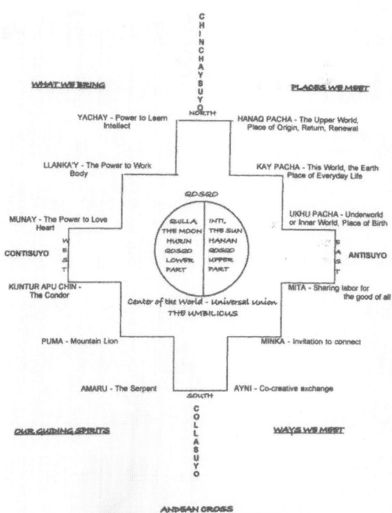

161

One of the things that drew me to shamanism was the myth of the flood which permeates cultural mythologies worldwide, even infusing the ancient beliefs of remote South American tribes prior to any western contact. Subsequently, one of the strong attractions to joining the two year study program was its broader focus on all aspects of shamanism back to its prehistoric roots regardless of its geographical location or historical origins. Two additional gems of knowledge we learned about were elements of African and Chinese shamanism.

In African shamanism the four chambers of the heart contain a vast storehouse of wisdom. One chamber relates to reliability which ties into doing things in a whole hearted way. Another chamber associates with having an open or closed heart. An open heart represents unconditional love which manifests as forgiving yourself and others without carrying grudges, resentments, and retaliations. Feelings of hurt and shame turn into anger and anger turns into retaliation. When you judge, your heart contracts and when you embrace acceptance it expands. Anger always comes from disappointed expectations. A third chamber relates to having a strong heart which manifests in being courageous, brave, and being in integrity through honesty of character. What you do in the face of conflict is a great catalyst for transformation.

As an aside, one of the core truths of fiction writing is that character reveals itself through conflict.

The fourth chamber correlates to a clear heart. Clarity is the ability to speak in a forthright manner stating the essentials and it inspires safety in others and confidence.

African shamanic wisdom is also thought of as four rivers that convey four questions to ask yourself at the end of the day and to guide you in how not to join the "procession of the living dead".

The first river is inspiration.
Who and what has uplifted and expanded me today?

The second river is challenge.
What has invited me to grow beyond my comfort zone?

The third river is surprise.
Where was I delighted by the unexpected?

The fourth river is love.
Where was I touched and moved to open my heart?

There are also four questions to ask if you lose heart.

When did I stop singing?

When did I stop dancing?

When did I stop being interested in my own life story?

When did I stop being comforted by silence?

Chinese plant and animal medicine and acupuncture are rooted in ancient Chinese shamanism. In traditional shamanism there are four primary elemental spirits; earth, air, fire, and water. Chinese medicine has five primary elemental spirits; wood, fire, earth, metal, and water.

Wood represents the liver and gall bladder. Its color is green, its direction is East, and it is where we store anger. To heal the liver, talk to the elemental of the tree.

Fire represents the heart. Its color is red, its direction is South, and it is where unconditional acceptance and joy are felt. The drum is its heartbeat and it also represents the small intestine. To heal the heart work with the elemental sun and fire.

Earth represents the stomach. Its color is yellow, its direction is the center, and it is where anxiety is felt, and it is able to put out the fire. It also represents the spleen. To heal the stomach work with the elemental earth.

Metal represents the lungs. Its color is a silvery metallic white, its direction is West, and it is associated with sorrow, grief, and inspiration. It also represents the pancreas. To heal the lungs lie on the elemental of a rock.

Water represents the kidneys. Its color is blue-black, its direction is North, and it is associated with instinctive fear and fight or flight. To heal the kidneys sit by the ocean or another elemental body of water.

In Chinese medicine the left side of the body is Yin, the feminine, and the right side is yang, the masculine. The thumb is connected to wood and the liver, the index finger is fire and the heart, the middle finger is earth and the stomach, the fourth finger is metal and the lungs, and the pinkie finger is water and the kidneys.

The last two little gems I gleaned is that we reflect during the first half of life with moon energy and give off life radiating with sun energy the second half of our life.

Finally, Ayahuasca is thought of as the Mother of the voice in the ear which I was due to intimately connect with in the near future during another plant dieta.

When I returned from the Andes Penny acted out in an explosive rage and attacked me by hitting me and pulling my hair. When she was lost in this emotionally disturbed state I didn't recognize who she was and her attack made my open heart collapse in on itself.

Among other things I believe her assault came because she resented the fact that I was travelling and having adventures which was the essence and purpose of my life, writing and learning while she had to work and stay home with her kids.

This trauma pointed to something deeper that I couldn't see because I was blinded by my own deeper commitment to my flawed lifelong myth of riding in on my white horse and saving the day.

TWENTY SIX

Picaflor Flirts First

Less than a month after my magical Andean adventure I left for the Amazon again on Friday October 10th, 2003. The morning that I left for the jungle I commented to Penny on the hummingbirds I saw at the fountain I had rebuilt in our yard. I carpooled to L.A. with Dog the chiropractor who I had met the previous year. We stopped at the Getty museum on the way to a friend's house I call Otorongo where we planned to spend the night so we could get an early start to the airport in the morning. Dog and I passed on the tram and walked up the hill to the museum. While walking I mentioned the hummingbirds I saw that morning. Seconds after I spoke a hummingbird darted in and flew around in front of us for a moment and Dog and I looked at each other with mild amazement.

When we got to Otorongo's house we ate and at Dog's urging, he, his new Japanese girlfriend, a gifted feature film director we called Coyote, Otorongo, and I did a hit of 5MEODMT to send us off on our adventure.

Nineteen people met us at LAX which seemed like too many, but my Canadian friends had returned and I adjusted. A total of eleven people were returning and I noticed how much calmer, subdued, and accepting I was of things in comparison to my three prior years, and would continue to gauge my overall growth and changes when I returned each successive year.

After the eight hour flight from Los Angeles to Lima and the one hour hop from Lima to Pucallpa, we sat in a large second floor echoing concrete hotel room above the streets of Pucallpa amid the cacophony of two stroke rickshaws, beeping horns, and the smell of exhaust punctuated by the sound of kids and the scents of cooking food.

Twenty of us sat in a circle while Ronaldo gave us the fine points and specifics of our upcoming dieta translated by Yoda. I recorded this talk and edited it, but like other translations spellings may be incorrect from phonetic translations and many are Quechua or Shipibo in origin. Much of this information was covered in past dietas, so I edited to remove redundancies except where reiteration adds to the importance of the subject. Rolando always went out of his way to convey this information in depth to make sure everyone was as fully informed as possible. Here is what he shared this time.

"The *dieta* is a time devoted to entering a place of relative isolation where you spend time taking plants with a suitable guide in the right place in the right context. One plant like Ayahuasca is psychotropic. Some of the other plants are slightly psychotropic, and some are not psychotropic, but have a different effect on you. Within the world of plants Ayahuasca is the most potent and the most known in this area of the world.

When you take it, it gives you visions and certain feelings, but around and beyond Ayahuasca there exists many other plants that are also teacher plants that have a different form of teaching. In order for us to ingest them they need a certain protocol so we can experiment with what they have to teach us. Within this group of other teacher plants in addition to Ayahuasca they produce several different types of effects.

For example when you take certain plants they ground, center, and connect you within Mother nature. In some cases the external form and shape of the plant gives some indication as to the effect the plant will have on you.

In the case of Ayahuasca it is considered a double plant as it is a tall vine that creeps up trees thirty or forty feet high and blooms up there. At the same time it has a very elaborate root system into the ground. From that you can say that Ayahuasca is a plant that takes you into high visions into the divine sky. At the same time it has strong roots in the earth.

Bobinsana lives on the edges of the rivers and has an elaborate root system and its branches open out. In the winter rains make the waters rise and it sometimes covers the whole plant keeping it underwater for three or four months but its elaborate root system keeps it in place. In a similar way to how we talked about Ayahuasca visions, Bobinsana tends to ground you and creates an internal flower like opening within you which is like the shape of the plant and its open branch structure, so it has the effect of grounding you while opening you internally.

There are another group of plants which are basically cleansing, purifying plants. When you ingest any of them you are cleansed by vomit, diarrhea, or sweating. Tobacco is one and Yaguarpanga is another. If you take Yaguarpanga and vomit repeatedly before drinking Ayahuasca you will vomit a lot less after drinking the Ayahuasca. When you purge this way, it is much more than just undigested food in your stomach, it is also an energetic purge that is similar to opening and untying a knot. Sometimes when you take Ayahuasca you can become aware of and see what you are energetically vomiting in the form of vermin, squirming worms, snakes, and other representatives of negative energy.

There is a different group of plants whose purpose is to strengthen you physically, emotionally, and spiritually, like Chuchuwasi. Essentially the plants that provide strength are not bushes, but large trees. Usually the bark is used as a tea or infusion or sometimes it is just ground up bark in water.

There are some plants whose function is to produce dreams.

One plant in particular called Japushatini grows on the surface of the water. You harvest the plant from there, dry it, and blend it with another plant and smoke it. It's not addictive and produces an effect opposite to tobacco which contracts the lungs. This dreaming plant expands them.

There's another group of plants that deal with the emotional aspects of a person. The effect is to produce emotional results like an open heart. Ushpawasha is one of these. Sometimes it produces a change in the state of consciousness. It often has the effect of opening up a chest of emotions that have been boxed in that you begin to feel. It's sometimes called the plant of rejuvenation.

There are many other plants with other uses, but what is important is that these plants all need to be taken within a certain context while following rules and conditions which have been developed through generations of trial and error. The dieta that we are doing here is to bring us as close as possible to the traditional context that has been handed down without deviating from it.

One of the rules is the need to do the work in an isolated place away from the city and the noise, smoke, fumes, and any other contamination. We also need to be isolated from each other. When you start the dieta you stop taking salt which is the gateway into the diet and in the act of breaking the diet as the gateway out at the end. One of the reasons the diet is the way it is, is that rice, quinoa, unripe plátanos, chicken, and fish are all bland with no flavor or odor.

It is important to follow the diet exactly as prescribed to gain the benefits it provides. When you ingest a plant drink you are taking in more than just a water infusion or preparation, you are ingesting the essence or spirit of that plant which infuses your whole body. This practice is not compatible with foods that are not on the diet. The diet and context that it happens in creates a special container that makes the Ayahuasca sessions more intense.

The cleansing and healing will also be more intense because we will be disconnecting from the rest of the world for ten days and will have a chance to experiment and find out what it was like in ancient times doing a traditional shamanic diet and how to learn from the plants. In line with this practice it is also recommended not to use soap, toothpaste, deodorant, lotions, makeup, perfumes of any kind, and anything that has any scent or flavor of any kind."

The following morning we took the two hour ride to the village where we boarded long canoes for the two hour ride upriver to the shaman's camp. Once we reached it I had mild competition for my tambo at the end of the line, but I asserted myself with a little seniority as this was my fourth dieta.

After my mind blowing experience with the elemental wind at the Pachamama temple on Amantani one of my primary intentions was to consciously work with the energies of this most special place in the jungle by practicing Qi Gong which is considered an active prayer. As part of my preparation I did an offering to the four directions and the land I was on with tobacco smoke from a cigarette called a mapacho, which I had been learning to work with in my two year study. I also blew smoke all over my tambo and mosquito net as added protection. A mapacho is rolled from Nicotiana Rustica, a jungle plant in the family Solanaceae which is a potent variety of tobacco containing up to nine times more nicotine than the common species of Nicotiana tabacum prevalent in North America.

As my teacher plant I would be working with Uña de Gato known as Cat's Claw, a diuretic that cleans your liver and kidneys, and bolsters your immune system while realigning the energies of your body. Our last full meal on Sunday night consisted of chicken soup, bread, olives, cheese, rice, and vegetables.

I awoke on Monday morning from wild dreams after sleeping deep as a result of being sleep deprived with all the travelling we had done. I also knew that the place where I was stimulated dreaming as well. My previous year's dieta with Ushpawasha was strongly connected to dreaming and my profound life changing Santa Teresa dream and visions from my first year's dieta with Bobinsana made my dreams and visions play off of each other, which carried great significance.

Uña de Gato was not known for influencing dreams and visions and these dreams were wild, nonsensical, chaotic, and fragmented. I didn't see any value in recording them except for what I thought might be any significant details.

At one point I awoke moaning from a trapped place and heard disembodied voices saying, "What are you doing in my house?" When I realized I was in the jungle I said, "How can they haunt an open air hut?" All the voices and interruptions went away and I fell back to sleep.

Breakfast was a bowl of rice. Penny's emotionally disturbed explosive rage and her assault on me when I returned from the Andes weighed heavy on me. I was reading **In Search of the Miraculous** by P.D. Ouspensky a Russian esotericist known for his expositions of the early work of Gurdjieff. I hoped to help Penny and I grow more, hopefully past this kind of trauma. One passage I read got my attention.

To awaken for man means to be dehypnotized. In this lies a chief difficulty and in this also lies the guarantee of its possibility for there is no organic reason for sleep and man can awaken. Theoretically he can, but practically it is almost impossible because as soon as a man awakens for a moment and opens his eyes all the forces that caused him to fall asleep begin to act upon him with tenfold energy and he immediately falls asleep again, very often dreaming that he is awake or is awakening.

I returned exhausted from our first session and did my routine plant bath and journaling on my recorder. I found out later on a plant walk that we were working with black Ayahuasca.

The ceremony was incredible, and as usual beyond description. We had twenty three people total in the circle and in this session I flew with Condor and energetically visited Penny and her kids, checked up on the house, and checked in on my Mom who had been battling colon cancer for a number of years now. My experience became uncomfortably intense at times, but overall it was blissful which I thought of as a gentle welcome from the Mother.

I did not purge and felt no fear going in. I attributed this to the work I was doing with my two year group which made a big difference in all my experiences. A number of people mentioned the big change they saw in me, confirming how much calmer, subdued, and accepting I was of things, validating my self perception of growth when I returned each successive year.

I ended up taking two doses. After the first one I flew through beautiful surreal snowy white rainbow-hued dimensions interspersed with browns and colored arabesque patterns and visions. At one point the preternatural white light completely filled me, at first feeling soft and furry like the effect photographers get with gel filters, then they became electric, transcendent, and luminescent.

We were also blessed by the presence of Amelia, a Shipiba curandera with a beautiful voice. A lot of people had a hard time in this first ceremony, something I was spared. While flying through my bliss I got lots of insights about my historical novel **Land Without Evil**. I also went through a process of catching myself judging people, calling myself on it, and redirecting my thoughts until my second dose kicked in and I took off again.

While journaling my experiences it started raining and everything became bright, so I thought dawn might be breaking or the moonlight was extra bright. Either way it was a unique and surreal magical jungle moment that did in fact brighten into dawn. One of Yoda's pearls of wisdom from the ceremony stuck with me, which was a saying from Buddha.

"The seed of compassion planted within the web of humanity grows into a tree of self realization."

He also told us a story about a Mayan ruler.

One of Cortez's lieutenants conquered and killed all the Mayan warriors and imprisoned this ruler in a big circular hole in the ground and shut him into darkness. The hole was divided into two sections.

The ruler was put in one and they put a jaguar in the other. The ruler was kept in darkness until mid-day when they took the cover off and lowered him food.

He spent years trying to understand it all and contemplating the meaning of his life. There was a legend that the creator had put the answer to the secret of life hidden in one sentence that had the power to transform and destroy everything and take over. They searched all the books and all the records and scrolls but never found it. The ruler drove himself crazy trying to figure it out, but couldn't. Years passed and he grew old and had the same routine of an hour of light a day when he was given food. All he ever saw when the mid-day light came was the jaguar, so he studied and contemplated it because that was all he had.

One day he found the sentence written in the spots on the jaguar and in a moment of revelation knew that if he uttered it, it would bring down the walls of his prison, free him, and cast destruction on his captors, but he decided not to do that. Instead, he made peace with himself and chose to keep the secret and not destroy everything and he died, never uttering the sentence.

In the later part of the ceremony Amelia the Shipiba healer sang to those having a hard time, then she came and blessed me singing sweet songs and blowing Agua de Florida on my head and hands, rounding off a blissful night for me. While others had a rough ride with strong emotions and purges I flew with Condor seeing multitudes of awesome colors and patterns while gaining insights about my relationship with Penny and her unsettling emotional issues.

I also travelled into my past and revisited situations as a one step removed objective observer which fed into the process of writing **Spirit Matters**. I so appreciated Ayahuasca for the way she helped me with that and the way it effortlessly dovetailed into my storytelling process.

I thought that the reason I had such a gentle, loving, informed journey was because of the tobacco offering I did before the ceremony and my new love, respect, and connection with the elementals. I was incorporating all of the things I learned in the two year study into this which enhanced the overall experience immensely. I also experienced increasing instances of telepathy where I would have a thought, then José would speak it in the next moment echoing my numinous Apinaré connection and blessing from my 2001 dieta.

TWENTY SEVEN

A Deepening Animal Spirit Connection

I slept hard for a few hours and was pleasantly surprised to get chicken, rice, and plátanos for breakfast along with a third of a pitcher of Uña de Gato. I downed the first glass which left a bitter aftertaste and took a mud bath after that.

Later that morning some butterflies landed on me. If that had happened a few years ago I would have panicked from the thought of bugs touching me, a fear that came from my mother who was terrified of them. Now free of any fear I corralled my energy and didn't move, something I was learning more about when it came to connecting with animals physically, psychically, and emotionally. I had come to understand that any communication or connection with them had to be on their terms.

As my studies of shamanism unfolded my first experience of what I can only describe as a deep telepathic connection with an animal, and the calm fearless receptive energy it required was taught to me by my friend's cat Sparky. I called him the psycho Charlie Manson cat because of his behavior and the fact that when he looked at you his eyes bounced back and forth like one of those old cat clocks with a pendulum tail on steroids.

When my friends took off for vacation they asked me to look in on him and every time I showed up to feed him he hissed and acted demented and aggressive toward me which puzzled me as I had come to feed him. He never liked me and I always gave him a wide berth. I was visiting these friends one night and had been working with 5MEODMT for a few years and for a reason I cannot remember I decided to take a 5MEO journey there.

To my amazement, when I came to from the short journey, Sparky was in my face, loving me up, and for a few minutes I felt like I fully embraced his essence. The lesson he taught me was that he had to be in charge to communicate and connect and it unquestionably had to be on his terms. After that mind boggling experience I understood the nature of the energy I needed to cultivate connecting with animals and it opened the door to more connections.

One day while bike riding with Penny I saw a dove on a fence. When I looked over at it, it flew off the fence and across the street to land on my shoulder for a brief moment before flying back to its perch to look at me in what I thought of as a loving manner, as if to say, "How about that?"

On another occasion I was preparing to join an Ayahuasca ceremony at a nature reserve. I stepped outside to a parking area at dusk, that magical time between the worlds and spotted a fox about thirty feet away. I grew excited but remembered to keep my energy even and receptive. To my amazement the fox came over to me and spent a minute or so rubbing himself back and forth against me the way cats do when they show affection. I exploded inside with excitement at the magic of it and resisted the urge to reach down and pat him while keeping my energy even. After thoroughly rubbing me in what could only have been affection and ownership, he trotted off and stopped at the spot where I originally saw him and gazed back at me with an expression that appeared to be the same loving one the dove had, as if to also say, "How about that?"

After my butterfly connection I was reading **In Search of the Miraculous** which was written around nineteen sixteen and had the revelation that it was the same teachings we were learning in the two year study. I couldn't wait to share this discovery with my teachers, who confirmed it when I told them.

Dinner that night consisted of brown rice and a plátano. I went to bed with a headache and drifted off to sleep, waking a short time later from a sharp pain in the side of my head. I surrendered, took a couple of aspirin and tried to sleep again, but couldn't. Soon after my stomach became upset and the dual pains drove me harder, so I took a third aspirin and finally fell asleep, waking some time later that morning from disjointed, chaotic dream fragments. I realized from my last few years of experience that my first jungle dreams were typically chaotic, as if my subconscious was cleaning out the clutter to go deeper, so I recorded a short summary of them.

The main theme of these dreams was about moving as I was spending a lot of time thinking about my mother's impending death and the fact that I was her executor. Part of me dreaded the challenge of clearing out her house after she died. I wanted to take her on a cruise before that happened as she had expressed a strong desire for that.

I went to look at the first house I owned to find the fences broken down, the windows broken, and lots of other things destroyed. I thought someone had broken into it, but nothing was missing and a lot of items were still there that I thought I had already dealt with. Some new owners came to remodel it and I had a number of possessions that I still had to move which presented an ongoing nightmare related to issues I had to face when I let go of my bigger house before moving into the smaller duplex with Penny and her kids. I tried to call her and discovered that the cell phone I had wasn't mine, so I found another person who gave me a cell phone that wasn't mine either. I tried to call on still another phone, but could not get through to Penny, then I was driving in a car trying to find her to let her know what was happening, but I couldn't find her. One of the items in question was my Mom's bedroom set that she wanted me to have in real life, but I could not take it as I had no place to keep it.

That night I came back from our second session saying it was unlike any other session I had ever been in before. It had been extraordinarily quiet and gentle in comparison to the first night when most of the people had loud raucous disturbing trips with the exception of me and one or two others, but it was powerful nonetheless with lots of insights. This stark contrast reinforced one of the things I loved most about Ayahuasca which is its unpredictability.

In his usual fashion Yoda shared a quote by Aristotle, which said, "The way to figure out and know if you have chosen the right path for your life is to gauge how much happiness is in your life."

After drinking a full dose my visions came on dark and uncomfortable as if some invisible force weighted me down, but it wasn't dark in the sense of hellish visions, just intense with dark visuals. Condor came and my crossed legs flapped like wings, but when I moved around she left which made a deep impression on me and taught me to be open, calm, and to cultivate the same receptive energy needed to connect the way I had with the butterflies.

When this revelation sank in, Condor came back and my leg-wings flapped hard, bringing me back to my past, showing me about the spirits of other birds. I revisited a shameful experience from when I had been seven years old. Some friends found some baby pigeons and threw big rocks on them, killing them. I got caught up in the madness and joined in the killing frenzy, then felt awful about it when it was over, realizing how senseless and stupid it was, then I revisited a similar incident from when I was in the Air Force. I bought a shotgun from a biker friend and went into a field and shot at a group of crows up in the top of a tree, instantly feeling guilt again, this time stronger from the mindless killing when three of them dropped to the ground. After beating myself up over this I rationalized that the slaughtered crows and pigeons gave their lives so I could learn the hard lesson, so I honored them and all other forms of life ever since.

When that experience passed I flew through exquisite colored visions and patterns as if being rewarded for the lesson. I visited Penny and her kids and I went to my Mom who had a dying wish of going on a cruise, something I intended to make happen.

After finishing my audio journal I went to sleep and woke up on Friday morning refreshed. I usually never dream after a ceremony, but on this morning I awoke feeling like I was in an unusually strange inexplicable emotional place that terrified me until I accepted it, then it felt exquisite. When I did Qi Gong that morning the biggest Hummingbird I have ever seen stopped in front of me and hovered there for a couple of seconds before zipping off.

I contemplated how I had woken up from wild chaotic dreams not worth recording. I didn't feel that they added anything of substance that would contribute to the narrative of my adventure.

The Uña de Gato they brought that morning was noticeably stronger and tasted more like Ayahuasca to me which made it harder to get down. I followed up with Qi Gong, a mud bath and a swim. Breakfast was quinoa and a plátano. After that I spent the day resting as our third session was coming that night.

I returned from a powerful mid-point session in the wee hours of the morning once more struggling to convey what I experienced when I sat down to journal after my plant bath.

I felt good and strong going in and didn't have the headache and body aches that had been plaguing me. I thought a chiropractic adjustment I had gotten from Dog combined with the Qi Gong enhanced my endurance along with the cumulative strengthening effect of the Uña de Gato.

Yoda gave us a few pointers before the ceremony. One of the things he said that got my attention was that Ayahuasca finds your weakness and exploits it. If you are fearful it will take you to a hell of sheer terror and show you your weaknesses. If you are angry you will get angrier and it will amplify your madness.

I thought about taking a second dose but didn't need it. I punched through and flew far, wide, hard, and fast thinking that Ayahuasca was showing me my power. Along with this intimidating show of power, I hoped and half expected to find a jaguar because of its power being revealed to me, then I realized that any connection would have to be on its terms, so I couldn't hunt it. It had to hunt me. As my journey continued, I received a steady flow of insights related to me and Penny's emotional disturbance amidst beautiful and intense visions, places, and dimensions with indescribable colors and hues, among them a beautiful brilliant emerald green forest, all guided by the sweet icaros of Carlos the apprentice who was coming into his own, and Amelia the Shipiba curandera.

Later in the session Yoda told another wonderful jungle story.

A man and his wife lived in the jungle moving around from place to place where the man hunted, the woman gathered, and they farmed together. One day the man woke up and while lying in his hammock said to his wife, "I don't feel like going out and hunting for food today. Would you go out and hunt for me?"

She said, "Okay," and left for a couple of hours coming back with some game, so they ate and everything was good.

He liked that, so the same thing happened the next day. Once again she went out and came back with game and they ate. He grew to like this new arrangement and it became the daily routine which went on for quite some time, allowing him to nap and relax all day while his wife kept him fed, content, and growing fatter.

One day while sleeping peacefully he opened his eyes to find himself face to face with a massive jaguar lunging toward him, mouth open, terrifying him to no end. In that instant he surrendered, knowing that his death had come and in that brief flash of awareness he felt remorse for his laziness and for what he had done.

The jaguar pounced onto him, its gaping maw driving toward his face and at the moment it closed its jaw on his head it transformed into his wife, who said, "Never, ever, ever, send out a woman to do a man's job."

He told another story in first person by an unknown Spanish writer that went like this.

I knew that one day my enemy would come and I spent the days of my life waiting for him. Many years passed with the knowledge that he would come.

One day I was in my house living on the side of a mountain. I looked out and off in the distance came the figure of a man and I knew he was my enemy. As he came closer I saw that he was bent over and the closer he came I saw that he was an old man struggling up the side of the mountain, stopping frequently to catch his breath.

After his long laborious climb I heard a knock on the door and opened it to a frail, trembling, barely breathing emaciated old man who said, "I almost killed myself climbing up this mountain and I need to rest. Can I lie down on your bed?"

I felt compassion so I let him, then I leaned over him and said, "What can I do for you?" When I did I saw a bulge of sharp metal under his robe and realized it was a gun.

He said, "I am your enemy and I have come here to kill you. I came under the guise of an old man as a ruse to get into your house to kill you."

I didn't know what to do. He had the gun and he was getting ready to kill me and there was nothing that I could do. I was totally helpless. All I could think of was to talk my way out of it, so I started talking, saying, "I am very sorry. Why do you have to kill me? I confess that earlier in my life I abused a young boy and now I am very sorry for that."

My enemy said, "That's too bad because I am the young boy you abused and I am here to kill you."

I didn't know what to do, then I realized that a miracle was happening because I was getting repentance for my past sins. I was still going to die, but death seemed unnecessary because I had repented for my sins. I said, "I am so very sorry for what I did and that was so many years in the past. Why can't we just let it go? Can we just move on with our lives and live in peace with each other and forgive and forget?"

My enemy said, "No. I can't. I'm here to kill you." As I was getting ready to die, I realized that *I* was the young boy that I had abused and the enemy was myself.

TWENTY EIGHT

Shamanic Story Time

I felt good when I woke up on Saturday morning and took a mud bath before a breakfast of runny oatmeal and a plátano. Later that day Ronaldo took us on a walk to learn more about the teacher plants which Yoda translated from Spanish. A couple of plants I described from prior plant walks have been left out and some descriptions of them overlap previous ones, so I included them for a more comprehensive understanding of their uses.

"A variety of Renaco that we use the bark from is cooked, boiled, and drank, and is great for muscle and bone problems, rheumatism, and the circulatory system. The external shape and form of the plant is what causes the effect on our body. The Renaco needs the base of a palm to grow and support it in a symbiotic relationship. If you look up you can't see its top.

In the same way Renaco engulfs the palm tree it takes us over when we drink it giving us strength and stability. The energy at the curing level gives you the kind of strength demonstrated metaphorically with the statement that not any wind can blow you over. In general Renaco finds a host and grows like a little innocent plant, then it overtakes its host. The curanderas say that the palm has a feminine spirit and Renaco has a masculine spirit.

Another smaller teacher plant of water is called Yakusisa. Yaku is a Quechua word that means water, and *sisa* means it is either standing up or pointing. It generally grows over rocks and is similar to a small Bobinsana in its physical effects as well as its energetic effects. There are several varieties of Yakusisa and the part that is used is the root which is cooked. The plant and its roots grow over rock and it grows taller in the winter. It always stays in its place when the rushing water comes through. The energetic level of the large roots are sustained in the harsh context of the rocks.

In general water plants allow us to go deeper within our dreams and can be mixed with Bobinsana. In the same way it opens up from its roots, it opens us up when we drink it.

Guayusa that we use for plant baths can also be drank in a dieta using the leaves and part of the bark which are cooked. Its role is to return courage on an energetic level to the person who drinks it."

When I first went to the jungle I did not know any Spanish and every time they checked in on me, I responded saying "Bueno bueno," twice because it was all the Spanish I knew and that became my nickname which sticks to this day. On this plant walk Ronaldo showed us the Supaicasha palm, known as Thorn of the Devil, which I described in a previous year's plant walk. When Ronaldo showed it to us this time I said, "No bueno! No bueno!", which cracked him up.

Anthropologists and historians say the Inca didn't know about Ayahuasca, but the people in the jungle who work with plants believe they did because of the imagery in the visions they see.

We had what I call jungle chicken some of which was too tough to chew for dinner that Saturday night with rice and a plátano.

I woke up on Sunday morning feeling drained and the *Uña de Gato* was extra strong which upset my stomach and created a lot of gas that had me belching repeatedly and I was on the threshold of a headache making for a challenging day that fueled my burgeoning irritability. I drank a second glass and the discomfort continued, then I forced myself to drink the last two remaining glasses. Dinner before the ceremony was rice and a plátano that I had to force myself to eat because of my stomach upset.

I came back from our fourth session on Sunday night reporting it as powerful, chaotic, and a real doozy. Ronaldo led the first three sessions before he had to leave, so José led this fourth one. He gave me an extra large dose and did a lot of work with tobacco.

My visions came on with a dark electric violet in the middle of my forehead, which I perceived as a combination of the rose color of love, the electric blue of power, and the gold of wisdom, confirming for me that I would be getting a great lesson in power.

I hadn't purged for the last three sessions, but on this night when

Amelia sang I had a massive purge including snot from my nose, tears from my eyes, and a gut wrenching purge that sent me flying off into a bright red paisley infused psychedelic realm. I launched so hard and so far that I lost any sense of being physically present in the jungle. When I returned from that timeless journey I felt a disturbance deep in my gut and hustled to the latrine where I exploded out my back end.

Needless to say this activity dissipated my burgeoning irritability, making me feel relieved and much lighter. As had become my custom, I flew far and wide, energetically checking in on close friends and family and I spent a lot of time working on myself. At one point someone made bird calls. When I heard them my legs started flapping on their own, sending me off again through stunning, beautiful, intense neon-fluorescent emerald green realm of colors and patterns with yellow and red accents beyond anything I had ever seen in the physical world.

They had been doing individual healings throughout the sessions and called me up for mine on this the fourth night. I went and sat in front of the altar and José joked with me about no bueno, no bueno.

He sang over me with the rhythmic whisper of his palm leaf chacapa and blessed me on my head, chest, and back with Agua de Florida. He blew it into the top of my head, down my shirt, and across my back twice which felt both healing and exquisite. When he finished I felt lit up and humming with energy. No words can describe the depth of this multilayered visual, emotional, intellectual, spiritual synesthetic experience. I opened my eyes at different points throughout my experience and when I closed them saw the exact same thing I saw with them open.

No difference.

Later in the session when things stabilized Yoda regaled us with another story.

"There was a very wealthy man who had a big house on a large estate with properties, groundskeepers, servants, possessions, and all the trappings that go with wealth. One day he had to go on a trip and left the house in the care of his staff.

He went away and kept sending money to keep the household running in his absence and was gone for a year, then another year, then for ten years and more. Over these many years he continued to send money and he had left orders for everybody, so they all knew what to do.

Over so much time the staff began to forget their orders and things started falling into disrepair with the exception of his bedroom and personal items and papers which remained safe the way he had left them. As more time passed the staff forgot more and more of what their jobs were, then some of them started to die off and new staff were hired, but they didn't quite know what to do.

So much time passed that all of the staff running the house forgot everything and they wanted to sell the house because they didn't know who their master was anymore. When an interested buyer wanted to see the deed they couldn't find it because they didn't have it. It was in the bedroom but nobody dared go in the bedroom because they had come to respectfully treat it like a temple, so they continued taking care of the household and the money continued coming regularly while more years passed. No one ever went in the bedroom and the staff forgot about the bedroom door and began thinking of it more like a mural on the wall than a door.

Finally the master returned and knocked on the door and the people in the house answered asking, 'Who are you?'

He said, 'I am the master of the house.'

They said, 'We don't know who you are and we can't let you in,' so they locked the door and wouldn't let him in the house.

The moral of the story is: Don't go away from your house for too long because you will be forgotten."

When the ceremony ended I felt physically beat and wrung out from all the purging, flying, and other Ayahuasca induced stresses, but I also felt lightened, unburdened, and energized at my core.

Monday morning after a few hours of deep sleep, Qi Gong and a mud bath I had quinoa and a plátano for breakfast. In spite of my hunger I had to force it down and deal with finishing off a half a pitcher of Uña de Gato and get myself ready for our last ceremony that coming night. Yoda came to check on me and left me a handout titled: On Seeing, Thinking, and Living. I recorded the following part which held great relevance for me.

A past misfortune becomes through habit the accepted order of things. The inner image of an outer restriction from the past distorts our seeing of the spaciousness in the present, then the habit functions like conscience instead of seeing what is and we substitute an inner image of what is already past as though it were still present.

I choked down the last of my Uña de Gato, ate rice and a *plátano* and went to my last session in the aftermath of a rainfall, eventually returning to my tambo on Tuesday morning around 4:00 to record the night's events.

Our last session did not disappoint and was intense, physically demanding, and I got an incredible lesson in power. I felt strong and clear going in and flew with Condor through spectacular colors and beauty in multiple dimensions, among them a preternaturally effervescent bright white realm infused with brilliant rainbow hues, insect-like creatures, plant life, and an assortment of otherworldly spirits. Amelia sang powerfully, bringing me a solid purge and in the midst of that experience I realized that the power of the energy and the personal transformation I came back from the Andes with had intimidated Penny, causing her attack. I came back at peace with myself and some shadow part of her attacked me wanting to destroy it. I had yet to see the full face of the monster which would rear its ugly head in the years to come.

As her madness escalated people asked me why I stayed with her after the abuse and I quipped, "Because she is a worthy opponent!" Looking back, in spite of all the pain, suffering, heartbreak, and disappointment she brought me, I am thankful for the lessons I learned through those horrific experiences.

Mother Ayahuasca showed me my growing personal power which came from all the intense inner work and learning from *all* of my shamanic studies. Along the same lines I was shown that the very people who worked for me who I had taken under my wing and taken care of turned on me because of their fear and envy, even after I had gone to bat for them. I was dealing with those very same dynamics, but it would still take years and intense emotional pain before I figured out the puzzle of those disappointing betrayals.

One thing I was shown is how much I intimidated people without consciously doing so, a protective habit that was deeply ingrained in me from growing up in Dorchester. I cultivated this in my earlier years, then had fun exploring it writing horror. In my later years it was all done with a bit of tongue in cheek, but it was so deeply ingrained as an instinctive behavior that I didn't realize people outside of me sometimes took my words and actions at face value. I consciously made an effort not to intimidate people, but that shadow part of me remained hidden and elusive which played in to the series of betrayals I experienced from the people I helped the most and I was absolutely clueless about the underlying dynamics.

It took some time to realize that the more I grew in personal power the more intimidating I became to people. My inner power grew at an accelerated pace while my deepest shadow aspects remained stubbornly hidden. I needed to get better control of my power by turning it up and turning it down at the right times and keeping it more under wraps by curtailing my words and actions, something I was learning and being coached on in the two year study. Along those same lines I was being taught how to put up protection in those trying moments when I was expanded, vulnerable, and needed it.

It was a fascinating paradox learning that the more powerful I became, the more cool and reserved I needed to be. I also saw that the more powerful I became and the more out of integrity anyone who came in contact with me was, the more extreme their reaction would be whether out and out hostility, or ego flattering praise and ass-kissing.

In the latter part of the ceremony Yoda told us the story **The Library** by the Argentinian author Jorge Borges reproduced here with his emphasis and embellishments.

"The library is a hexagon with hexagonal rooms with four walls covered with shelves. All the books are exactly the same on each bookshelf with the same number of words with the same twenty six letters put together in different ways. Nobody knows what they really say, but the hexagonal rooms have two doorways. A doorway goes out and connects to another hexagonal room which has identical books and shelves lining four walls like the first one. This hexagonal room is connected to another and another and another and when you go through the second doorway you see that they are all connected to spiral staircases that go up and down endlessly in all directions to infinity. There are librarians there, but not as many as there used to be because some have died off from famine, disease, attrition, and competition with each other, so there is a librarian for every five or six hexagonal rooms to take care of things.

In some rooms it is rumored that there are young men who kiss and worship the books with salacious homosexual attention. If you go through a door and fall down a spiral staircase you continue to fall until your body rots and decomposes into nothing. It is also rumored that all these hexagonal rooms and spiral staircases are contained within an infinite circular sphere and nobody really knows its boundaries. Some librarians think that their hexagonal rooms are better than other hexagonal rooms, but every room is the same and no one knows the information that is contained in them.

The library is called the universe.

Though the vast majority of the books in this universe are pure gibberish, the library also contains every coherent book ever written, or that might ever be written, and every possible permutation or slightly erroneous version of every one of those books. The library contains all useful information, including predictions of the future, biographies of any person, and translations of every book in all languages. Conversely, for many of the texts, some language could be devised that would make it readable with any of a vast number of different contents.

Because of this glut of information, all books are useless to the reader, leaving the librarians in a state of suicidal despair. This leads some of them to superstitious and cult-like behaviors, such as the Purifiers who arbitrarily destroy books they deem nonsense as they scour through the library seeking the Crimson Hexagon and its illustrated, magical books. Others believe that since all books exist in the library, somewhere one of them had to be a perfect index of the library's contents. Some even believe that a messianic figure known as the Man of the Book has read it, and they travel through the library seeking him."

I survived this physically hard and painful journey and its beauty was literally out of this world while flying hard with Condor.

In his final words of wisdom Yoda ended with this gem titled Places to Avoid.

"The first place to avoid is entrapment. The best way to avoid entrapment is to not let it happen, so you need to keep your eyes open. If you do find yourself entrapped and think that there is nothing you can do, the way out is to move to free yourself from it.

The next place to avoid is an entanglement. An entanglement is different from an entrapment because in an entanglement you are stuck and the more you struggle with an entanglement the more stuck you become, so you can't move or fight your way out of an entanglement because like a spider's web, the more you struggle the more stuck you become. The only way out of an entanglement is to cut your way out.

The next place to avoid is ensconcement which is a little different. With ensconcement, it comes to you, moves in, and you become beholden to it. It doesn't go away and it gets your attention and it wants all your attention. It essentially takes you over and you continue to give to it as it and you think it is everything, and you give yourself to it all. It traps you in that way because you are stuck with it. You have to free yourself from ensconcements by getting away from them, and of course there is the other side of ensconcements where you become the ensconcement. You think you can help everybody and you are there for everybody and you want all the attention from everybody, and you are stuck in the same way. With ensconcements you must assert and free yourself from them.

The research into places to avoid continues.

TWENTY NINE

Shepherding Goddess Royalty Across The River Styx

My mother told her friends that I was like her best girlfriend because she could tell me anything and she is the only person in my life who ever gave me true unconditional love. I had no awareness of it growing up, but now I see that she was the embodiment of what I call the Cosmic Feminine, blessing me in the form of a loving, nurturing mother. I have spent a lifetime trying to find that same effervescence in a partner, but it only haunts me and has never materialized. This longing has deepened the love and appreciation I have for my mother and the special bond and blessed time we had together, and I can say without reservation that if not for her influence I would surely be dead or in prison.

I documented the depth and magic of our connection in *Spirit Matters*. The love we shared transcended the physical world, culminating in a life changing experience that altered the course of my life.

My brother and sisters all had children, and though I was not keen on having any the decision was partially made for me because I spent most of my life helping my traumatized older sister, her kids, and eventually their kids, especially in my early twenties when I would have been dating more in search of a partner.

My life situation played into my mother's decision to ask me to be her executor when she died. The way she arranged things, she helped my older sister get her own house in Florida so she could help my mom with the demands of her sickness, and my older brother along with my mother helped get my sister a new car. My sister took excellent care of my mom up to her moment of death and I took over as executor once she passed which was a wise decision on my mom's part as both roles had their own demands.

When I questioned my mom about why she asked me over my older brother and sister, she told me part of her decision came from the fact that I didn't have any children of my own. She also said that when she left her second husband I was the only one who showed up to help her move to Florida from Massachusetts, which confirmed to her that she had made the right decision.

Over the course of my life my abused older sister often cut my brother and I off and refused to talk to us, sometimes for years. On one occasion she left with no warning leaving me to pay storage on what she left behind for seven years. My brother and I puzzled over her actions, but we did what we could when we could and realized that the extent of the hell she and our nieces had been through early in her life at the hands of the worst abuser ever had inflicted irreparable damage. Over time we realized that envy lurked beneath it all motivating her resentment toward us and my sister in law.

My mom's arrangement called for me to be her executor and for my older sister to be her caretaker which meant we needed to communicate, but my sister was not talking to me. When my Mom's cancer progressed I finally called my sister and said, "Are you ready to put all the bullshit aside so we can take care of business for Ma the way she wants us to regardless of what you or I think or feel?"

After a short hesitation, she said, "Yes."

I found out later that she also resented my brother and I because she was the one taking care of Mom in Florida while my brother and I were in San Diego and were not present for any of the day to day challenges.

A couple of years before my mom's death I planned to spend Easter with her so she could meet Penny's kids, but a few days before we left she ended up in the ICU with collapsed intestines. Everything had been arranged so we continued with our plans. When I visited her then, I brought Agua de Florida which I anointed her with. She loved the scent of it and it had a calming effect so I left her with the bottle.

Visitation was restricted and they didn't allow kids in because of the lowered immunity issues that went with the cancer. Penny ignored the rules and brought the kids in anyway, creating a confrontation that was one of the worst situations in my life when my sister launched at her horrifying me and my poor mother. My mother did not want to meet the kids being barely conscious, looking like a monster hooked up to the maze of tubes, sensors, and monitors. To her credit once she recovered she flew out to California specifically to meet the kids.

Her last birthday was in May 2003 and I always tried to do something special for that and for Mother's Day which came in the same month. When that time came in the final year of her life I puzzled over what to get her as material possessions seemed useless at that stage of the game. After much thought I sent her a monarch butterfly farm that came with a clear mesh caterpillar cage and a butterfly life cycle poster to honor her upcoming transition and transformation. She was always skittish about bugs but she accepted the challenge and raised the monarch chrysalises into butterflies and found great joy when they emerged as fully grown monarchs which she released into her back yard.

A couple of months after that I spent a week with her going over all the details of her affairs which she had meticulously planned out. She showed me a small fire resistant safe which she said held my inheritance and offered to show it to me, but I declined. We also visited a lawyer securing power of attorney for me and she took me to see her burial plot which no one else would visit with her. While there she said, "I don't expect you to visit me here."

I said, "Don't worry about that. You won't be here and I hope and expect you to come and haunt me."

I did all I could to prepare myself spiritually, mentally, and emotionally for what was coming, but no one can ever adequately prepare for the inevitable mystery of death when the reality of it hits.

Her colon cancer had progressed over a five year period and she longed to go on a cruise in her last days, so armed with the settlement money from the lawsuit from my unethical employer I came back from my fourth shamanic dieta in October, determined to make that happen.

At this point in her illness her liver was failing and her stomach swelled with backed up fluids which needed to be drained by a huge needle inserted into her stomach every ten days. Part of the deal with Penny's custody of her kids was alternating holiday times and this year Christmas was with their father, so we planned a Christmas week cruise. My mom arranged things so she would get drained before the cruise and after she returned. By this time she could no longer walk, so she rented a bright red electric three wheeled scooter for the cruise.

My mom was never one to ask for anything, but one thing she hoped for on this cruise was a room with a balcony that she could look out from which I happily reserved. She insisted that Penny and I go on all the shore leave activities we could and was happy to stay behind and enjoy her alone contemplative time. I had her thinking about doing some psilocybin mushrooms following a friend's protocol from his groundbreaking study treating terminally ill cancer patients for death anxiety, but the setting, my mom's stomach problems, and the at sea situation did not provide the right circumstances for that to happen.

We left Fort Lauderdale on the December 21, 2003 solstice on Royal Caribbean Cruises with ports of call in Key West, Cozumel, and Belize before returning on Saturday December 27th which allowed my mom time to get home and resettled in time for her Monday morning fluid draining.

Penny and I had fun visiting Key West where we rented bikes, visited Hemingway's house, harassed flocks of seagulls, and explored the town. The following morning we docked in Cozumel where we snorkeled and fed fish and that night we feasted on a fancy Christmas eve dinner where we dressed up. My Mom, who never wore red, dressed in an outfit that matched the red of her scooter.

We arrived in Belize early Christmas morning and the ship had a magical feel to it with a huge Christmas tree in its main lounge and waiters everywhere serving egg nog. On my mom's insistence Penny and I took a bus and did an underground cave river tour on truck innertubes with a scrumptious arranged lunch half way through it. Before heading downstream we took some psilocybin mushrooms which added to the connection with nature and we had childlike fun that day. That night we had an extravagant Christmas dinner with my Mom that ended with a dozen ballroom waiters doing an elaborate dance, each with a cake balanced on his head.

After that highlight the ship cruised straight back from Belize getting us to Fort Lauderdale on Saturday where I helped my Mom get on her flight home to Ocala before taking my own flight back to San Diego.

On January 6, 1974 I got a little tipsy with my mom at the airport in Warwick Rhode Island when I left for Air Force basic training in Texas. Four years later on January 6, 1978 I received my honorable discharge in Nebraska and drove to Boston first before turning around and heading West to San Diego in my van driving my traumatized older sister and her abused little girls to take them under my wing.

January 6th took on special significance for me as the day I left home with an emotional departure with my mom, and my discharge four years later with my sister and nieces in tow, so every year I called my mom on that day. When I made the call on January 6, 2004 my sister picked up and my mom didn't come to the phone. I knew things were serious and when I asked my sister if I should fly out she said yes without hesitation.

I felt the energy and saw the signs when I arrived at my mother's house. The kitchen looked like a bomb had hit with a sink of overflowing dishes, cluttered counters and everything else in disarray, including a near empty refrigerator. I found my sister in my Mom's bedroom sitting beside a hospital bed next to my mom's bed where she had been for days, exhausted from keeping a constant bed side vigil shortly after our mom came back from the cruise.

The bottle of Agua de Florida I left my mom in the ICU sat waiting for me at her bedside which gave me small comfort as other family members didn't know what to make of my shamanism, and some had ridiculed it, but I knew that my mom was on board.

Seeing that bottle purposely left there for me to use empowered me to embrace the profound spirit connection I had with my mom that came to fruition at the end of my first plant dieta when my heart opened and filled me with divine Cosmic Feminine love, confirmed by the exquisite shared blessing from the spirit of Santa Teresa De Avila. I knew what to do as if on autopilot to pass through the uncharted territory of grief, loss, finality, and acceptance confronting me, and in that passage I would discover the full realization of the deepest Cosmic meaning of Mother.

I suppressed any reaction I might give when I saw my emaciated mom withered down to skin and bones less than two weeks after our cruise. She was still lucid and I was grateful to spend a little more time with her. We had already gone over her affairs, so most of our time consisted of comfort, companionship, and some odds and ends details that confirmed her wishes.

After spending time with my mom I settled into the room beside hers and tackled getting the kitchen and the rest of the house in order as my older brother and younger sister would be coming with their families for my mom's final days. At the peak of it thirteen family members filled the house to pay their respects.

I spent a month at my Mom's house without leaving and I have blank spots in those memories related to my grief which had its own agenda, but some memories stand out and the major events of her transition are indelibly tattooed in my mind and spirit. I struggled with all the people in the small house and tried to find ways to keep them occupied. Based partially on all the talks with my mom, I expected some family members to give me more trouble. Some expected troublemakers turned out to be the most helpful and others who I had hoped for more support from made things more difficult than they needed to be, but I understood that the grief and confusion surrounding death brings out unpredictable reactions from people.

I was smoking cannabis at the time and when I ran out, my nephew who lived locally scored some for me which I really appreciated. Another nephew knew I liked Zone bars, so he bought some and hid them in a cookie jar, then pulled me aside to tell me he had hidden them there specifically for me so no one else would eat them. Those thoughtful gestures really touched me.

In a moment of inspiration I sent my nieces to the store and my youngest niece cooked an amazing dinner which my mom ate like a bird and it turned out to be her last meal on earth. Most of the family had gone when she slipped into a coma, leaving me, my older sister, brother, and my ever supportive sister in law.

We began our death watch and paid close attention to the rhythm of my Mom's breathing when she slipped into unconsciousness. She tried to stand a few times as if she needed to go to the bathroom, but once standing with our help she appeared lost as if trying to remember what she was doing, then settled back into the hospital bed where she remained until the end, breathing long, slow, and steady.

For three days I played gentle meditative music, lit candles, burned incense, and anointed her from time to time with Agua de Florida and lavender which I found out from my sister was mom's favorite scent, something I had not known. I have no idea what prompted me, but while she was still conscious I shared the haunting melody of **The Lord of the Dance, Celtic Dream** by the band **Enigma** with her, thinking that she might like the new age kind of music. She brightened when she heard it, recognizing it as one of her favorite pieces from **The Lord of the Dance** show which I knew nothing about. This combined with the synchronicity of my urge to share the song with her had a powerful impact on me because she had been a dancer and an acrobat and this became her transition theme song that I played frequently in those last days. It still haunts me every time I hear it.

I have no memory of any dreams during that time except one where I remember looking down at my feet. I was wearing sandals with long straps shepherding royalty across the river Styx as a temple priest accompanied by the temple priestess which I understood was my sister. Whether there is anything to reincarnation or not, this sole dream seemed appropriate as my mom always had a thing for ancient Egypt which also had great significance in my life, research, and thinking.

At one point during this time early on in the process I took a hit of 5MEODMT before going to sleep. I thought of its overwhelming effect of surrender and ego dissolution from forces bigger than me as a "dress rehearsal" for dying and advance scouting for the imminent moment of my mom's passing.

My mom continued breathing in long, slow, steady breaths for three days until the rhythm of her breathing became deep, heavy, and labored. I think she engineered things in spirit for me and my older brother and sister who were all close in age to be there. Together we sensed that the moment had come, so we all took her hand and held on as that last powerful exhale signaled her exit at 2:45 on Monday morning, January 19, 2004, Martin Luther King Jr. Day.

In that ineffable moment of her passing an owl hooted outside her bedroom window announcing her passage and her stereo turned on by itself blasting Frank Sinatra, her favorite singer that she had worked with and whose music she had loved for most of her life.

We spent a little time honoring her in that resting state before I called the funeral home to take her to be cremated, which was her wish, then everyone went to bed to get some much needed sleep and the house grew quiet.

With dawn breaking I slipped out the front door and stretched out on a lounge chair on my mother's front porch where I inhaled and held in the biggest hit of 5MEO I could. In the same way that a Star Trek ship flashes into warp drive I disintegrated into nothingness, surrendering to the void of non-existence to accompany my mom as far as I could on her return home into the Great Mystery.

A mourning dove cooed from a nearby tree when I came back into consciousness announcing my return, signaling an expansive emotional mixture of joy, awe, grief, and release when I felt my mother's spirit in every cell of every blade of grass, leaf, branch, and root on a nearby tree, as well as in all the birds, bugs, bees, animals, and anything else that harbored consciousness. I felt like I had escorted her into the Great Mystery in the most meaningful way that I could.

In that massive revelation of that returning to consciousness moment I fully understood the deepest meaning of Mother as the Face of the Cosmic Feminine in ways I never could have imagined in the most expansive expression of connection to the greater cosmos I ever experienced, much less comprehended.

For the next five years I set an alarm to awaken me and I took a hit of 5MEO by myself at the time of my Mom's passing to commemorate that moment until it felt like that ritual no longer had any emotional charge.

I had met a wisdom filled older man at the Santa Barbara Writers Conference prior to my Mom's death and our discussion went to my mom and her cancer. Toward the end of our chat he said, "A man never truly becomes a man until after both his parents have died."

Now that I was an "orphan", I understood the depth of his words.

THIRTY

Death Comes Knocking Again

A few days after my mom passed I did a ceremony with my sister using a combination of psilocybin mushrooms and MDMA called a Hippie Flip. We focused on the spot in her bedroom where her spirit left her body which I thought of as a portal. In the month that followed I had to deal with her house, possessions, and other items to settle her affairs which ultimately took a year to complete. I didn't know what to do with a lot of what she had, so I let members of the family pick select mementos and with the help of my sister donated the remaining items where they could be put to good use to help others.

When things settled down and I was alone in the house, I opened her portable safe to discover my inheritance which was $6000.00 in twenties that gave me a little giggle at my mother's foresight regarding taxes. I was doubly thrilled because this matched what I spent on the cruise, making the energetic balance perfect in my mind. She also had a watch with extra large numbers on its face with a beautiful silver band set with turquoise which she stressed over and over again that she wanted me to have. I gladly accepted this treasured item which held deep meaning for me. She had also given me gold and silver necklace chains through the years, but I never wore them. With her death she gave me one more and I vowed to wear it every day which I did for close to a decade until it nearly fell apart.

I left Florida in mid-February and drove her van with the last of her remaining possessions back to San Diego in a haze of unpredictable outbursts of grief and an underlying numbness that lasted for months.

Soon after returning from Florida some friends asked Penny and I to join them on their vacation at a time share resort in Cancun in March with our rooms already paid for. All we needed was to cover air fare. My heart was not in it as I was still in a fog, but I accepted. Based on my shamanic experiences throughout Peru and Mexico we had a great adventure visiting the Maya ruins of Tulum and Chichén Itzá under the influence of mushrooms.

In May of 2004 my two year group went on an extended camping trip to and around Four Corners, the only point in the United States shared by four states; Arizona, Colorado, New Mexico, and Utah. While in the area we had a Huachuma walkabout throughout Monument Valley followed by two more Huachuma journeys. The first of these was in an area full of petroglyphs dating from 1300 to 1600 AD, carved into dark volcanic rocks. We had the second at Chaco Canyon in the ruins of the largest, most advanced ancient villages in the Southwest built along the floor of a shallow, sheer walled canyon in a remote part of the high desert of northwest New Mexico.

Aside from the experiential downloads I received during this trip my teachers continued with their teachings. Among them were the **Four Agreements** from the book of the same name by Don Miguel Ruiz which are listed here in order.

- **Be Impeccable With Your Word** is the most important, most difficult agreement to honor. Ruiz said that the word "impeccable" comes from the Latin word peccatus meaning "sin", and the "im" at the beginning of impeccable is the Latin prefix that means "without". A sin is anything that goes against yourself and being impeccable with language means to take responsibility for your actions and remain without judgment against yourself and others. This agreement focuses on the significance of speaking with integrity and carefully choosing words before saying them aloud.

- **Don't Take Anything Personally** is how to deal with hurtful treatment from others and stresses the importance of having a strong sense of self without relying on the opinions of others to be comfortable with your own self-image. This also helps to understand how everyone has a unique worldview that alters their perceptions. Their actions and beliefs are a projection of their own personal reality. Anger, jealousy, envy, and sadness will all dissipate once someone stops taking things personally.

• **Don't Make Assumptions** is about how assumptions lead to suffering, and why you shouldn't be making them. Assuming what others are thinking creates stress and conflict because you believe your assumption is the truth. A solution to overcoming making assumptions is to ask questions and make sure the communication is clear between everyone involved. You can avoid misunderstandings, sadness, and drama by not making assumptions.

• **Always Do Your Best** is about making progress toward your goals in life and comes from integrating the first three agreements into daily life and living to your full potential by doing the best you can which changes with different situations and circumstances. If you avoid self judgment and do your best in every moment you can avoid regret and live a life free from sorrow and self ridicule.

Among other things we also learned that the purpose of ceremonies and the importance of places and emphasis on something makes it possible to transform more energy and work on power which signals a transition and makes something important. Altars represent a portable center of the universe and is populated with sacred objects and honors the four directions. Bowls represent the feminine and carry the sharp masculine. Flowers and scents like Agua de Florida are feminine and stones are masculine.

All ceremonies have a beginning, middle, and end. The elemental sprits, totems, allies, and the four directions are brought in through prayer by moving clockwise through the East, South, West, and North, and end by moving counterclockwise through the North, West, South, and East. We were told to bring in a quality, ally, or a power place into a ceremony, inhale to the left and blow in the requested energy three times from left to right and when you take a dose of medicine invite it in with respect and talk to it with the intention of dynamically working with it.

A shaman manifesting full power embodies the roles of leadership, ceremonialist, storyteller, artist, healer, protector/warrior, and a person of knowledge. There are twelve support positions that a shaman moves through in doing shamanic work; child, mentor, discipline, knowledge, anchor, enlightenment, beauty, compassion, love, muse, healer, and humor.

Another gem of wisdom we were given was the Four Fold Path as a way to success in life.

- Show up fully.
- Pay attention to what has heart and meaning.
- Tell the truth without blame or judgment.
- Be open to the outcome rather than be attached to it.

In addition to this we learned an ancient Zen master's four step answer to every problem we might encounter.

- Too many thinking.
- Put it all down.
- Only go straight.
- Keep "don't know mind".

In July of 2004 I took Penny and her kids to visit with my jungle friends up in Nelson, British Columbia where I did one of the best American Indian sweat lodges ever on top of Crystal Mountain which is considered a major power spot. I had a strong reaction to the powerful energy of the place, something that occurred more frequently after my timeless, literal mind blowing elemental wind experience at the Pachamama temple on top of the island of Amantani.

Two months later I headed South again to the Peruvian Amazon, this time with my two year group. Our adventure started in Iquitos, a Peruvian port city and gateway to jungle lodges and tribal villages of the northern Amazon. The Plaza de Armas in Iquitos is surrounded by European-influenced buildings dating to the area's turn of the 20th century boom in rubber production. We spent a couple of days exploring the jungle around Iquitos with the two Shipibo shamans who had accompanied us in the Andes. We spent an afternoon with the Bora tribe who welcomed us with songs, dance, and a variety of handcrafts, among them blowguns, bracelets, necklaces, and other adornments of teeth, fur, feather, and seeds. We also visited a jungle zoo full of an uncaged collection of animals that you could hold and engage with. They had a huge anaconda, an ocelot, monkeys tied to ropes that would interact with you, macaws, a three toed sloth, tortoises, other snakes, and an alligator.

We left Iquitos and headed South on small boats down the Amazon River to where it split into two tributaries, the Marañón, which is Peru's second longest river, and the Ucayali. There we spent an afternoon swimming at this confluence of three rivers and enjoyed the company of Amazon pink freshwater dolphins as well as an epic sunset, then we proceeded further South to a jungle compound with a large screened in maloca, a community kitchen, and men's and women's screened open air huts.

Once we settled in the Shipibos tattooed us on different parts of our bodies based on our nature and their intuition creating Ayahuasca patterns seen on their pottery and embroideries using the dark blue juice from unripe huito fruit that they also used to dye textiles and color their hair.

We did three Ayahuasca ceremonies there led by the Shipibos and I felt the unbridled energies of the tropical jungle intensely in the way I now felt elemental energies in radically different environments. As if to confirm this my friend was crossing an open space where chickens foraged and heard a loud squawk of surprise. She turned to see a massive anaconda shoot forward and capture a chicken in one bite and swallow of its huge open mouth.

Adding to the powerful energies of this place, at one point in our first ceremony a hideous, slavering alien looking serpentine demon materialized in front of me opening its huge maw as if to swallow me with multiple sets of jagged teeth. I studied it a moment, then looked straight at it and said, "Fuck you!" in a dismissive tone. It vaporized into a beautiful woman who swayed back and forth like a hula dancer and giggled before disappearing.

In the second ceremony I experienced what I now realize was my first hummingbird encounter beyond a mere flirtation. I didn't make the connection at the time. One of the Shipibo shamans overreacted and panicked blowing Agua de Florida all over me like something was wrong when my "wing" legs started flapping faster than ever before while my body twitched and my head bobbed. I flew through a neon pastel colored bliss that I wished could have lasted forever.

My stomach grew upset and acidic by the time we left the compound, causing me to belch repeatedly. We stopped at a couple of villages on the uncomfortable boat ride back North and purchased weavings and handicrafts from the locals. When we made it back to Iquitos I was belching nonstop and nursing a headache. We checked into the most disgusting hotel on the planet where I fell into bed feeling sicker and sicker and soon had diarrhea that kept me running back and forth to my shared room's bathroom that had a toilet that gushed shit infused water where the toilet met the floor every time I flushed it.

Welcome to hell.

I struggled down to a corner store and bought a couple of containers of kefir which I drank, hoping that I might restore microflora which I thought might be related to the upset, but only grew sicker. When my companions saw my condition the called in the shamans who did all kinds of healing work on me but nothing helped. In my sickness I thought I had taken on the energy of my mother's colon cancer when our spirits merged and needed to send it back into the earth.

My stomach settled some, but I didn't feel right and my energies were lagging the next day when we took a large open air diesel powered boat down the Ucayali River to Pucallpa. Families and hammocks covered the decks but we were lucky to get sparse cabin rooms to keep our belongings from being stolen. My belching subsided some as we traveled through the rest of the day and overnight until we reached Pucallpa, but I still felt under the weather when we settled into the shaman's long house in the Shipibo village of San Francisco where we did more Shipibo led ceremonies interspersed with nature walks.

In these teachings we were told that shamanic thought had three building blocks that make up the unstable universe which is what makes it dynamic.

- Truth, which is intelligence manifested in the intellect.
- Love, which is magnetism manifested in the emotions.
- Energy, which is manifested in the moving body.

As mentioned earlier these energies align with the Inca reality of the rose colored upper world of the Condor, the electric blue middle world of the jaguar or puma, and the gold lower world of the serpent, all of which needed to be brought into balance through mastering these dynamic energies to gain power. Our teacher referred to the path of shamanism as the power path and on this adventure he gave us what he called the ten rules of power.

1.) Power is whatever cannot be taken away from you and is inherent in your potential or capacity. Shamanic work is done to increase capacity to gain more power.

2.) Everything in the universe is seeking to become more powerful. More powerful objects make it possible for lesser things to become more powerful. Associate with people and forces that are more powerful than you are to become more powerful.

3.) Power is associated with inspiration, simplicity, exchange, and conception.

4.) Power is neutral and is not good or bad. It is how it is used that matters.

5.) There is always a price to pay for real power.

6.) Power can only be manifested when you focus your attention and intention in the present.

7.) Power can be hunted and gained in ways similar to the hunt using patience, observation, timing, neutrality, and by being psychologically, emotionally, and spiritually prepared.

8.) Power must be ridden like a surfer rides a wave using balance.

9.) The path of real power is the path with heart.

10.) The smaller the degree of separation, the greater the power available through removing barriers.

You can lose personal power through money, politics, and by allowing someone to take it from you by not paying attention. If you are not impeccable you can lose power in the area you haven't mastered and you can appear to lose power if something arises that beats up on you.

As if emphasizing my heartbreak, mental fog, and recurring grief from the beginning of the year, this last point relating to losing power became apparent to me when I returned to the United States feeling depleted with an escalating loss of energy and focus accompanied by sweating clamminess, a struggle to focus my vision, and mental confusion.

I went to the hospital where they ran a battery of tests and told me they could find nothing wrong with me. I sat with this for a few days puzzling over how they could find nothing wrong with me when I was becoming increasingly incoherent. Feeling lost, coupled with a sense of desperation, I could barely concentrate on the simple task of punching in the numbers on my cell phone to call my acupuncturist.

I will never forget the look on her face when she examined me, which frightened me more than anything else. She told me I had a combined bacteria and virus, and my heart, lungs, kidneys, spleen, and liver; in short all of my vital organs were in the process of shutting down and were presently operating between 20 to 30 percent capacity.

I have had many acupuncture treatments over time and am used to the tiny pinprick of inserted needles, but I never felt the kind of pain I did with this treatment along my meridians which felt like highly sensitized bruises getting stabbed. In addition to this treatment she prescribed bovine hormone pills and a number of other Chinese herbal pills and had me return every other day for treatments for a week before finally ridding me of the sickness.

Shortly after I ran myself into the ground from lack of sleep at the week long Santa Barbara Writers Conference and I relapsed, but I went right back for treatment from her when I returned home and it cleared up swiftly, then I gave myself proper rest and recovery to make sure it did not come back.

Another friend of mine in our group was a nurse who developed the same symptoms. The hospital she worked at insisted on admitting her as a patient and soon after she slipped into a coma and died.

THIRTY ONE

Mama Coca Welcomes Me To The Jungle

We left LAX on Friday afternoon, October 1st, 2004 for my fifth dieta and had our first talk in a hotel in Pucallpa about the plants we would be working with on Sunday night. Twenty of us including my chiropractor friend Dog listened which made things more crowded than I would have liked. Our first session would be on Monday night and our added teacher plant would come the following day.

I had agreed to do a study for a microbiologist friend who wanted to analyze daily samples of my saliva during the course of the dieta to measure stress levels and other indicators. Dog agreed to participate to give her two sets of samples and we planned to meet once a day to complete this task.

Once I settled in to my tambo my regularly scheduled headache came so I didn't waste any time taking aspirin to try and knock it out early. After going through this every time I did a dieta I finally figured out that my headaches came from caffeine withdrawal from stopping drinking coffee.

After a long night's sleep I awoke from a vivid dream that set the tone for a series of escalating conflicts that passed me between restless dreaming and waking that tested me more with each successive episode.

I was with an Air Force buddy who was also from Boston who was reading my book, which must have come from the fact that I was editing the part of **Spirit Matters** *that he was in. Next I was holding a basketball very high up in the air, and half realized I was dreaming while plunging toward the ground, afraid of how*

I would hit. I consciously slowed down time and nearly froze it to make adjustments to how my body would land. I didn't land the way I wanted, but I landed okay, then I jumped back up and shot the basketball into a hoop.

Next I went with some people to a room full of drug dealers selling crystal meth and heroin. There was a lot of trouble when they said, "Okay, we're going to kick the door in and you're going in with a gun."

I held an automatic weapon so I pushed the door in and waited. A group of people turned, getting ready to draw their guns. I kept waiting wanting them to draw on me first and once they did I fired away until I killed them all.

I had many dreams throughout my life with guns that wouldn't shoot. They would jam, I couldn't find the bullets, I had the wrong ammunition, or some other frustrating way. This dream started like that, but I got this gun working.

I talked to someone afterward and said "I have no guilt or bad feelings about blowing them all away and I take full responsibility for my actions," and thought that the subconscious message was not about the killing, but the fact that I succeeded with the gun and the bullets after a lifetime of failure with them.

They brought quinoa and a plátano for breakfast and Ronaldo came by to discuss my second teacher plant which to my surprise was Coca, a plant I already had a close relationship with. I was actually wearing a turquoise and silver Coca Leaf on the silver necklace my mom gave me when she died to honor her spirit, the spirit of the mother plant, and the spirit of the Cosmic Mother in the expansive emotional mixture of joy and awe when I felt my mother's spirit in every cell of every plant and animal that harbored consciousness after "escorting" her to the other side.

I did not expect to work with Coca here in the jungle as it is from the Andes. Ronaldo told me I would be working with the *root* of the Coca plant as opposed to the leaves which I sensed would be extra powerful because I thought of the root as being the heart of the plant.

I returned from our first ceremony around 4:00 on Tuesday morning reporting it as good and powerful. I took a full dose which altered me, but didn't really come on, so after an hour, most if not all of us took a second full dose from a different brew and I took off, flying far while William the musician sang with José and played guitar, flutes, and panpipes.

At the beginning of the ceremony the glowing electric violet spirit energy that I associated with my mother and what I had been told represented a balance of love, power, and wisdom blossomed in my mind's eye. It stayed with me which felt powerful and affirming. I also became aware of the fact that my inner chatter had diminished considerably since my first dieta five years ago. It often came and went and I told it over and over again to shut up which it did for awhile before sneaking in again. In this session it was almost nonexistent which allowed me to embrace my experience more and travel further.

I wasn't trying to interpret everything with my monkey mind chattering away and it made me think of the words of wisdom that say if you are always transmitting, you can't receive. In my diminished transmitting I received more contributing to the difficulty of articulating my experience. At different times of the night a harmonica sounding instrument, a digeridoo, and their vibrations made me dissolve into indescribable primordial realities.

Condor checked in with me which was now a regular thing and once we connected in essence, Condor let me know that wherever you want to go, I am here to take you, then I flew, travelling and visiting people and places. Though not yet fully aware of its true nature I felt a little hummingbird energy and thought I sensed some sweet playful jealousy between the two bird energies. At one point it felt like I had both of them with me which fascinated me. I worked with the dance of different energies. Hummingbird moved faster at a higher vibration than the bigger, slower moving Condor and I later discovered an Inca myth where Condor changes into Hummingbird.

I flew through vistas of colors, patterns, and realms and checked in on friends and family while emanating loving, protective energies and embraces. I also went to a plethora of unexpected places, at one point losing touch with my physical surroundings for an unknown period of time. I felt overheated and poured sweat when I was aware of my body, then I had a purge that erupted out of nowhere that came so strong that it hurt my throat.

Exquisite color filled rainbow hues enveloped me, erupting within a scintillating preternatural white background before playing out in an alternate velvety black background. My color travelling tied in with music that guided my journey, overwhelming me to the point where I couldn't remember parts of it. As William and José sang to the plants and animals I felt like I absorbed their spirits on deeper levels and disparate visions came each time they called in different spirits. Some of them brought in diverse colors, patterns, emotions, and other things of an inexplicable nature, but I didn't see any specific beings like I had in other sessions. I felt like I was travelling through the astral world.

Later in the ceremony I was thinking about the microbiology study Dog and I were contributing to. It struck me as being holographic in nature as the stress and condition of the whole organism and other indicators from our saliva could determine the condition of our whole body by analyzing a single cell.

In the moment I thought that, Yoda told a story that felt tuned in and telepathic about a huge clay Buddha in Tibet someone made that sat for many long years. Over time it developed cracks and as more time passed the cracks grew bigger. One day somebody decided to investigate it with a flashlight and found pieces of mica and similar substances, so they took a sample, did an analysis, and found the image of the whole Buddha within the tiny samples they took.

His story blew my mind as I was thinking about holograms in that same moment he chose to tell the story.

Feeling tapped out after my pre-dawn journaling, I crawled under my mosquito net for a good night's sleep and the following morning I did Qi Gong to raise my flagging energies before a breakfast of a solid plátano and a mashed plátano mixed with water.

That afternoon they brought my first infusion of Coca root. I poured a glass, expecting it to be nasty and bitter like other plants I had worked with, but it went down easy, almost tasting sweet in comparison to what I expected. They started me with a pitcher of about five glasses and told me they would bring me a fresh pitcher the following day with more.

I awoke from a nap a little later when they brought a dinner of oatmeal and a plátano and I remembered a funny dream I had about a lawyer named Perry Mason from a famous sixties TV show.

I was trying to record a message for Penny and Perry Mason sat next to me trying to discredit what I was saying. I said, "Don't believe him, he's a liar." He started arguing with me, calling me a liar, then I said, "Hey, he took all your money. How can you believe him?"

Perry Mason started justifying that and I made him look me in the eye, saying "You're a fucking liar! Admit it!", but he wouldn't.

I thought it might be related to misconceptions Penny had about me that led to many of our conflicts because I was trying to get the real truth of the matters under discussion realized and accepted.

I awoke from more disjointed dreams on Wednesday morning that seemed to have some continuity, so I recorded them in hopes of finding underlying patterns.

I was with one of my nephews on the way to get some cannabis with another guy in a house that turned into a bank that the guy who brought us wanted to rob. He started robbing it right then and there and it turned into a hostage situation, but my nephew and I were not hostages, the people in the bank were.

The cops came and there was no way we were escaping. I walked across an open lot to a group of detectives and F.B.I. agents. One of them said, "If you're going to get out of here, you better get out of here now!" Cops were everywhere so I went back to the bank where the guy still held everyone hostage with his gun.

I returned to the open space and saw a hole in the fence. Nobody seemed to be looking so I peeked through, surprised not to see any law enforcement, so I slipped through and escaped. I walked a lot of blocks back around and returned to find out that the robber and my nephew got busted together and were going to court for it.

*I felt bad, thinking that if my nephew got convicted I would turn myself in because he was innocent, but we came up with a weird strategy. The bank robber started saying something about being part of a strange religious thing. He started making up a crazy story but the gist of it vindicated my nephew who somehow got my book **Land Without Evil** involved.*

*I looked through a door and saw book displays, posters, and promotional materials and everyone was talking about my book. I wasn't sure what was happening and was listening when I heard Larry King, a talk show host talking about **Land Without Evil.** I listened as much as I could, then I wanted to go home to watch the rest of it on television but I wasn't sure how much I would miss and didn't know how to get it on the radio.*

*I walked down the street and saw a girl who asked me about **Land Without Evil.** I was going to tell her she was talking to the author when she pulled out a copy of it and said, "Hey, I know you're the author," and showed me where I had signed it.*

She wanted my address but I had a hard time writing it so I went to her apartment. She had two male roommates that I thought I knew and I felt like I knew her from before too. I kept trying to write down my address and messing it up. I couldn't do it no matter how hard I tried. I'd get to the end of it or I'd miss the zip code, or misspell something.

Next I was at a business run by young military guys who had big electronic radio bags with all kinds of electronic gear on them. They had microwave equipment and one of them was cooking bread and other things in one. I walked by, slipped on the floor, and almost fell, then I walked into a huge demonstration where people stood up to show themselves as part of their movement. One of them was a lady from my two year study group. Someone else was beside her and I was supposed to be going next to show my solidarity. One of the guys I used to work with was there doing strange things like backflips, standing on his head, and saying weird things, trying to make them laugh. They weren't supposed to laugh because the lady from my two year group was pleading for help.

Next I was at a place where a band played and people performed and sang. They marched toward us and marched away. I ended up at a huge factory for humanoid robots like the assembly line in the kid's movie Monster's Inc., and the movie A.I. One of my teachers from the two year group was there and we talked about the difference with the way the movies were edited, the plotting, and how long the scenes were before we got pulled into the assembly line by a suction cup contraption that came down on our heads. We got pulled high up like the scene in one of the Star Wars movies of a clone assembly line.

My teacher said, "Oh man, the part where they put the brains in is really gross."

I got pulled along thinking that if I was in a movie preview and I got hurt, I was going to sue somebody. I went so high my head almost hit the top of a pipe, then I went through the whole assembly line process and got dropped off like I was a young android similar to the little boy in the movie A.I., and something didn't seem right.

My new parents who weren't my real parents were waiting for me. I knew it wasn't right when they took me outside to the street. I saw my forearm smoking and said, "Look, my arm is smoking! My arm is smoking!"

They tried to ignore what was happening and looked at my forearm which opened up. A wisp of smoke came out above my wrist on the inside exposing sparking and buzzing electronic circuits. My spirit in the form of ectoplasm came out of my arm crying and screaming while floating up out of my arm, dying.

The dream ended there and I drifted in the hypnogogic state between waking and dreaming when I heard a distinct Spanish female voice call my name, "Mateo!" from somewhere to my right, jarring me awake to find no one there.

I fell back asleep after a while and heard a Spanish male voice call, "Mateo!" this time from my left and jolted awake again to nobody.

THIRTY TWO

The Color Of Expansive Love Power

It rained all day Wednesday and came down hard on and off all night, so I spent the night in the maloca to avoid walking the treacherous muddy trail in the dark while altered. I returned to my tambo at 7:00 on Thursday morning for a plant bath before making my recording and getting some much needed sleep.

José led a mind-boggling ceremony under a new moon combined with a solar eclipse and the medicine came on sweet with colors and patterns which I enjoyed until I got whacked hard out of nowhere. Even Yoda was out of it for an hour or two along with most of the rest of us.

An extraordinarily beautiful white light enveloped me infused with green neon pastels and other colors that felt like *all* the plant spirits and entities came to me at once. This barrage of extreme visions kept unfolding bright, beautiful, infinite, and eternal. While enraptured within brilliant preternatural white light deep in this vision I thought, I have to do something with this, so I embraced it wanting to be a channel for it. I consciously opened my heart and pulled in Penny and her kids in close, then family members, starting with those I had helped the most, particularly my sister and her kids. I kept pulling more people in, opening my heart and extending further outward until I became overwhelmed in the rush of it and lost myself. It felt tremendously powerful, but the most astonishing part came after the ceremony ended.

My friend Geramy sat on my right and my Canadian buddy Jim sat to my left. Geramy leaned over to me and said, "You are such a warrior. I can't believe how you opened your heart and brought all those people in."

Jim on the other side of me confirmed it, saying, "Yeah it was incredible. We felt it."

Their words flabbergasted me. I had been far off in my visions and had not spoken a word. If I ever had any doubt about telepathy or the magical energies of Ayahuasca transcending the physical, the people on each side of me felt and confirmed its reality. They continued blowing my mind, talking about how powerful it was and Geramy said, "It's obvious that Pachamama and Pachatata really love you."

It dawned on me during this exchange that when I woke up that morning hearing voices, I first heard a female on my feminine right side, then a male on my masculine left which combined with the synchronicity I now heard from friends on both sides of me creating a powerful validating overlapping experience.

When José played sweet music on his charango I flew with the hummingbird, still not fully aware of what it was, up into the white light with her and felt absolutely in love with her energy while we had a great time bathing ourselves in the music that I came to understand that she loves so much. I felt so integrated and overwhelmed with blissful energy that in the middle of my rapture hummingbird left and I never knew when. She had been gone for some time before I realized it which amazed me because of the intensity of our closeness and her departure which I was completely unaware of. Looking back, this paradox of full absorption followed by a vacancy I never noticed felt oddly fitting because in spite of the ineffable gift of its power, I still didn't recognize the depth of my attachment and intimate connection with Hummingbird.

My instances of telepathy increased. Twice now I wondered when Dog would come to do our saliva test and as the thought completed itself I heard his flute and saw him come up the trail. The same thing happened with Geramy when I thought about him and turned around to see him walking up the trail.

We took a plant walk later that day, most of which I already covered from other plant walks. Toward the end of it Ronaldo showed us Yaguarpanga. While watching and listening to him I knew I wanted to experience it. When that thought completed itself Ronaldo looked up at me and said, "Do you want to try it?"

I said, "Yes, next year?"

He said, "Next year."

Later that evening I felt energized even though I had only slept a couple of hours and awoke around 6:30 on Friday morning from a wild and incredible night that included what I thought of as a visitation. I thought Qi Gong might have had something to do with it, but the stronger influence came from the Coca root I drank every day.

I was reading around 9:30 on Thursday night and decided it was time to try and get some much needed sleep, but I ended up lying there wired and awake. While fully conscious the exquisite electric violet hue associated with love, power, and wisdom formed in the third eye spot between my eyes growing brighter and brighter, pulsing and flickering as it grew still brighter. Though formless, it reminded me of expanding wings and felt so powerful that I opened my eyes, thrilled to find that it remained unchanged whether my eyes were open or closed.

It continued getting stronger and brighter, infusing and enveloping me before it slowly faded back before surging once again, flickering like wings that spread out like my entire mosquito net was lit with it. Points of light flashed inside it that could have been fireflies, but I couldn't tell for sure in the overwhelming brightness. Even though I knew I was having a subjective experience it felt like if someone was watching from a distance they would see my whole mosquito net glowing like a giant otherworldly electric violet lantern.

I didn't want it to ever stop. Instead of remaining intense and flickering in one spot it spread out and filled everything, then faded back and returned a third time, once again growing brighter like flickering wings that almost made my ears pop in the way it came so powerfully. It made no difference whether my eyes were open or closed throughout the whole experience and before it ended that stunning magical color bathed me in its energy like I was in a cocoon or a womb. It felt like my bed, mosquito netting, and my whole body immersed in what I can only describe as a bright electric violet spirit, then I slipped off to sleep and dreamed an active nonstop conflict filled dream that seemed to continue all night.

I knew this heralded the stirrings of my shadow and I wanted to deal with it from a watchful awareness that didn't include harsh judgments of people popping up at every opportunity. I worked steadily at developing a mindfulness practice of shooting judgments down as soon as they popped up in the same dismissive way I banished the slavering serpentine demon in my Iquitos visions. It rained heavy that night and tree branches broke off partially waking me from time to time and like the rain these dreams felt chaotic, nonsensical, and continuous to the point where I awoke jumping and twitching many times throughout the night.

In the beginning I had a minor disagreement with my mother over something she didn't understand, then I was with my shamanic friend Hawk who showed up with liquid medicine in long tubes with needles on them. We put the needles in our mouths without piercing the skin and squeezed the substance into our mouths to drink it. I felt bad doing this because I was supposed to be on the plant diet. Hawk told me that this substance cost $450, then he said $275, then he said $80. I told him I would think about it, then I found myself in a store in Boston.

Some Mexican guys grabbed me by the arm and demanded money from me and I said, "Forget it, I'm busy." I had a Spanish dwarf with me and these guys kept hassling us. The dwarf winked at me and acted like he was passing out. I said, "Oh, man, he's fainting!" I picked him up and carried him past the Mexican guys who didn't bother us when I went past them.

Next I went down a street past a yard behind a building. A few younger guys were yelling at and challenging us. I thought about fighting them but didn't want to. I wasn't afraid of them, I just didn't want to fight, so I passed them and climbed a hill to get away. They started throwing rocks and other things at us. I wanted to throw something back and engage them, but I didn't. I managed to get away by cutting through some back yards until we came to a friendly middle aged guy in his yard. I said, "Man, it's nuts tonight! What's going on with all these nuts around?" He laughed.

Next there was a new Zorro television show with an actor. Hawk said to me, "This is really good and we have to watch it."

I became part of the show, caught up in an involved plot. First it was a movie, then it turned real. The actor playing Zorro had a secret identity, a cape, a mask, and a beautiful black horse. They were lying down together on the ground putting their heads together. Thunder and lightning filled the air which felt powerful and it seemed like the opening of the show.

I became one of the characters in the show and played the son of some guy. There were four or five of us who stayed at his house as brothers, then bad guys came and caught him. He had a wound on his side from a horse and they pulled him out without any clothes on. A battle erupted and they tried to burn down the house but we ran in and stopped them. I chased one guy down and beat him.

A nasty woman insulted me by calling me names and I gave it back to her worse. People were getting killed and running back and forth. Me, Zorro, and a couple of other guys all ran and hid together, then we found a car to get away in. I was half way to it when the nasty woman caught me and I ended up on the ground having a hard time moving with her insulting and kicking me. I tried to play dead but she wouldn't stop, then I got up and saw that she had a bag of chips or peanuts. I grabbed her, threw her down, and poured the bag over her head, then I got in the car and drove to some place like the Pennsylvania countryside feeling like an escaping family. We drove by movie theaters where space movies were playing and came across a guy in an airport with a giant jet fuel truck surrounded by people, threatening to blow everybody up.

He was a big guy and I got behind him, jumped on his neck, grabbed him, and pulled him back choking him to stop him from blowing everybody up and I asked him why he was doing it. He became friendly and offered me the possibility of a new job. He showed us a workshop where he let us do what we wanted, then it turned into a hardware store. People there were doing mechanical drafting using pencils, then somebody was trying to fix what looked like training wheels on a motorcycle and asked me to come help, which I did. We left and were hanging around with some gangs, and found another gang like ours that had been chased out. We were acting like guerrillas and they wanted to join with us, so we decided to have our own little war games with them and split up.

A huge guy came up to me brandishing a big linoleum knife which he put to my stomach. I wasn't afraid because I was figuring out as the dreams unfolded that I had to confront this conflict in the right way, so I said, "Who are you and what are you doing this for?"

He turned friendly and he was my buddy who said he was there to help us out.

I understood that the key to these situations when faced with conflict from my dreaming shadow selves meant I had to face them, but I had to do it in the right way. Sometimes I had to defeat them and sometimes I had to befriend them, and as I discovered here, sometimes all I had to say was "What is your problem?" I knew that what they were looking for is acknowledgment. My last two biggest conflicts came at the end of this long sequence which indicated to me that I was figuring it out.

The whole power of the Inca rose color of love, the electric blue of power, and the gold of wisdom combining into the beautiful electric violet hue was the brightest I had ever seen when it fully enveloped me. My sense of it was that Mother Coca came and protected and fortified me, preparing me for the battles I needed to go through and as they unfolded I got it together more and more and I triumphed in the right way when I wasn't fearful. When I jumped on the big guy's neck who threatened to kill everybody I wasn't trying to hurt or kill him, I just wanted to stop him. When the last big guy at the end had the knife to my stomach and I asked him what he wanted, he changed into an ally.

While lying there contemplating my marathon dreaming I realized that in the beginning of my dreams the threats came from smaller younger guys like teenagers or in their early twenties. The guys hassling us at the store were scrawny looking and as the dreams progressed, the last two guys I overcame were huge, almost seven feet tall. I could barely get my arms around the neck of the guy who wanted to blow everyone up.

In the aftermath of it all I felt like I had passed a test that the combined love, power, and wisdom from Mother Coca fortified me to go through the trial. I kept thinking as I went through each escalating confrontation that I had to confront each one and overcome it in the right way.

During the whole time the violet light infused and enveloped me Ronaldo's icaro went through my head. I didn't remember the exact words of it, only the melody, but looking back I discovered it was Ikaro De Las Tribus, the calling of the tribes that played in my head throughout the whole experience.

THIRTY THREE

Two Ayahuasca Firsts

I returned from our third Friday night ceremony at 3:00 on Saturday morning talking about the continuing revelation in my visions from my Thursday night dreaming marathon. The electric violet energy of the combined energies of love, power, and wisdom strengthened me for the escalating conflicts I evolved through dealing with aspects of my shadow in my dreams and I had faced similar confrontations with the same fearless dismissive energy I banished the slavering serpentine demon with in the jungle outside of Iquitos.

In this mid-session I experienced another Ayahuasca first. After I took a full dose I waited for about an hour. I was in the zone, but I wasn't flying, so I went up for a second dose. As soon as I got there I started belching and my body said No! No! No! They gave me another half dose which I forced down while it tried to come back up. I thought I would puke on myself, so I hustled back to my spot and sat with it as it went up and down up and down in my throat until it came back up and I puked into my bucket.

I sat there pissed that I couldn't keep the dose down trying to figure out what to do. After a few minutes, I thought, Fuck it, grabbed the bucket, tipped it up, and downed it. It still tried to come back up but it went down easier than the first time.

I soon flew off into beautiful worlds full of engaging plants, people, and beings which were all invisible. All I saw were the outlines of everything like pictures in coloring books. These magical worlds were both invisible and full of gorgeous colors bursting with different plant and people colors, yet I could see through everything.

People, spirits, and plants moved around while I passed through them like a first class tour of an entire astral realm that I had glimpsed many times before, but never fully immersed in, and in typical fashion I never wanted it to end.

They played music and sang icaros as the night went on and when William played his guitar hummingbird came to me and we flew through a multitude of places together. I tried to reach out energetically to Penny and her kids again holding them in my heart to channel the blissful energy I was travelling through, then I felt my mother's loving presence, and nothing could top that.

I woke up later on Saturday morning anticipating the second consecutive ceremony that coming night. During the day a friend came by and read me something by Paulo Coelho the Brazilian author of **The Alchemist**. This translated and abridged *Hymn to Isis* honors the Cosmic Feminine and came from the foreword to Coelho's book **Eleven Minutes.**

Hymn to Isis

For I am the first and the last
I am the venerated and the despised
I am the prostitute and the saint
I am the wife and the virgin
I am the mother and the daughter
I am the arms of my mother
I am barren and my children are many
I am the married woman and the spinster
I am the woman who gives birth and she who never procreated
I am the consolation for the pain of birth
I am the wife and the husband
And it was my man who created me
I am the mother of my father
I am the sister of my husband
And he is my rejected son
Always respect me
For I am the shameful and the magnificent one

I returned after 5:00 on Sunday morning from Saturday night, our fourth ceremony exhausted from a physically demanding session singing icaros that I did not know the words to, but felt the lingering power of, as well as the energy from the ceremony. It had been another remarkable night where I took three doses, another first for me, and with three doses I felt like I had been on three separate journeys.

I first flew into an incredible green plant space filled with white light infused with polychromatic hues while I sang and drummed along with José and Ronaldo, adding my energy to the individual healings they did. I felt fully present drumming, singing, and giving my energy to the healings at the same time experiencing an effortless, natural sense of bilocation. I felt totally absent from the present moment while exploring and moving through other incredible realms and experiences throughout cosmic, color laden multidimensional textured worlds that defied logic. In these journeys I travelled back into the past and dealt with some of my father's, mother's, and grandfather's issues while experiencing a cornucopia of remarkable nonverbal teachings.

Yoda, José, and Ronaldo kept taking more doses and Yoda seemed to be pushing everyone to drink more. I took my first dose and was two or three hours into it when my Canadian buddy Jim took a second dose. After he came back and sat down I found myself struggling with the possibility of taking a second dose too. I said, "The hell with it," did so, and took off again, launching into more spectacular colors where beings came touching and checking in on me in the form of multiple eyeballs that came from everywhere.

Yoda took still another dose and I got it into my head to take a third, which I did. When the session ended and the circle closed I was still way out there in other realms still experiencing full bilocation. I talked to people while remaining present in the ongoing physical reality while flying in the other energetic ones which signaled my arrival at a whole new level of experience.

This phenomenon brought me back to the first time I worked with José when he seemed to be gone from the room while still being present when I thought, Where is José? I looked up to where he was and saw a black void of nothingness and thought again, Where is José?, then realized that his awareness was everywhere in the room. He was everywhere and nowhere at the same time. This experience was similar with my awareness being fully aware in other multidimensional worlds while being totally present in the circle drumming and singing.

I woke up later Sunday morning after sleeping about four hours feeling worn out with an Ayahuasca hangover that included a mild headache. I forced myself out of bed to do Qi Gong hoping it would energize me, which it did. I went down for a nap around 2:30 that afternoon and awoke filled with an ethereal green light similar to what you might see by shining a light through a leaf. My head felt swollen with building pressure that tracked with the increasing brightness that bordered on uncomfortable, like someone had turned on bright lights that weren't quite blinding. The green stayed for some time, lighting me up from within, then it faded and I thought I had better get up because dinner would be coming. When I completed that thought the helpers came over the hill bringing it to me. I thought the green light I experienced had to be the spirit of Mama Coca.

José and Ronaldo's icaros continued non-stop in my head before going to bed that night. I stayed quiet, closed my eyes and I could see the beginnings of the otherworldly starting to form.

THIRTY FOUR

A Marathon of Light And Dark

I awoke on Monday morning from a wild, challenging night of restless sleep and dreaming anticipating our final ceremony that coming night. I had spent much of the night dancing between agony and ecstasy. The magical electric violet light came throughout the night at different times energetically recharging me over and over again for all of the alternating dark, morbid, chaotic dreams and passages I was plunged into.

I was at a gathering with my brother and other people along with Penny having a hard time trying to connect with her, then we connected.

We went to visit Jim and my other Canadian friends and tried to bring in bags of different things but came to a road blocked by construction and had to stop the car, get out, and carry everything. I wrestled with all of it to get to Jim's house and realized that a lot of what I was carrying shouldn't have went to their house, it should have gone to a friend's house. I took everything and struggled back to their friend's house alone and got to the top of some stairs where I discovered that I had a lot of the wrong things that I should have brought to Jim's house. I tried to sort through it all and felt like I couldn't do anything right, then I tried to unpack the bags and figure out what was what.

These friends of my friends were understanding while asking me questions I couldn't answer in the right way. I tried to talk to them with a lot of things in my mouth so I spit them out and tried to unpack the bags and separate things, but I couldn't figure out what belonged to who.

Next I played with a black puppy that playfully bit me while I wrestled with him. Somebody came and had me turn on my computer because they wanted to give me a web page. We didn't think there was internet but we had wireless so I looked though the web page they gave me and it had all the answers I needed. I was trying to figure out how to get some software to work when another guy came and tried to force everybody into another room. I went along with it, but I said, "You know, we got a bad ass here." I looked at my friend Jim, who said, "Yeah." He was trying to make a phone call while this guy tried to force us into a room to do something. I started making fun of him, saying, "Oh please no, I want my mommy."

Jim and our other Canadian friend Terence did the same thing. This guy was being obnoxious and threatening until a group of Jim's other friends came who were all pretty tough guys. They grabbed the troublemaker, dragged him out and gagged his brother who was in a wheelchair. The first guy wasn't so tough anymore and was whining, saying, "Where's my mom?" I was verbally confronting him and was going to physically confront him, but Jim wanted to take care of it and his friends said it was their job to take care of it, so they took him out.

Next I was with a cat with a muzzle. I took the muzzle off and played with the cat, then kept trying to put the muzzle back on, but I couldn't put it on right. Every time I tried I did it wrong and messed it up, so my friends took care of it for me and helped me out. Throughout the dream every time I tried to do something I couldn't do anything right. The main theme of the dream came from conflict with bullies. In this case I let others take him away so he was no longer a problem.

My last longest stretch of dreaming was the hardest. I had to go to a funeral with my mom, brother, sister, and the whole family. It seemed like it was for my mom's baby. She was having a tough time with it and wanted me there to help her, so we went into the funeral parlor to look at the body. My mom took me by the hand and held it because she was scared and nervous about the whole thing. The baby looked like a little extraterrestrial, but not the kind with the big eyes and big head. It looked alien with rainbow colors around its head which I thought was not so bad to look at.

I saw a stack of mass cards and pictures of the baby and it was my job to send them out to the right people, something that seemed to be an issue throughout the dream. We were figuring out whether we were supposed to drive or get in a limo to take us where we needed to go and decided on the limo. I went to get in the first limo with my mom, who now had black hair. My sister jumped in ahead of me into the front seat. There wasn't any room for me so I went in another limo and rode along in a motorcade to the cemetery which was the final resting place. On the way there in the limos a couple of beautiful girls who were members of the funeral director's family sang funny inappropriate songs to entertain us.

In the next moment it wasn't the baby's funeral anymore, it was my mother's. I was grieving, thinking this was the place where she was going to rest, the place where her body meets the earth, which was the same thought I had in Florida when I was dealing with her ashes from her cremation.

We went to a huge funeral home that was like a multiplex with a dozen funerals going on. I was one of the last ones in and couldn't find my way to my mom's ceremony. I wandered around among drunks falling down stairs and people drinking at a bar. I saw some of the guys who had worked for me and they saw me, but I didn't talk to them, then I slipped and fell. I couldn't find my mom's funeral ceremony anywhere, then I found my brother being loud and obnoxious getting drunk at the bar. He knew that the ceremony was downstairs in another hall so I found my way down through an elevator that didn't go up and down. I went out the back elevator door into a huge underground hall where they waited for me up front. I went along the side to the front to where somebody wanted me to sit beside them, but I said, "No, I need to sit right up front." The whole front row was taken, so I sat front and center a few rows back and the ceremony started.

People kept asking me questions and there was the issue of who was going to get the mass cards sent to them. I spoke to the whole assembly saying, "Your name is on the list so you'll get a card and if you don't give me your information." One of the guys went up the aisle and I followed him before realizing that I didn't need to be doing that because it was his job.

I went back and heard some noise from a problem off to the side. I went and saw that someone had committed suicide by hanging himself and cutting his own throat. It was really bloody but it was off behind the doors. My buddy Otorongo was there and he said, "Hey, you watch the door and don't let anybody in or out and I'll take care of it."

I said, "Okay," and watched the door. Otorongo took care of everything while I tried to find a funeral director. I went back, slipped and fell again, and grabbed on to a funeral director, then I let go, hit the floor and stood again to find more issues about the mass cards and pictures being sent. There were family members and distant relatives there that I didn't want to have anything to do with and never wanted to see again and I was glad that I never would have to see them again.

My brother got excessively loud and started talking about some of our childhood friends who had gotten out of prison and started a bar in Chicago that was doing really well. It seemed very much out of place and I thought, jeez, he's talking so loud and ma's dead. I guess he really wants her to hear him.

At the end of the dream everything turned into a jungle and some guys came after us with machetes. I had a machete and a .45 and Otorongo, myself, and others chopped back plants to clear a path. We had to make sure that the space in between us stayed clear and we kept moving forward while these guys kept coming. The dream ended when they came close to my friends and I went for my .45. I was getting ready to blow them away when I woke up, but while in the process of waking I wanted to make sure that I shot the bastards, and I did.

While experiencing these dark disturbing dreams I felt my body twitching and shaking the entire time they unfolded. The same thing had happened in my first night of marathon dreaming. In this dark passage and subsequent breaks I felt the electric violet fortifying me in the intervals between each extended dreaming episode.

My first dream with Penny was self apparent and in the second dream in Canada with the bully who made everything wrong, my friends and their friends took care of him, even though I could have confronted him. I think because I was in Canada I didn't know people and my friends did because it was in their territory. I didn't know if the bully was putting us on or not, but sensed that all of these confrontations were with different aspects of myself. The idea of not being able to do anything right, messing things up and seeing this theme continue into the third dream where I kept pushing to get through it made sense because I sensed that I was responsible for everything. Obviously I was still dealing with my mom's death, particularly in the last dream.

I had my last pitcher of Coca root infusion on Monday morning which was very dark and strong. That night in the ceremony I recorded the healing José did for me when he sang the spirit of the Coca plant into me as well as other plants and reported in from a great last session feeling exhausted at 5:00 Tuesday morning.

I flew fast and furious after taking one full dose and embraced colors, patterns, downloads, and reiterations of what I learned that week. In these ceremonies Ronaldo did most of the healings, but when it came my turn José did mine which held a special emphasis for me as I was following up on my mom's death and my own near death from my Iquitos adventure.

All of this swirled through me as he shook his chacapa over and on me. It felt like he was sweeping these energies out of me in a big whirlwind like a leaf blower. I also sang, rattled, and drummed with José as he sang throughout the ceremonies and did healings on everyone.

Later in the evening Yoda shared a passage from William Butler Yeats which had a powerful effect on me.

My fiftieth year had come and gone,
I sat, a solitary man,
in a crowded London shop,
an open book and empty cup
on the marble table-top.
While on the shop and street I gazed
My body of a sudden blazed
and twenty minutes more or less
it seemed, so great my happiness,
That I was blessed and could bless.

He also told us a story by Scheherazade from **One Thousand and One Nights.**

There was a man in Egypt who had a dream one night. In the dream he was told that a treasure would lie in wait for him in the Persian city of Islahan which in antiquity was very far from Egypt. The dream was so strong that the next day he decided to start on a journey to Islahan. He had to traverse Christian and Muslim cities, deserts, mountains, and all kinds of things and finally exhausted, he arrived in Islahan. He was so tired that he went to the yard of a mosque and fell asleep.

That night bandits came and robbed the people sleeping in front of the mosque, then soldiers came and arrested everybody and took them to jail for disturbing the peace, including this man from Egypt who had nothing to do with the robbery.

The next day they took him before the judge who said, "What is your story?"

The man from Egypt told the judge why he was there, what had happened, the dream he had, and that the treasure was waiting for him in Islahan.

When the judge heard the story he laughed and said, "You poor man. You followed these silly dreams. There is no treasure in Islahan. I dream often and practically every night I dream the same thing, that there is a treasure waiting for me in a garden that has a sun dial and a fig tree and the treasure is under the fig tree, and you know what? I don't pay any attention to these things. Take this man away and give him five lashes for idiocy and send him back home."

The man went back to Egypt. In his garden there was a sundial and a fig tree. He dug under the fig tree and sure enough in his back yard there was an enormous treasure waiting for him under it.

Later, my friend Geramy shared some verses by Kabir, a 15th-century Indian mystic poet and saint.

I Just Laugh

If I told you the truth about God, you might think I was an idiot.
If I lied to you about the Beautiful One you might parade me through the streets shouting, "This guy is a genius!"
This world has its pants on backwards.
Most carry their values and knowledge in a jug that has a big hole in it.
Thus having a clear grasp of the situation if I am asked anything these days I just laugh!

Also by Kabir is one of my all time favorites that has great relevance for me.

See If They Wet Their Pants

The words Guru, Swami, Super Swami, Master, Teacher, Murshid, Yogi, Priest, most of those sporting such a title are just peacocks. The litmus test is hold them upside down over a cliff for a few hours. If they don't wet their pants maybe you have found a real one.

When I went to sleep early that morning after the night's session it took me a little while to get to sleep. When I did my consciousness instantly dissipated like I had taken a hit of 5MEO. My whole spirit and energy accelerated like a big aperture of consciousness had slammed shut and I was getting pulled out of there at light speed off on a wild flight until I woke up a couple of hours later.

This experience struck me as a fitting ending to the dieta.

THIRTY FIVE

My Psychic Surgeon

In early 2005 a friend of mine told me about a personal coach he was working with over the phone, but she was very expensive. Even though I had made great progress working with plant medicines, I knew I had deeper issues that I hoped someone outside of me with a feminine perspective might help me work through. This was a major first for me as I had never asked for help from anyone before this and thought a second set of objective feminine eyes could help me refine things.

Initially we had an audition where she spent forty five minutes with me on a phone call. When we finished I asked her what I owed her and she said that I didn't owe her anything for that first call, but she gave me a homework assignment which was to do something nice for little Matthew. I thought long and hard about this and remembered how much I had loved the space program when I was little so I bought myself the *From the Earth to the Moon* DVD set and enjoyed watching it. This began a five year series of weekly phone calls where we delved into wounds deeply buried in my subconscious, then she sent me her notes every week so I could follow up on what we covered in the session.

When I saw the value in this work I had Penny start her own sessions in hopes of helping her overcome her demons which improved our situation for awhile before it all blew up. At one point I also paid for a number of sessions with my then thirty-something traumatized youngest niece who I had helped for all of her life. This too eventually blew up on me.

The primary focus of what my coach helped me see through our many sessions was that we all carry a primary wound of abandonment that began at birth when we were forced out of the womb. As we evolve this translates into the false perception that we are not worthy of being loved and this deep rooted falsehood generates coping strategies that color and corrupt our thoughts and actions.

As we develop our unique personalities we add layers on top of this this primary wound like the proverbial layers of an onion. The core of this this compounding wound is obscured by the fact that our initial experiences are non-verbal and emotional which form the basis of our shadow. This creation occurs in the pre-intellect stages of the still forming brain, so there is no verbal recollection, and many of the neural connections are still being pruned, refined, and formed to adapt to inner and outer environments.

I was already aware of this phenomenon through the groundbreaking work of Stanislav Grof, known for his early studies of LSD and its effects on the psyche in the field of psychedelic therapy. Grof constructed a theoretical framework for prenatal, perinatal, and transpersonal psychology where powerfully emotional experiences are mapped onto early fetal and neonatal experiences into what Grof called a cartography of the deep human psyche. Following the suppression of legal LSD use in the late 1960s, Grof developed a theory that many states of mind could be explored without drugs using a breathing technique known as Holotropic Breathwork.

Though I was aware of Grof's four Basic Perinatal Matrices, known as BPMs, my coach guided me through the nuances of my hidden not feeling worthy of being loved wound and helped me uncover the secrets of my self defeating behaviors which went back to my entry into this world and possibly beyond that. She didn't refer to Grof's work in our sessions, but what she helped me uncover dovetailed with it and is worthy of further elaboration within the context of my overall growth.

According to Grof, the First Basic Perinatal Matrix is known as the Primal Union with Mother related to the intrauterine existence before birth. The fetus in the womb has no awareness of boundaries and knows no difference between inner and outer worlds which is reflected in experiences associated with reliving the memory of the prenatal state.

During episodes of undisturbed embryonal existence we

experience vast regions with no boundaries and can identify with galaxies, interstellar space, or the entire cosmos. A related experience is that of floating in the sea identifying with aquatic animals, or even becoming the ocean and it appears to reflect the fact that the fetus is essentially an aquatic creature. Positive intrauterine experiences are associated with safe, beautiful, unconditionally nourishing archetypal visions of Mother Nature like a good womb. Visions of fruit-bearing orchards, fields of ripe corn, agricultural terraces in the Andes, or unspoiled Polynesian islands are hallmarks of this. Mythological images from the collective unconscious that appear in this context portray celestial realms and paradises often described in mythologies from different cultures.

When we relive episodes of intrauterine disturbances like memories of the "bad womb," we sense a dark ominous threat and often feel poisoned. We might see images portraying polluted waters and toxic dumps reflecting the fact that many prenatal disturbances are caused by toxic changes in the body of the pregnant mother. These sequences can be associated with archetypal visions of terrifying demonic entities or a sense of insidious all-pervading evil. Those who relive episodes of violent interference with prenatal existence like an imminent miscarriage or attempted abortion usually experience some form of universal threat or bloody apocalyptic visions of the end of the world that reflect the intimate interconnections between events in our biological history and Jungian archetypes.

The Second Perinatal Matrix is referred to as the Cosmic Engulfment and No Exit, or Hell where we feel like we are being sucked into a gigantic whirlpool or swallowed by a mythic creature. We can also experience what feels like the entire world or cosmos being engulfed which can engender images of devouring, entangling archetypal monsters resembling leviathans, dragons, whales, vipers, giant snakes, tarantulas, or octopuses. The sense of overwhelming threat can lead to intense anxiety and mistrust bordering on paranoia. Another experiential beginning of the second matrix is the theme of descending into the depths of the underworld, death, or hell which Joseph Campbell described as a universal motif of the hero's journey.

In the first stage of birth uterine contractions constrict the fetus and the cervix is not yet open. This part of birth feels like being caught in a monstrous claustrophobic nightmare of agonizing emotional and physical pain coupled with a sense of helplessness and hopelessness where feelings of loneliness, guilt, absurdity of life, and existential despair can reach metaphysical proportions. Someone in this predicament is often convinced that it will never end and there is no way out, evident in a sense of dying, going crazy, and never coming back.

Reliving this stage is often accompanied by people, animals, and mythological beings in painful, hopeless predicaments similar to the fetus caught in the clutches of the birth canal. It can appear as a medieval dungeon, a torture chamber of the Inquisition, a smothering, crushing mechanical contraption, a concentration camp, or an insane asylum. This suffering can also take the form of pains of animals caught in traps or dimensions that are archetypal. We can feel the intolerable tortures of sinners in hell, the agony of Jesus on the cross, or the excruciating torment of Sisyphus rolling his boulder up the mountain in the deepest pit of Hades. Other images that have appeared in sessions dominated by this matrix include the Greek archetypal symbols of endless suffering, Tantalus and Prometheus, and other figures representing eternal damnation like the Wandering Jew Ahasuerus or the Flying Dutchman.

While under the influence of this matrix we are blinded and unable to see anything positive in our life and human existence in general. The connection to the divine dimension seems irretrievably severed and lost. Life seems to be a meaningless Theater of the Absurd, a farce staging cardboard characters and mindless robots, or a cruel circus sideshow. In this state of mind, existential philosophy can be the only relevant description of existence. Going deeper into this experience is like meeting eternal damnation. This shattering experience of darkness and abysmal despair is known in spiritual literature as the Dark Night of the Soul, an important stage of spiritual opening that can be tremendously purging and liberating.

The Third Perinatal Matrix is The Death-Rebirth Struggle. Many aspects of this rich, colorful experience can be understood from its association with passing through the birth canal after the cervix opens and the head descends into the pelvis. In this stage uterine contractions continue, but the cervix is dilated allowing gradual propulsion of the fetus through the birth canal involving crushing mechanical pressures, pains, and a high degree of anoxia and suffocation. This uncomfortable, life-threatening situation brings intense anxiety.

Aside from interrupted blood circulation from uterine contractions and the compression of uterine arteries, the blood supply to the fetus can be compromised by other complications. The umbilical cord can be squeezed between the head and the pelvic opening or twisted around the neck, and the placenta can detach during delivery or obstruct the way out. In some instances the fetus can inhale biological material encountered in the final stages of this process further intensifying feelings of suffocation. This stage can be so extreme that it requires intervention like the use of forceps or an emergency Cesarean section.

Aside from the realistic reliving of different aspects of the struggle in the birth canal BPM III involves copious imagery from history, nature, and archetypal realms. The most important of these are associated with a titanic fight, aggressive, sadomasochistic sequences, deviant sexuality, demonic episodes, scatological involvement, and encounters with fire. Most of these associations can be related to anatomical, physiological, and biochemical characteristics of the corresponding stage of birth.

When we encounter the third matrix we experience streams of energy of overwhelming intensity rushing through the body, building up to explosive discharges. At this point, we might identify with raging elements of nature like volcanoes, electric storms, earthquakes, tidal waves, or tornadoes. This experience can also portray technology involving tanks, rockets, spaceships, lasers, electric power plants, thermonuclear reactors, and atomic bombs. The titanic experiences of BPM III can reach archetypal dimensions and portray battles of massive proportions like the cosmic battle between the forces of light and dark, angels and devils, or gods and titans.

Aggressive and sadomasochistic aspects of this matrix reflect the biological fury of an organism whose survival is threatened by suffocation as well as the destructive onslaught of uterine contractions. Facing this we can experience cruelties of astonishing proportions manifesting in violent scenes of murder, suicide, mutilation, self-mutilation, massacres, bloody wars, and revolutions which often take the form of torture, execution, ritual sacrifice, self-sacrifice, bloody man to man combats, and sadomasochistic practices.

The Fourth Perinatal Matrix is The Death Rebirth Experience related to the final expulsion from the birth canal and the severing of the umbilical cord where we complete the difficult transition through the birth canal, achieve explosive liberation, and emerge into light. This is often accompanied by concrete, realistic memories that can include anesthesia, the pressure of forceps, and the sensations of other obstetric maneuvers and postnatal interventions.

The reliving of biological birth is not experienced as a simple mechanical replay of the original biological event, it is also a psychospiritual death and rebirth. Because the fetus is confined during the birth process and has no way of expressing the extreme emotions and reactions to the intense physical sensations involved, this memory remains psychologically undigested and unassimilated.

Our self-definition and attitudes toward the world are heavily contaminated by this constant reminder of vulnerability, inadequacy, and weakness experienced at birth. In many respects we are born anatomically, but have not caught up with this fact emotionally. The "dying" and the agony of the struggle for rebirth reflects the actual pain and threat of the biological birth process. The ego death that precedes rebirth is the death of our old concepts of who we are and what the world is like which were forged by the traumatic imprint of birth and maintained by the memory of this situation that stays alive in our unconscious.

As we clear these old programs by letting them emerge into consciousness they lose their emotional charge and in a sense die, but we are so identified with them that approaching the moment of ego death feels like the end of our existence or the end of the world. As frightening as this process is it is healing and transforming. While only a small step separates us from an experience of radical liberation, we have a sense of all-pervading anxiety and impending catastrophe of enormous proportions. What actually dies in this process is the false ego or personality that we have mistaken for our true self. While losing all the reference points we know, we have no idea what is on the other side, or if there is anything there at all. This fear creates enormous resistance to completing the experience and without appropriate guidance people can remain psychologically stuck in this problematic territory.

Experiential completion of reliving birth takes the form of psychospiritual death and rebirth, giving birth to a new self through integrating our shadow selves in what Jung referred to as individuation. This is also the basis for the dismemberment, decapitation, or being swallowed by the jaguar in the shaman's journey to the underworld that lies at the transformative core of Joseph Campbell's Hero's journey.

When we overcome the metaphysical fear encountered at this important juncture and decide to let things happen we experience total annihilation on all levels including physical destruction, emotional disaster, intellectual and philosophical defeat, moral failure, and spiritual damnation. Everything important and meaningful in life seems to be mercilessly destroyed. Following the experience of annihilation and hitting "cosmic bottom" we are overwhelmed by visions of white or golden light of supernatural radiance and exquisite beauty that appear numinous and divine.

Having survived what feels like total annihilation and the apocalyptic end of everything, we are blessed moments later with fantastic displays of magnificent rainbow spectra, peacock designs, celestial scenes, and visions of archetypal beings bathed in divine light. Often this is the time of a powerful encounter with the archetypal Great Mother Goddess, what I have been referring to as the Cosmic Feminine in her universal form or in one of her culture specific forms which in my case was my revelation of Santa Teresa de Avila facilitated by my birth mother.

After experiencing psychospiritual death and rebirth we feel redeemed, blessed, and experience ecstatic rapture with a sense of reclaiming our divine nature and cosmic status resulting in being overcome by a surge of positive emotions toward ourselves, others, nature, and existence in general.

Much of this embedded subconscious and traumatic material is uncovered, and in many ways defines the content of visionary journeys hosted by none other than the Great Mother Goddess herself, Ayahuasca. My coach had other clients who worked with Ayahuasca. She told them to stop working with it, but she encouraged me to continue. I spent years struggling between these two conflicting approaches until I worked though the paradox and resolved what ultimately became complementary approaches aimed toward the same goals.

In the case of Ayahuasca this long buried material arises in barrages of complex nonlinguistic, visual, spatial amalgams of thought and emotion analogous to stirring up sediment and muddying the waters for filtering and analysis of its content. My coach had a way of zeroing in on specific issues instead of the mass of stirred up energies that Ayahuasca let loose, prompting me to call her a psychic surgeon because of her precision which delighted her.

Aside from the initial physical abandonment at birth that we all share, I had a second literal abandonment by my father at the age of five when he went to prison, further obscuring and exacerbating my wound and the wounds of my three siblings which left us all feeling unworthy of being loved.

These revelations tied in with the work I was doing with the plant medicines and with what I was learning in my two year study which broke everything down to the two basic fears we all have that trace back to the binary core of our perinatal experiences; abandonment and entrapment. While sharing this with a lady friend she pointed out that males generally fear entrapment and females fear abandonment. This led to the further realization that fear is contraction and love is expansion, something that goes back to our primal mammalian beginnings and still further back to the roots of our survival instincts.

This inner shadow work is painful, unpleasant, terrifying, and a full blown ordeal when you face it head on in an Ayahuasca jungle plant dieta, but if you can navigate the self imposed psychic obstacles and pass through the darkness, the results are more than worth it.

Our loyal subpersonalities representing the face of our buried traumas are members of the shadow community we created and they are elusive, cunning, and will go to great extremes to complete the job that we created them for. As much as we might think we are aware of this, we still miss their presence within and the emotional depth of their commitment to the purpose we gave them. We are the Creators of this holographic realm that stands in contrast to those around us, reflecting those same aspects of who we are as part of the bigger Cosmic hologram that makes up the Great Mystery.

When I started this detailed shadow work with my coach she gave me a set of ground rules and warnings about what to expect and how things might unfold. Chief among these are what I called her prime directive which was a simple admonition.

Tell your secrets.

When you do this with someone you might have previously judged and projected your shadow onto, you are taking responsibility for your creations. There is no perception of blame because you are pointing the finger at yourself, effectively disarming them from becoming defensive. After many years I still have to remind myself to do this as I still catch myself in small lies by a lifelong habit of misrepresenting and exaggeration.

She also told me that I needed to become vulnerable in order to expand, which was hugely challenging for me. I grew up defending myself and others, and as I did the work to become more open and vulnerable, I paid a heavy price for lowering my guard on this lifetime defense mechanism. Tied in with this, she warned me that if I stayed true to my path people would filter out of my life and it could very well fall apart in many ways which also turned out to be true.

As hard as this was to accept I understood that if I was going to change my internal dynamics and come to terms with my inner conflicts and false assumptions of my elusive shadow selves, then my shifting inner relationships would be reflected in my outer world. This also turned out to be true, but the falling out with people and the dissolution of my life as I knew it came in dramatic ways I never could have predicted.

I have always learned the hard way which is how we learn our most difficult lessons. Our primary wound of not feeling worthy of being loved engenders learned and invented behaviors calculated to get us the love that we lack. The problem with this approach not only makes it conditional, it makes it false. *Real* love is unconditional, evident in the required vulnerability. This counterfeit fabricated agenda aimed at attracting love holds within it with the unspoken expectation of acknowledgement and reward.

Among other widely held cultural practices, martyrdom which we think of as an honorable trait is rampant in our belief systems and has been drilled into us through long standing myths similar to the Christian one that Jesus died for *our* sins and *you* will be rewarded in heaven for the sacrifices you make in your lifetime. This belief which is considered honorable has an agenda that creates the hope of a reward in the afterlife identical to that espoused by jihadists, assassins, suicide bombers, kamikazes, and the like.

Like the continuously flowing energy from the sun, true unconditional love has no expectations, and once it is fully embraced it results in real freedom. This is no easy task in a world where the majority of its people have no conception of real meaningful sacrifice.

Until my downfall I spent most of my life giving and sacrificing my time, money, and energy for my sister and her kids thinking I was doing the honorable thing until I saw how deeply embedded I was in this twisted ancient dynamic that played out endlessly through my life and still plays out in the lives of family members and others.

Thinking I was doing the right thing, when everything was said and done I did what I thought was my best when I gave up everything I had for Penny and her kids to provide a safe loving environment for them.

I became consciously aware of my misguided actions through the passage of time when I saw that the more I did for Penny, the more displeased she became, and the more I tried the worse she got. This was at odds with my intention to please and with these recurring moments of nonappreciation for all I did, I found myself puzzling over other incomprehensible quirks in her behavior like her physical and verbal assaults and lack of support on those rare occasions I was looking for it.

I finally saw the truth of my hidden agenda one afternoon after spending the day doing yard work and was particularly happy with the manicure I had done on a badly overgrown tree in the side yard. When she came home that afternoon she became disproportionally upset with me for trimming the neglected tree and the reality of the dynamic snapped into place.

While assimilating this burgeoning reality I fully grasped the wisdom of something I learned and from Andean cultures that resolves any hidden expectations of reward for giving.

Ayni refers to the concept of reciprocity among people of Andean mountain communities. As a noun, the law of ayni states that everything in the world is connected, and is the only commandment that rules daily life in many Andean communities. As a verb it refers to the cooperation between members of a community. When one member gives to another, he or she is entitled to receive something back. Well-known practitioners of Ayni include the Quechuas, and Aymara as well as other tribes that live in Peru, Ecuador, and Bolivia.

THIRTY SIX

Soaring From Blue Deer To Condor Mountaintops

In March of 2005 the Condors, our two year study group traveled to Mexico to participate in an all night Huichol Peyote ceremony. After flying and a long car ride we spent a night in a sparse, barely habitable hotel in the town of Wadley in Central Mexico close to Wirikuta. The Huichols believe the sun made its first appearance in this sacred desert high in the mountains of central Mexico between the Sierra Madre Oriental and the Zacatecas ranges, near Real de Catorce. Out of respect for the Huichol our teacher made it a point to bring us there for our ceremony during a time outside of the Huichol pilgrimages.

The Huichol make these yearly pilgrimages to Wirikuta between October and March following the journey of their deities to the Cerro Quemado where the Sun appeared guided by Tatehuari, Grandfather Fire. There a Deer used his horns to rise the sun to the sky, illuminating the world. The pilgrimage helps seekers find greater health, awareness, understanding, and meaning, enabling them to "find their lives". To follow the sacred journey every year Huichol shamans travel 250 miles from Jalisco to San Luis Potosí collecting peyote along the way following the belief that it enables them to commune directly with their ancestors and deities.

After the work is done they eat enough peyote to have visions and through their visions the Huichol believe that their shamans speak to the gods and ensure the regeneration of the Huichols' souls. At the end of their ceremonies they collect peyote and take it home, recreating life's cycle.

Groups travel under the direction of a leading shaman who advises participants on their ingestion of peyote and other behavior. Participants abstain from sex, and limit food, water, and sleep. Early in the journey they participate in a rite of public confession and purification to prepare them for more healing and growth which involves a retelling of their transgressions in front of the group. The most significant transgressions are theft, murder, and adultery and confessions include the public recitation of a full sexual history. The intention is to create an experience of cleansing and renewal free of jealousy, shame, or blame. A fire invokes Tatehuari while a Maraka'me hits each speaker's legs with a stick so they remember correctly.

Huichol beliefs consist of four principal deities, the trinity of Corn, Blue Deer, and Peyote, and the Eagle, all descended from the Sun God. They believe that two opposing cosmic forces exist in the world, an igneous one represented by Tayaupá, Our Father the Sun, and an aquatic one, Nacawé, the Rain Goddess. Eagle Stars, their Father's luminous creatures, hurl themselves into lagoons and Nacawé's water serpents rise into the sky to shape the clouds.

According to Huichol belief the Sun created earthly beings with his saliva in the shape of red foam on the surface of the ocean's waves that flow from Our Father the Sun which has a heart. Its forerunner adopts the shape of a bird that came from the underworld and placed a cross on the ocean. Father Sun was born and climbed up the cross killing the world's darkness with his blows.

The day after our arrival in Wadley and older man with a beat up pickup truck drove us out to Wirikuta with a few staples, among them oranges which we would snack on throughout the night to neutralize the alkalinity of the peyote helping to avoid stomach upsets. We did a peyote hunt with the admonition that we had to eat everything we gathered and were shown how to cut the buttons off at ground level, leaving the roots intact which allowed more buttons to grow back in bigger numbers. We peeled the skin from these and removed the spines leaving the inside which had a texture similar to, but a little denser than cucumbers. I collected nine good sized ones and found this first experience with fresh buttons easier to get down than the dried ones I had worked with before. Though bitter, something about their freshness made them more tolerable. They told us not to take them all at once but to eat them throughout the night as the ceremony progressed. We drummed at sunset honoring the passage of the sun from the day and welcoming the cooler desert night. When darkness came we sat together in a circle around an unlit fire and ate buttons as the night progressed.

I felt the effects of the buttons after awhile and saw mild colors and patterns like I saw in the Sacred valley in Peru, but more powerfully and sensed the distinctive power of Wirikuta with a new awareness of elemental places poignantly made evident to me on the island of Amantani. Although every aspect of the desert was the opposite of the jungle, and in many respects opposite to Amantani in the middle of Lake Titicaca, I felt a deep inner personal connection with the spirit of Wirikuta in its own idiosyncratic way.

We lit the fire at midnight to honor the sun's place on the other side of the planet as if it shone through from the other side following the Huichol tradition honoring the spirit of Tatehuari, Grandfather Fire. This reinvigorated the energy of our ceremony and drove my awareness deeper within in what I can only characterize as a more intimate, revealing, welcoming way. I finished my nine buttons and discovered a great affinity to them, so when someone else could not finish theirs, I gladly took them. My experience felt perfect in its own way and I could have eaten more buttons for a lot longer period of time.

After an enchanted gentle night compared to my many Ayahuasca ordeals, I felt open, connected, and part of the land similar to the way I did from Ayahuasca dietas as if no separation existed between me, the energy, and the spirit of the place. Like all the plant, animal, and other spirits I worked with in the mountains, jungles, and other deserts, I knew Wirikuta would stay with me permanently, even if I never returned and never ate another button.

Our host came the next morning in his battered pickup and drove us back to his house where he treated us to a breakfast of scrambled eggs and fried nopal cactus. After eating we headed to Real de Catorce, a historic mining town constructed by the Spanish in the 1700s which is now a sparsely inhabited village, but still a pilgrimage destination for the Huichol.

We spent the night in a rustic hotel made out of stone, like an ancient church, and the following morning rode horses about 10,000 feet up to the top of Mount Quemado to honor the sacred site where the Huichol say the sun was born and what we honored in our ceremony with Tatewari, Grandfather Fire in Wirikuta. Mount Quemado itself represents the head of the Blue Deer god, Kauyumari.

Once there everyone ate a peyote button as a sacrament similar to

Catholic communion and made offerings to Tatawari, the Sun god at the temple to Kauyumari, the blue deer. About the size of a modest house, a macabre display of deer skulls, skins, antlers, and other deer parts and representations covered the walls of Kauyumari's temple. After spending meditative time there we rode our horses back to Real de Catorce and celebrated the completion of our pilgrimage with a well deserved and much appreciated dinner.

Some of the Condors went from the Mexican Mountains and deserts in March to the Peruvian Amazon in May to spend a couple of weeks in the Shipibo village of San Francisco on the Rio Ucayali outside Pucallpa Peru where I had visited many times. I brought balsa planes, a couple of frisbees that lit up at night for the boys and soap bubbles and hair clips for the girls which were big hits. I had fun swimming with the kids in the Ucayali picking them up and throwing them into the water. When Enrique the older shaman saw me doing this he named me Honi Kushi, which means strong man in Shipibo.

We took nature walks to learn more about their favorite plants and uses, and held a number of Ayahuasca ceremonies in the village with the Shipiba shaman Herlinda who had accompanied us through the Andes and our ceremonies outside of Iquitos. Toward the end of our visit the younger members of the tribe performed traditional storytelling dances and musical performances. I paid special attention to my contact this time as I did not want to contract another deadly virus and avoided kissing babies thrust toward me. With this new awareness I saw that many people handled our food and a constant flurry of snot-nosed kids ran everywhere along with free roaming pigs, chickens, and mangy dogs.

The Shipibos neglected the flea infested dogs that ran freely, scavenging, and barely surviving on food scraps and garbage. My teacher who had been there before thought ahead and brought flea and tick shampoo and we had fun with the kids giving one cute little half starving mutt a bath.

In contrast to the neglected dogs, the Shipibos raised their children communally. Everyone, including aunts, uncles, and older children looked after the younger ones all the time. They still remained close to their parents, but were not attached or spoiled and received equal attention from everyone. As a result I saw no jealousy, favoritism, sibling rivalry, bickering or envy. The love was shared equally everywhere. It was both heartbreaking and heartwarming at the end of our visit when some sweet young girls I had become close with cried openly when it was time to leave.

I felt honored when my teacher asked me to join him for another week on a trip to the Andes after the rest of the group departed from the jungle. We flew through Lima to Arequipa, the "White city" located on the tectonic fracture of the Earth's crust called Ring of Fire, or Cadena Del Fuego in Spanish, known for its frequent volcanic eruptions and earthquakes. Framed by 3 volcanoes, Arequipa is the colonial-era capital of Peru's Arequipa Region filled with baroque buildings made from sillar, a white volcanic stone. We spent a night in its historic center by the Plaza de Armas, a stately main square flanked on the north by the 17th-century neoclassical Basilica Cathedral. The plaza also has a number of vintage shops with excellent goods at reasonable prices. While there I purchased some beautiful silver jewelry inlaid with turquoise and other stones and a high quality leather wallet.

The next day we took a five hour packed bus ride full of locals headed for Colca Canyon, a habitat for the giant Andean Condor at the Cruz del Condor overlook where Condors rose up every morning on thermals and descended again in the afternoon.

This canyon of the Colca River is about a hundred miles northwest of Arequipa and is Peru's third most-visited tourist destination. At an altitude of 10,730 ft Colca Canyon is one of the deepest in the world and covers a 43 mile stretch. The Colca Valley is a colorful Andean valley with pre-Inca roots and towns founded in Spanish colonial times, still inhabited by people of the Collagua and the Cabana cultures. The locals practice ancestral traditions of cultivating pre-Inca stepped terraces called andenes. The Spaniards under Gonzalo Pizarro arrived in 1540 and in the 1570s the Spanish viceroy Francisco de Toledo ordered the inhabitants throughout the former Inca Empire to move to a series of centrally located settlements in a process called "Reductions" which remain the principal towns of the valley. Franciscan missionaries built the first chapel in the valley in 1565, and the first church in 1569. The Colca River feeds into the Majes River which the Incas believed flowed directly into the Milky Way and often put sacrifices and gifts to the gods in it to flow to them.

My teacher and I felt the beginnings of altitude sickness in

Arequipa which set in stronger along with an upset stomach over the course of our bus ride. It was full blown by the time we reached a hotel in the town of Chivay midpoint in the Colca valley. 11,500 feet above Chivay agriculture turns to livestock consisting of alpacas, llamas, sheep, and cattle. Small villages are spread out over 35 miles within the deepening valley downriver between Chivay and the village of Cabanaconde.

It was fascinating to visit towns and markets where three cultures of differing dialects communed and traded. The Kollowas occupied the eastern region of the river basin, the Cabanas in the eastern region of the Colca river, and the Caccatapay lived in the deepest area of the center of the Colca River canyon. Apart from its rich agriculture, local churches have remarkable architecture and valuable pieces of religious art that shows the culture and traditions of each community.

We did everything we could to alleviate our sickness including trying to sleep, but spent a mostly sleepless night. Thinking it through, we figured that coming from the oxygen rich jungle to the thinner dry Andean air made things harder than they needed to be and would travel in the opposite direction if we made this kind of passage in the future.

In spite of feeling sick we hired a cab to take us to the Cruz del Condor overlook, stopping first at the town of Yanque. A large group of dancing women in colorful intricately patterned dresses danced in the open square there within sight of beautiful, centuries old perfectly preserved churches and a beautifully dressed woman stood stoically, looking picture perfect with a large hawk on her arm.

We left Yanque and headed to the Cruz del Condor overlook in time to witness Condors rising on the morning thermals. I looked forward to this, not only to honor the Condor spirit who I considered my primary totem, but to extend that blessing out to the rest of our two year group, the Condors. The closer we got to the overlook the more my headache and stomach ache diminished and they disappeared when we got there.

I attributed my escape from head and stomach pain to Condor healing mojo, but the fact that I felt like a joyful overstimulated three year old when we arrived may have contributed to that, or it was simply part of the positive energy. We made tobacco offerings and scrambled all over the place for a couple of hours exploring different viewpoints. I got dizzy from moving in slow circles taking hundreds of pictures of the magical air show that we witnessed close up beneath the wings of soaring Condors. On the way back that afternoon we stopped to marvel at ancient mummy bundles covered with rocks stuck to the side of sheer cliffs like massive prehistoric bird nests.

Whether Condor mojo or not, my headache and stomach upset returned after we left, less severe than before and it gradually diminished a few hours later. After returning to Chivay we toured a small museum on the outskirts of town that showed local medicinal plants, primitive weaving looms, and other ancient ways of dressing and lifestyles that didn't look much different than what we saw in the present day.

THIRTY SEVEN

The Magical Embraces Of Sting And Picaflor

I finished my two year shamanic study with the Condors in mid-2005 and went into 2006 riding a high point in my life. Penny and I were getting weekly sessions with our coach and seemed to have found peace after five years of struggle. I had been working with Yoda doing ceremonies and jungle dietas for four years before joining the Condors and averaged thirty Ayahuasca ceremonies a year for those two years as well as a plethora of other substances, chief among them 5MEODMT.

Acknowledging the depth of my experience my two year study teachers asked me to lead ceremonies with them, so I continued working with them while taking a stronger role doing ceremonies with Yoda while branching what I had learned across both disciplines.

One afternoon while preparing for a ceremony I was sitting with my friend Lorenzo when someone popped their head in the door and said, "Sting is here!"

Disbelieving my ears, I asked Lorenzo what he heard and he said, "I thought they said, 'It stinks in here!'"

Intrigued, I got up and poked my head out the door and my eyes met Sting's from across the way. I admit to being a bit star struck, but I wanted to respect his privacy and avoid being a "fan boy". Another person there did not show the same respect and latched onto him, but to his credit he handled it tactfully.

When we were introduced Penny didn't know who he was, which he thoroughly enjoyed and I felt blessed to participate in an all night ceremony with him and thirteen others. Needless to say Penny was mortified when I played a Police album for her and she realized who he was. When we stated our intentions prior to the ceremony, he said he was tired of the whole Sting thing and would have liked another name, and in that moment another friend and I looked at each other and in the same time said, "Stung!"

Not only did he participate in the ceremony, but when it was over he could have slept in a more exclusive room, but to his credit he slept on the floor with most of the rest of us. I ran into him face to face coming back in the room after the ceremony and after asking him how his journey was I said, "You're the last person I expected to see here and because of that much of my journey was a retrospective of your career, and I have to tell you, you were awesome in **Quadrophenia.**

He brightened and said "Thank you!", then he hugged me and kissed me on the cheek. It struck me that yoga had paid off for him as he was solid muscle. Stunned by his sincerity I went back to Penny in a mild daze, and said, "Sting just kissed me on the cheek!"

Her eyes widened and she marched off to find him to say, "Matt, said you kissed him on the cheek."

He graciously hugged her and gave her a kiss on the cheek too.

The following morning he had to leave early for four hours of dental work, which I admit to being in awe of after participating in an all night Ayahuasca session. I knew he had been a high school English teacher and was sympathetic to indigenous people, so I signed and gifted him a copy of **Land Without Evil.** He studied the back cover and saw the endorsements I had and said, "Thank you, I'm really looking forward to reading this."

I love telling people, "I met Sting. Ask me if I got his autograph."

When they play along and ask, I say, "No, he got mine."

In another indicator of how down to earth he is, before leaving in a surely sleep deprived state for his dental ordeal, he went up three flights of stairs and searched the upstairs hall to find Penny to give her a goodbye hug.

Meeting and connecting with him and sharing an intimate Ayahuasca ceremony was a magical highlight of my life, but in some respects it paled in comparison to another enchanted encounter I had in that same series of ceremonies.

At some point deep in my visions my usual Condor "wing" legs started flapping faster than ever before and I became overwhelmed in an experience that felt outside of time and infinite. My body twitched and my head bobbed while I flew through neon pastel colored bliss into sublime, exquisite high frequency luminescent realities while my body quivered at a high speed that I did not think possible.

I felt honored by the attention from what I thought of as a playful conflict that hinted at jealousy between the slower energy of Condor and this higher energy and at one point it felt like I held both energies within me. Fascinated, I worked with that dance of energies until the higher vibration took over and pulled me up out of the bigger, slower moving Condor without any urge to shit or puke. I felt pure joy and believe my body's energies had adjusted to embracing these high frequencies and raised up enough in vibration to handle and embrace them fully.

I felt exceptionally clear and open the following morning when we met to discuss our experiences and subsequent integration, and the full impact of what happened hit me when my friend Geramy said, "I knew we were going to have a powerful session because just before I came inside a hummingbird flew up to me and hovered in front of my face."

The moment he said that I realized I had embodied the spirit of hummingbird and in that same moment of revelation Penny exclaimed, "You were the hummingbird!"

I felt a profound shift inside of me in that flash of insight and a mystical inner rebirth and understood that I had reached a new level of awareness and would never be the same from that moment going forward.

Picaflor in Spanish comes from picar which means to *sting* and flor means flower. I felt deeply honored that Picaflor had chosen me and a little embarrassed that it had taken me so long to embrace this loving realization, but I don't think my body and its energies were ready for its full embrace before this which would explain its short flirting visits in life and in the jungle in my visions leading up to this momentous blessing. I had been loyal to Condor and believe that all my time with her cleared me out and raised my vibration to prepare me for fully merging and accepting Picaflor. Now after all these years Picaflor is my primary totem while my deep connection, respect, and gratitude with Condor remains and she still joins me from time to time in my visionary journeys.

Those who know me best in shamanic circles call me Picaflor.

THIRTY EIGHT

5ME-NO?

5MEODMT, short for 5-methoxy-N,N-dimethyltryptamine is a psychedelic of the tryptamine class found in a wide variety of plant species including Ayahuasca as well as in the Sonoran Desert toad. The first time I smoked it in May of 1998 I purchased it synthesized from a lab in China when it was not well known and still legal. The following year I got to smoke real toad venom and like ingesting pure Mescaline as opposed to Peyote and Huachuma, the difference from the effects of the pure psychoactive and the combination of other substances found in its natural form create subtle differences in its subjective influence the way mild spices change the taste of food.

The increasingly popular, widely touted toad venom comes from the Colorado River toad known as the Sonoran Desert toad found in northern Mexico and the southwestern United States and can grow to almost 8 inches long. It is the largest toad in the United States apart from the non-native cane toad and has a smooth leathery skin that is olive green or mottled brown. A bulging kidney-shaped parotoid gland lies behind its large golden eye with a horizontal pupil and below that is a circular pale green area that is the ear drum. A white wart by the corner of its mouth and white glands on its legs produce toxic secretions that are the toad's primary defense system. These glands produce a poison potent enough to kill a grown dog in the form of 5MEODMT and bufotenin which is named after the Bufo genus of toads.

When vaporized a single deep inhalation of this poison produces a strong psychoactive effect within 15 seconds. After inhalation the user usually experiences a warm sensation, euphoria, and overwhelming visual and auditory hallucinations, due to 5MEO's high affinity for the 5-HT and 5-HT serotonin receptor subtypes. In addition to bufotenin, *Bufo* secretions also contain digoxin-like cardiac glycosides. Ingestion of Bufo toad toxins and eggs by humans has resulted in several cases of poisoning and death.

The now defunct Church of the Tree of Life was founded in California in 1971 by John Mann who declared the use of 5MEODMT as a sacrament. Between 1970 and 1990 smoking of 5MEO on parsley was one of the two most common forms of ingestion in the United States.

Albert Most, founder of the Church of the Toad of Light and a proponent of spiritual use of *Bufo alvarius* venom, published a booklet titled **Bufo alvarius: The Psychedelic Toad of the Sonoran Desert** in 1983 which explained how to extract and smoke the secretions.

A 2019 European study with 42 volunteers showed that a single inhalation produced sustained enhancement of satisfaction with life, and easing of anxiety, depression, and post-traumatic stress disorder. Extracts of toad venom containing bufotenin and other bioactive compounds have been used medicinally for centuries in China. The toad was often depicted in Mesoamerican art which some have interpreted as indicating that the effects of ingesting *Bufo* secretions have been known in Mesoamerica for many years, but others doubt that this art provides sufficient ethnohistorical evidence to support the claim.

In addition to bufotenin, *Bufo* venoms contain digoxin-like cardiac glycosides. Digoxin is a medication used to treat various heart conditions like atrial fibrillation, atrial flutter, and heart failure and its ingestion from toads by humans has resulted in poisoning and death.

In 2006 I had been working with 5MEO for eight years, guiding hundreds of people through that experience, a responsibility I took seriously. I thought of myself as a portal keeper and ensured that anyone I sat with were in a safe, loving environment where I paid close attention to every breath, expression, or any other nuances of those taking the metaphorical leap in consciousness so they had a safe integration.

Like the 2019 European study suggested, I believe that a smoked hit of 5MEO with the right guide at the right time in the proper context at a certain point in someone's psychological evolution can blow open the doors of perception and open someone to a new level that can engender a dramatic shift in personality resulting in a profound sense of being reborn.

After eight years of smoking 5MEO I suspected that it had hidden aspects that I as well as many others had been blinded to due to its profound ego shattering effect and the expansive sense of open loving that followed. I noticed that the more I worked with it, the more I had sexual feelings cropping up amidst the expansive love I felt. Over time I discovered some definitive conclusions that I was absolutely convinced of from these journeys were not so definitive after all.

This observation reminded me of the man who asked the old Ayahuasquero about the nature and validity of what Ayahuasca teaches you when the shaman said, "One third of what Ayahuasca shows you is the truth, and one third of what Ayahuasca shows you is not the truth."

When nothing more was forthcoming the man asked, "What about the other third?"

The shaman simply shrugged.

My conviction of absolute truth and the glaring discrepancy of its questionable reality presented itself to me as a puzzle. I was becoming more aware of the combined ego and consciousness shattering effects of 5MEO and how it triggers a blast of neurochemicals that result in an expansive feeling of a loving heart opening. This concept and my growing observations supporting it evolved into a theory that I believe holds the underlying key to the whole phenomena.

Human consciousness is not specific to any particular function or system of the brain. All of its major systems participate in complex human behavior and specific systemic patterns of brain functioning are associated with distinct experiential states of consciousness. The relationship of brain physiology to consciousness is illustrated through an examination of how the physical structures of the brain and their associated activities relate to patterns of consciousness.

The human brain is layered with three anatomically distinct integrated systems that provide a range of behavioral, emotional, and informational functions. Our motor patterns, emotional states, and advanced cognitive and linguistic capabilities are primarily managed by brain systems that emerged sequentially in evolution in what is called the triune brain that provides a framework for the relationship between systemic brain activities and consciousness while relating to lower brain systems common with other animals.

Our hierarchical tripartite brain is based on neuroanatomical, structural, and functional divisions that break down into three strata starting with the reptilian, followed by the paleomammalian, and neomammalian brains. These three formations have different anatomical structures that mediate different psychological and behavioral functions with their own forms of subjectivity, intelligence, time and space sense, memory capabilities, and motor functions. Although the three segments are integrated, they provide the basis for different capacities and represent a hierarchy of information processing capabilities that facilitate distinct forms of consciousness.

The core reptilian brain is composed of the upper spinal cord, portions of the mesencephalon, or midbrain, the diencephalon thalamus-hypothalamus, and the basal ganglia. The instinctive reptilian brain regulates organic functions like metabolism, digestion, and respiration, and is responsible for wakefulness, attentional mechanisms, and the regulation and coordination of behavior.

The layer over that is the paleomammalian brain which is based on evolutionary developments in the limbic system that creates distinctions between reptiles and mammals, and provides the basis for social behavior and nonverbal, emotional, and analogical information processing. It functions as an emotional brain, mediating affect, sex, fighting, self defense, social relations, bonding and attachment, and *the sense of self that provides the basis for beliefs, certainty, and convictions*.

The neomammalian brain provides advanced symbolic processes, culture, language, logic, rational thought, analytical processes, and complex problem solving.

The reptilian brain provides the basic plots and actions of the body. The paleomammalian brain provides the emotional influences on thoughts and behavior, and the neomammalian brain uses enhanced symbolic capacities to elaborate on basic plots and emotions, integrating them with higher-level information processing.

The reptilian brain also provides primary awareness which is adaptation to the environment through reflexes, conditioned responses, and habituation, as well as through instrumental learning.

The paleomammalian brain provides for qualities of consciousness enriched by self, other, like society, and emotions, while the neomammalian brain encompassing the tertiary neocortical area, in particular the right hemisphere that is involved in cross integration and reorganization of perceptual modalities basic to symbolic cognition and self awareness.

The neomammalian brain consists of the neocortex and connecting thalamic structures thar represent the most dramatic evolution of the brain. The expanded neocortex's functions are based on extensive connections with the visual, auditory, and somatic systems, indicating the primary orientation of the neocortex to the external world.

If you consider Grof's layered perinatal matrices coupled with the effects of 5MEO and the fact that the poison in toad venom developed as a primal defense mechanism from a reptilian source, its impact on the human mind, hitting *its* reptilian core can be revealing. This rush of thought, emotion, and feeling bursts outward through the paleomammalian emotional brain; the part that mediates sex, social relations, bonding, attachment, and *the sense of self that provides the basis for beliefs, certainty, and convictions.*

If you contemplate the fact that this eruption flies up instantaneously stripping through all the accumulated layers of life experience, similar if not the same as "your life flashing before your eyes" reports from people having close encounters with death, then voila, you have a profound ego shattering effect and the expansive sense of open loving rebirth that follows.

I believe this lies at the core of the 5MEO experience and all of the problems of misuse that go with it and it became something that I was destined to see manifest and acted out in the worst way.

I had other friends doing their own versions of facilitating, among them Dog and my buddy Jacques, the first person to try it with me. A growing number of people were interested in it so the demand grew as did the frequency of our smoking it. At one point in this escalating number of people smoking or wanting to smoke it someone referred to 5MEO as hippie crack which annoyed me, but I was aware of my own addictive tendencies. The fact that it irritated me coupled with the "false positives" I observed told me there was something I needed to pay attention to.

Dog started hosting group events where everyone stretched out on his living room floor and took their hit at the same time to check out together. The people I did it with in his groups were experienced, so I didn't worry about re-entry for them, but I was concerned with the way Dog did things, particularly his lack of follow through with those he gave 5MEO to. It didn't sit right with me and his obsessive search for bigger and better experiences grew more outlandish as he tried to top himself each time. Planetary alignments, phases of the moon, meteor showers, and any other thought of possible cosmic alignment became reasons for group journeys.

He claimed to be a shaman and took on a sidekick I will call Puppy who emulated, supported, and reinforced everything Dog did, playing the role of Robin to his Batman. With Puppy's faithful support he collected his followers into a group he named the Love Tribe fostered by a wealthy couple who bought into and supported his "spiritual" leadership. The husband was the vice president of a well known international company and his wife was an attractive, apparently loving blonde who I'll call Cat.

They tried to convince me to be their shaman too but it all felt wrong to me. They had a big house in Southern California that became the focal point for frequent gatherings where Dog led increasingly bizarre "ceremonies". One of the things he did there that spooked me was "rebirthing" people by giving them a hit of 5MEO while they sat in a jacuzzi. His lack of follow through with someone who was struggling after this experience disturbed me to the point of leaving a Love Tribe party where this was happening.

When smoking 5MEO people often laugh, cry, scream in terror, or have any number of other unpredictable reactions, and like my buddy Jacques who let out a bone chilling scream his first time smoking it, they return with no memory of their terror and report feeling nothing but bliss. For me this psychological disconnect adds to the importance of being fully present for people when they return to full waking consciousness.

My own inner convictions and observations from my near decade use of 5MEO stood in stark contrast to Dog's "shamanism". I was becoming acutely aware of how this confusing attribution of mind altering substances could engender blissful, insightful glimpses into higher states of consciousness which were mistaken for true spirituality.

The expansive loving open hearted feeling typically reflected back to the person providing the experience carries with it a huge temptation to fall into what I refer to as guru-it is. This happens when the egotistic purveyor of the experience takes the adoration directed toward them as their own, when the truth of it was the blissful neurochemical experience that the 5MEO engendered as opposed to the actual loving compassionate spirit that the guru is deluded into being the spiritually superior source of.

In my mind the person seeking this and other entheogenic experiences comes to it willing to expose themselves to complete vulnerability and helplessness which requires a trust and integrity that I take seriously. I sensed that my own burgeoning sexual feelings without a focused sense of mindfulness could go unchecked and had the potential to violate this given trust.

My suspicions were confirmed one night after an Ayahuasca ceremony when we all felt open and loving. Dog came over and was lying at our feet when he started to suck on Penny's toe, which I immediately put a stop to with a warning to back away. This violation put me on alert to make sure he stayed away from her and it made me acutely aware of his wandering eye which indicated a lack of integrity.

THIRTY NINE

The Devil Made Me Do It

One night Dog wanted a group of us to go see Alex Grey and his visionary artwork at an exhibit in Los Angeles. I have a life long history of exploring altered states and am considered a "hard head" because I have a high tolerance to mind altering substances and on this night I decided to match Dog dose for dose to get some insight into what drove him. We started early with a dose of LSD. While we were dosing I looked at him and what came out of my mouth was, "You're a hedonist, aren't you?"

I will never forget the empty look in his eyes that defines the expression "the lights are on but nobody's home" when he affirmed it without hesitation. The next surprising thing that came out of my mouth was, "I guess that makes you Satan." He gave me a mirthless smile and I felt uncomfortable being so direct, so I followed up with, "I guess that makes me Satan's little brother."

From that point on, my joking references to him being a hedonistic Satan continued coming out of me as if someone or something else spoke through me. As if on autopilot I added, "I must be Satan's little brother." to cover my tracks and the fact that I was partaking of the same substances which made me guilty by association.

About an hour after doing the LSD we took a dose of MDMA which is called a Candy Flip. It kicked in strong and we took boosters throughout the night. After the exhibit we went to someone's house and walked into a room packed with about thirty people. Dog was in the middle of it, the 5MEO Pied Piper shaman-priest, ensuring that everyone launched, and again I was troubled by his nonexistent follow through.

When dawn broke we went to a restaurant in Venice Beach for an early breakfast. After that Dog was pushing to do more LSD and go to a church service where they sang and danced. I was physically and mentally burned out and knew I would need to quadruple my dose of LSD to have any effect on my poor abused brain cells, neurochemistry, and exhaustion which struck me as not only a waste, but beyond simple hedonism if that was possible.

Thankfully he relented when I refused to take more and we had an uncomfortable ride back to San Diego from Los Angeles filled with nuttiness and Dog's repetitive "spiritual" music that wore on me and Penny. We blissfully escaped his hedonistic insanity when he dropped us off later that morning for much needed relaxation and recovery.

After this episode Penny expressed her discomfort with Dog, Puppy, and his Love Tribe which I shared, so we decided it was time to distance ourselves and get as far away from them as we could.

This lasted for about four months until we were on a family vacation in Northern California with friends when I received a phone call from Puppy confirming my worst fears when he told me, "Our beloved Coyote died by drowning in the jacuzzi and we are all gathering for a funeral and to support each other."

His announcement made me think of the *line spoken by Al Pacino when he played Michael Corleone in* **The Godfather: Part III**. He was about to do a big deal that would take him out of the family business that he never wanted to be part of and discovers that he's been double-crossed by his mafia buddies.

"Just when I thought I was out they pull me back in!"

I had to break the news to Penny who had been friends with Coyote and the kids picked up on something being wrong right away. We cut our visit short and drove eleven hours straight through to San Diego. Soon after arriving home one of the Love Tribe showed up at my house with a bag full of illicit substances and paraphernalia for safekeeping as Coyote's death by drowning in the jacuzzi put them in a delicate legal quandary.

We went to Dog's house and found everyone preparing for the funeral. We had no details of Coyote's death, so I gave Dog, Penny, and a few others some MDMA to ease their emotions. We were introduced to Coyote's sister who was unhappy and scowling as everything about Coyote's death didn't add up to the story she was being told. Dog went around reassuring everyone that everything was all right and all was perfection which everyone appeared to be going along with, but I sensed denial and a lack of responsibility which troubled me and Penny.

Everything was *not* all right.

Penny drifted off and came back a few minutes later to tell me that I needed to talk to Otorongo. After a brief discussion he brought up the idea of doing an intervention. The Love Tribe had clearly spun out of control and we agreed to set things in motion to make that happen. Skirting the questionable legalities of the whole situation, we realized that we had to handle things on our own, outside the law.

Cat's wealthy husband had been studying with Ralph Metzner, so I spoke with Ralph about the situation. He agreed with our intervention plan and gave me some great support and advice. To Penny's credit, she took the kids and left the house to us so we could have uninterrupted privacy while me, Otorongo, another close friend, and a renowned psychologist friend with psychedelic experience sat with Dog to convince him that he had lost touch with everything through his excessive use of substances, particularly 5MEO. We told him he needed to back off, dry out, and encourage his followers in the Love Tribe to do the same.

He listened with Zen-like humility giving us the impression that he was in agreement with us and in response to our concerns he shared a piece of personal history that sent me off into the Twilight Zone.

He told us that when he was eighteen he was given LSD by a man who called himself *Satan* and that instead of the normal twelve hours of feeling the effects of the acid he went on a multiple day convoluted journey that he felt like he never fully came back from.

My mind was obliterated in that moment by the implications of what he said and its impact reverberated deep within me.

After our private session with Dog we went and spoke to the roughly thirty members of the Love Tribe giving them the same admonitions we gave Dog and strongly recommended that they take a break from getting high so much. We did it in a way that Dog could save face, telling them that he was overworked and needed a break so he could get some much needed rest.

I felt repercussions from my encounter with Satan over the next few days. Penny and I saw flocks of noisy crows more frequently than in the past, and whether it was subjective or not, it contributed to the morbid Edgar Allen Poe pall that hung over everything. In the midst of those dark days a wounded coyote limped across our path on a walk through our greenbelt as if confirming the dark energy being communicated through the elementals. I discovered more details about Coyote's passing in the following days.

I was there when Dog first met Coyote and approached her in a humble, adoring, nearly worshipful manner and she quickly moved in with him. The Love Tribe started soon after that and they practically lived at Cat and her wealthy husband's house which became the home of the Love Tribe fostering a nonstop party atmosphere where everything ingested was sacred, and it all revolved around Dog, the enlightened shaman.

As Dog grew in prominence he became increasingly dismissive of Coyote and lavished more and more attention on Cat with sexual undertones which I suspect may have been realized. Coyote was Japanese and loyalty and honor were deeply imbedded in her psyche and Dog became increasingly rude in his treatment of her.

One afternoon Cat and Coyote were home alone and Coyote suggested they take a little time to bond with each other by taking a hit of 5MEO together in the jacuzzi. Cat agreed and Coyote, being a film director and videographer who constantly filmed everything, set up her camera and recorded holding hands with Cat, both of them taking the hit together, and submerging herself beneath the water.

When Cat came back to consciousness she saw Coyote under the water and thought she was submerging herself, so she waited until it dawned on her that maybe Coyote had been under for too long. When Cat finally became aware enough to check, Coyote was unresponsive.

Japanese culture has a long history of suicide as an honorable way out of this life.

A couple of weeks later Dog and Puppy called, begging me to join them and a few others on the beach that night for a special ceremony for Coyote. This went against my grain and felt wrong, but I decided to relent this one time as the shock and horror of the whole turn of events affected everyone, so feeling sympathetic I agreed to partake in this show of solidarity.

Not long after they called me to do it again and I declined, knowing where it was going and telling them I was not interested. In truth I had been done with them months before the disaster and had only gone back out of a sense of duty to provide damage control.

Puppy called me frequently, begging me to join them and he continued asking me to come visit with them at Cat's house. I eventually figured out that she was the one asking him to call. They dropped by my house one afternoon unannounced and double teamed me, trying to guilt me into joining them for a ceremony and I nearly physically threw them out.

When I say No, I mean No, and when someone continues coming at me and disrespecting what I said after I made my intentions clear it creates an immediate escalation inside of me.

In keeping with the dark Satanic undertones of the whole drama, I was up alone late one night deeply engrossed watching Hannibal Lecter, the ultimate villain in *Silence of the Lambs*. I had reread the book, read the movie script, and was watching the movie again with the script doing a shot by shot analysis of the adaptation for a project I was working on. I jumped when I heard a knock on the door at that late hour. I paused the movie and warily opened the door to see Dog and Puppy. I stepped out and pulled the door shut behind me as there was no way they were coming in the house. I didn't want anything to do with them.

They backed up when I stepped out and begged me to do a 5MEO ceremony with them which enraged me. I found myself clenching my fists and being forceful about not participating and getting ready to come to blows over it. They must have finally read me right as they backed down sniveling like a couple of beaten, still growling dogs. After they left, I realized that I was shaking hard, especially my legs, but I don't think they noticed.

That was the last time they ever dared darken my doorstep.

Soon after that I took my own advice. After eight years and hundreds of journeys I was not getting anything more from 5MEO than the fuzz out it brought. The Love Tribe tragedy brought things full circle indicating closure from that part of my life.

One afternoon when no one was home I did my own little ceremony and buried my pipe beneath the roots of a datura bush.

FORTY

Chiric Sanango

In October of 2006 I went into the Amazon with my original group led by Yoda to do my sixth plant dieta and for the first time I did not record my experiences. This year I would be working with a plant called Chiric Sanango which translates as chilly wood. Its scientific classification is Brunfelsia grandiflora, a flowering shrub in the nightshade family native to South America. It is a beautiful plant with purple, blue, white flowers that teaches you endurance. In English it is known as royal purple brunfelsia, kiss-me-quick, and yesterday-today-and-tomorrow.

The bark is rasped off the plant and steeped in cold water. It is very strong and only taken twice during the dieta. Some shamans mix it with a little tobacco. In the first few minutes after drinking it your lips, tongue, then your whole body gets numb before deep cold and shivering set in. It can be visionary. Once you are freezing you submerge in cold water and freeze more, then you get out, wrap yourself in a blanket and sweat profusely before passing out. Chiric Sanango makes you physically resistant to cold and heat. Shamans are very respectful of this plant. Too much can mess up your nervous system. Another way of preparing it can give males an erection.

I asked Ronaldo if I could work with other plants and without hesitation he told me that Chiric Sanango needed to be taken by itself because it was too powerful to work with any other plants.

On two mornings spaced evenly throughout the course of the *dieta* under close supervision I drank a glass of the infusion which did not taste bad, and as advertised the tip of my tongue, my lips, the rest of my tongue, and my whole body grew numb and I began to shiver. Once that set in I froze in what felt like even colder water for about five minutes. Thoroughly shivering, I climbed out of the river and hustled back to my tambo where I crawled under my mosquito net and wrapped myself in a blanket sweating profusely before passing out for the better part of twelve hours. I remained mostly unconscious during this time with no dreams. I had to get up to relieve myself once or twice during the experience and when I did I could barely walk. The whole world seemed tilted sideways and off kilter, and I felt really drunk trying to navigate by holding onto the railing of my tambo to relieve myself without pissing all over everything. I felt so incapacitated that I did not dare go any further than those few steps as I would surely have fallen over. After accomplishing that monumental task I crawled back into bed for more deep, dreamless sleep. I now understood why Ronaldo said what he did about no other plants and only doing it twice during the dieta.

In the aftermath of my long nearly comatose sleep, the effects of Chiric Sanango stayed with me for a few days like a diminishing mental fog of alcohol intoxication. I repeated the experience with all of the same sensations when I almost felt normal again, and the lingering after effects stayed with me throughout the rest of the dieta.

In contrast to my prior wild rides in the jungle with Ayahuasca and other plants this dieta felt subdued without any chaotic dreams and there were no interactions between them and my visions which were still strong and insightful, but held no major revelations worth recording.

Physiologically speaking Chiric Sanango hits your endocrine glands with a hard reset which explains why shamans are so respectful of it and why they stress how too much can mess up your nervous system. It also explains the excessive sweating and that fact that it can give males an erection.

Endocrine glands secrete hormones throughout the body which are absorbed into the blood rather than through a duct. The major glands of the endocrine system include the pineal, pituitary, pancreas, ovaries, testes, thyroid, parathyroid, hypothalamus and adrenals. The hypothalamus and the anterior pituitary gland are two out of the three endocrine glands and are both part of the hypothalamic–pituitary–adrenal axis referred to as the HPA axis which plays a major role in cell signaling in the nervous system.

Every teacher plant I worked with affected me in different ways. Some of them had strong physiological effects, while others like Ushpawasha, Coca, and Bobinsana had more pronounced psychological effects. The combination of all of these plants ingested in the context of an Ayahuasca cleansing dieta created cumulative changes in my body chemistry and physiology as well as major shifts in my physical, mental, and spiritual composition.

There's an old saying in neuroscience, "Neurons that fire together wire together". The more you run a neural circuit in your brain the stronger that circuit becomes. Working with different plants on more than one occasion and in differing combinations resulted in each of them reinforcing each other.

After my Chiric Sanango dieta marking my sixth year of plant dietas and my experiences with my two year study group I didn't feel the need to journal. My visions still came strong and insightful, but they dealt more with my ongoing day to day life as opposed to the deeper revelations discovered earlier.

In my October 2007 dieta, Ronaldo gave me a daily mixture of five plants consisting of Una De Gato, Chuchuwasi, Cumaseba, Renaquilla, and Icuja in a combination that was energizing, grounding, strengthening, and fortifying. Aside from that power boost combination, Ronaldo added two solo Ayahuasca sessions in my tambo in addition to the five group sessions in the maloca, which became a regular thing for me with each successive dieta in the years that followed.

With the tragedy of Coyote and other issues behind me and the work I had been doing with my coach and the upcoming publication of **Spirit Matters**, my life and dreams felt positive, hopeful, and primed for a big break which came in ways I never could have imagined.

FORTY ONE

Treasure Island

I met Marc and his brother Mike around 2000 through one of my best friends when they were looking for a drummer for their rock/blues band. I hadn't been in a band for years and had been jamming to CDs with headphones on, playing simply for the joy of it.

We had a solid set together when the bass player left so the band dissolved but the friendship remained and Marc and I hung out on and off for close to a decade. He often shared his enthusiasm for treasure recovery which I found interesting and he showed me an article written about him that described him as "possibly brilliant". I told him that I was waiting to see if he had what it took to move beyond the possibility and he told me about his current project that revolved around Cocos Island in Costa Rica, the inspiration for Robert Louis Stevenson's Treasure Island.

When I was five years old I spent a lot of time digging in my back yard in hopes of finding buried treasure and have no doubt that the story of *Treasure Island* inspired me along with all the pirate movies I had seen. I kept my loot consisting of key chains, coins, pins, marbles, and anything else I valued inside of a small metal treasure chest with a pirate on one side and a skull and cross bones on the other with a tiny working gold lock that I bargained for in a trade with my best friend Jack. I also owned a large plastic treasure chest bank that I hoped to amass a fortune in, but I never had any money to save in it. I loved it because it represented the possibility that anyone could find buried treasure regardless of who they were, where they came from, or how much money they had.

Cocos Island lies midway between Costa Rica and the Galapagos

Islands 300 miles off the coast of Costa Rica. First discovered less than half a century after the New World, Cocos is legendary for its natural and man-made treasures. Now a World Heritage Site, Jacques Cousteau called it the most beautiful island in the world and Michael Crichton wrote Jurassic Park with it in mind.

This 10 square-mile tip of an ancient volcano is the largest uninhabited island in the world. Precipitous cliffs tower over its craggy shoreline up to the 2079 foot summit of Mt. Iglesias, the island's highest peak. Cocos is home to dense tropical moist forests punctuated by scores of sparkling waterfalls that tumble from its heights. It is the only oceanic island in the eastern Pacific region with these kinds of rain forests and their characteristic flora and fauna. The cloud forests at higher elevations are unique in the eastern Pacific. Cocos was never linked to a continent, so its flora and fauna arrived from the Americas making it rife with a high proportion of endemic species.

Over the centuries before the Republic of Costa Rica assumed control of Cocos in 1869 pirates buried priceless artifacts and tons of gold bullion in its inaccessible hillsides. Many of these pirates died from disease, battles, or execution before they could ever return to Cocos to claim their loot and it remains there to this day. Its value is estimated to be in the billions.

The story of Cocos began in 1526 when the Spanish pilot Johan Cabeças first discovered it. Sixteen years later it appeared for the first time on a French map of the Americas, labeled as Ile de Coques which means "Nutshell Island" or simply "Shell Island". It appears that the Spanish misunderstood the French name and called it Isla del Cocos which means Island of the Coconuts which is a fitting name according to Dr. Lionel Wafer, the surgeon who wrote one of the earliest descriptions of Cocos after visiting it in the late 1600s with Captain Edward Davis, an English pirate.

Wafer wrote, "'Tis thick with Coco-nut Trees, which flourish here finely." So abundant were Coconuts that Wafer's shipmates on the famous *Bachelor's Delight* got carried away one afternoon, drinking 20 gallons at a sitting. According to Wafer: "That sort of Liquor had so chill'd and benumb'd their Nerves, that they could neither go nor stand; nor could they returned on board the Ship, without the Help of those who had not been Partakers in the Frolick..."

Over the next century Cocos became a haven where ships of all stripes rested and took on fresh water, firewood, and coconuts.

Whalers stopped there regularly until the mid-19th century when their industry in the region collapsed from overfishing. Captains with missions ranging from exploration to administration of justice dropped anchor in Chatham or Wafer bays, the island's principal harbors, but more than any, pirates made Cocos their home.

The Golden age of treasure burying on the island took place in a few years on either side of 1820, beginning in 1818 when Captain Bennett Graham, a distinguished British naval officer put in charge of a coastal survey in the South Pacific aboard the H.M.S. Devonshire abandoned his mission for a life of piracy. He was eventually caught and executed along with his officers and the remainder of his crew was sent to a penal colony in Tasmania.

Twenty years later one of the crew, a woman named Mary Welch, was released from prison claiming to have witnessed the burial of Graham's fortune, 350 tons of gold bullion stolen from Spanish galleons. She is reputed to have had had a chart with compass bearings showing where the so-called "Devonshire Treasure" was buried that Graham had given to her before being captured, thinking it would be safer with her instead of with him.

An expedition was mounted to hunt for the treasure and Welch went along. As an old woman she set foot once again on Cocos but in the decades since she'd been there the landscape had changed so much that many of her identifying marks, including a huge cedar tree that she had camped near for six months had disappeared and the expedition recovered nothing.

Another treasure still believed to be buried on Cocos is that of Benito "Bloody Sword" Bonito, who terrorized the west coast of the Americas around 1818, looting and burning Spanish galleons. In his most infamous exploit, Bonito, learning that Spanish gold was transported by uniformed guards from the Mexican cordillera to Acapulco captured the guards, put their uniforms on his own men, and loaded the treasure onto his ship without firing a shot. His most infamous mistake was to let two Englishmen from a British ship he hijacked join his band of pirates. Years later when the Brits were arrested and sentenced to hang they were released after leading their captors to Bonito's West Indian hideout where the blood thirsty Bonito was finally cut down. According to legend, the two Englishmen never returned to Cocos, and the "captain's cut" of Bonito's cache still sits there.

The most famous Cocos hoard of all is the "Loot of Lima", buried in 1821. Since that time more than 300 expeditions have tried to locate these and other treasures on Cocos. President Franklin Delano Roosevelt visiting on three fishing trips between 1935 in 1940 let his crew give it a whirl, but as far as public records go all of these efforts failed.

In 1821 when the Lima treasure was taken from Peru it was valued at anywhere from $12 to $60 million dollars. In today's market it could be worth over $1 billion dollars. For three centuries the history of Peru was also the history of Spanish South America. The Viceroy installed at Lima ruled not only the Vice-Royalty of Peru which included the present territories of Bolivia and Peru, but also held authority over most of the other Spanish governors of the continent. It was the Viceroy's duty to send to Spain the royal share of the precious metals mined in Peru and its subject territories. Aside from the silver mines of Potosí in present day Bolivia, gold had been mined on the remote slopes of the Andes since the days of the Incas. Emeralds were cut in intricate designs with great skill by Inca craftsmen. The first treasure taken to Spain by the conquistadores included emeralds. The annual transmission to Spain of this vast horde had always been fraught with danger and considerable risk.

In 1820 a rebel army under the leadership of the victorious José de San Martín and a fleet commanded by Admiral Thomas Lord Cochrane began an invasion from Chile. A year later San Martín entered Lima and proclaimed himself "Protector of Peru." With the sea routes to Spain in danger and eventually closed, the Viceroy in Lima had been unable to remit the King's annual "fifth" for a number of years. Bullion accumulated in the Lima mint and according to the most reliable records, some of it had been piling up for 11 years before San Martín invaded Peru. In spite of San Martín's success in Chile, the Spanish Viceroy did not take the rebel invasion of Peru seriously until he learned that San Martín and his victorious army were within 50 miles of the capital.

One of the Viceroy's first thoughts was for the safety of the vast hoard of gold and silver in his keeping that the King of Spain held him accountable for. A similar thought struck the church officials whose wealthy treasures were also in Lima. Every church in the city which numbered around fifty possessed immeasurable riches in the form of gold and silver utensils and ritualized objects used in church services, images, decorations, and reserves of gold coin.

A series of frantic secret midnight conferences were held between the Viceroy and the clerics and between them they saw only one possible way out of their dilemma which was to take the chance of shipping their combined wealth out of the country. With this plan in mind the mint and its storehouse of gold and silver were emptied; the churches were stripped of their gold and silver accoutrements; even the heavily laid on gold leaf on the church cupolas were removed to preserve it and give an air of poverty to the buildings. Several oxcarts of chests and rawhide bags of loot were deposited in the heavily guarded fort at Callao.

A British merchantman ship out of Bristol named the Mary Dear commanded by a Scot by the name of Captain William Thompson lay at anchor in the harbor. When the Viceroy approached Thompson with his plan the Captain agreed to help. They loaded all the treasure onto the Mary Dear and put out to sea where they could cruise out of danger until receiving word that it had passed. Thompson had no objection to the Spanish sending along half a dozen trusted men including a couple of priests to keep an eye on the treasure.

Records confirmed by an entry in Admiral Cochrane's diary dated August 19, 1821, state, "The Spaniards today relieved and reinforced the fortress at Callao, and coolly walked off unmolested with plate and money to the amount of many millions of pounds - in fact, the whole wealth of Lima which was deposited in the fort for safekeeping."

What Cochrane didn't know was that the treasure laden Mary Dear slipped out of the Port of Callao undetected, flying the flag of the Admiral's own country and before morning the gold hungry crew of the Mary Dear turned on the guards and the two priests, cut their throats, and dumped their bodies into the shark-infested sea.

After discussing their limited options it was agreed that the treasure needed to be hidden as soon as possible. Captain Thompson suggested Cocos Island, a nice sizable uninhabited island lying several hundred miles off the Central American mainland. After hiding it they planned to wait a year or two after the furor had blown over, then reunite at a prearranged rendezvous and return to Cocos to recover the treasure and get it back to England.

When they dropped anchor in one of the bays on the north side of the island the ship's heavily laden longboat made eleven trips from ship to shore to transfer all the booty to the island where it was buried in one spot selected after much consideration by the captain and mate, James Alexander Forbes. They kept only a small number of coins that they shared among the crew. One version of the waybill left by Captain Thompson regarding the Loot of Lima is an original document found in the museum of Caracas.

"We have buried at a depth of four feet in the red earth: 1 chest; altar trimmings of cloth of gold, with baldachins, monstrances, chalices, comprising 1,244 stones. 1 chest; 2 gold reliquaries weighing 120 pounds, with 624 topazes, cornelians and emeralds, 12 diamonds. 1 chest; 3 reliquaries of cast metal weighing 160 pounds, with 860 rubies and various stones, 19 diamonds. 1 chest; 4,000 doubloons of Spain marked 8. 5,000 crowns of Mexico. 124 swords, 64 dirks, 120 shoulder belts. 28 rondaches. 1 chest; 8 caskets of cedar-wood and silver, with 3,840 cut stones, rings, patents and 4,265 uncut stones. 28 feet to the northeast, at a depth of 8 feet in the yellow sand; 7 chests: with 22 candelabra in gold and silver weighing 250 pounds, and 164 rubies a foot. 12 armspans west, at a depth of 10 feet in the red earth; the seven-foot Virgin of gold, with the Child Jesus and her crown and pectoral of 780 pounds, rolled in her gold chasuble on which are 1,684 jewels. Three of these are 4-inch emeralds on the pectoral and 6 are 6-inch topazes on the crown. The seven crosses are of diamonds."

Soon after, the Mary Dear was picked up by a fast Spanish Man of War. The commander of the Spanish ship knew about the Viceroy's deal with Thompson and wanted to know what happened to the treasure. Since no satisfactory answer came the Mary Dear and her crew were taken prisoner and brought to Panama where Captain Thompson and his crew were put on trial for murder and piracy. Everyone from Captain Thompson down was sentenced to hanging, beginning with the lowest member of the crew, working its way up to the mate Forbes and the Captain. By the time the last member of the crew had been hung Thompson and Forbes offered to make a deal with their captors. If their lives were spared they would be guaranteed freedom provided that they led the Spaniards to the spot where they had buried the stolen treasure.

The two survivors led an expedition to Cocos Island to recover the treasure. They anchored in Chatham Bay and the prisoners were taken ashore with half a dozen armed guards. Pretending to take bearings and measurements the captain and Forbes disappeared into the thick tropical jungle that grows down to the water's edge. The guards fired their muskets at random into the bush and the ship remained at anchor for several days while an intensive search was made but the two prisoners were nowhere to be found.

Eventually the ship had to leave them behind and Forbes and Thompson remained on the island for several months living on coconuts, bird eggs, fish, and small game. Finally, sometime in 1822 they were rescued by a British whaler which stopped at the island for fresh water. Thompson and Forbes told the captain of the whaler that they had been shipwrecked on the island. The whaler put in at Puntarenas on the Costa Rican coast a few days later. In all the stories and legends about the Cocos Island treasure, the mysterious mate Forbes disappeared from the scene at this point.

In 1831 James Forbes arrived in California on a whaling ship and a few years after arriving he married Ana María Galindo, daughter of the majordomo of Mission Santa Clara de Asís in 1834. The Forbes family lived on Rancho Potrero de Santa Clara, a 1,939-acre Mexican land grant near San Jose received from Governor Manuel Micheltorena in 1844. The rancho and cattle were sold in 1847 to Commodore Robert F. Stockton for $10,500, a high price for the time. The couple had three daughters and nine sons. In 1851 James Forbes persuaded the Jesuits to establish a school at Mission Santa Clara to educate his sons. This school formed the basis of what became Santa Clara University and five of the Forbes sons were part of the first class at Santa Clara College.

In 1850 Forbes noticed there was no local production of flour and purchased about 2,000 acres of Rancho Rinconada de Los Gatos from José María Hernandez with the intent of building a mill on Los Gatos Creek. In 1853 he raised the money for the construction and in 1854 the mill was built. After many delays the mill started grinding flour on December 1, 1855, but the location Forbes chose only had enough water in the creek to power the mill during the winter months. This coupled with the delays in its opening allowed competitors into the market which dropped flour prices from $50 a barrel to $5, so it wasn't generating enough income. Forbes was forced into bankruptcy and he was evicted due to non-payment of the loan in 1858, but a town sprang up around the mill which was known as Forbestown before changing its name to Los Gatos.

Los Gatos historian William A. Wulf described Forbes as "a suede-shoe man", a term used to portray a devious individual. He was bright and better educated than most men in California when he first arrived but he was a bad man who ended up losing control of circumstances. When the Jesuits arrived from Oregon to Mission Santa Clara they asked him to move out of the mission which he did, but not before getting $11,000 from them. He used the money to build a mansion right behind the mission and later sold it to a group of nuns, neglecting to tell them there was a $20,000 lien on the house. According to the Hernandez family Forbes never paid $8,000 he owed for the Los Gatos rancho.

When Forbes died in 1881 in Alameda he gave a treasure map to his son Charles H. Forbes who was an attorney in Los Angeles, urging him to go to Cocos Island to find the treasure. Charles was already wealthy and had no desire to go. He kept the map in a safe until he died and passed it down to his son, James Alexander Forbes III who had the same adventurous spirit as his grandfather but he died before ever making it to Cocos Island to look for the treasure.

In 1939, the map was passed on to his son, the great grandson of the Mary Dear mate, James Alexander Forbes IV who dedicated a major part of his life and money trying to locate the treasure. After six expeditions to Cocos Island, James needed more information which he received from a relative, allowing him to organize a final expedition with John Ford, the legendary film maker.

After reaching Cocos while standing over the location of the treasure they decided not to recover it when they spotted two boats full of men with rifles and machine guns. On the way home, Ford suggested making a movie with John Wayne recovering the treasure on film, but Ford and Forbes passed away soon after their return.

In 2004, William B. Forbes, the fifth generation descendant of the Forbes family shared his story with my buddy Marc, president of Adventure Quest. With a combination of historical documentation and advanced technology, and potentially profitable true story documentary markets, Forbes and Marc agreed to jointly recover, film, and market the "Loot of Lima" and the Cocos Island legend. William passed way in 2006 and entrusted the map and the Cocos Island Project to Marc.

In February of 2009 Marc approached me with a generous offer of 10% of Adventure Quest and a position of Senior Vice President for the Cocos Island Project which promised a six figure salary. He made the offer based on our friendship, my trustworthiness, and what he knew of me. From what he told me it seemed like a perfect fit that drew upon everything I had done in my life, including my 35 year technical career and my writing.

When The Cocos Island Project presented itself I knew it would take a tremendous effort, but with the right support I could end up financially secure for the rest of my life as well as the lives of Penny, her kids, my sister, and my nieces. I spent hours discussing it with Penny, asking if she could give me the support I needed and she told me she supported the dream, so I accepted Marc's offer.

When I started, The Cocos Island Project had been going for six years and was at a standstill and at that point, one and a half million dollars had already been put in by seed investors.

Marc had twenty five years in the business, so I relied on him to tell me what I needed to know. He said he owed lawyers twenty six thousand dollars. When I asked him if that was what was needed to get the funding, he said that if we had the twenty six thousand, we could be funded within thirty days. He also had a couple of DUI charges that needed to be dealt with so because of this I drove him everywhere and I knew just the person who could help him.

I thought long and hard about what was needed to get funded. After one and a half million in seed money and meeting many of the investors, I thought that twenty six thousand meant we were close. Marc had most of his possessions in hock which showed me that he was committed. He told me that it would cost about seventy five thousand dollars to get it all out. Based on what Marc told me I figured one hundred thousand dollars was the magic number needed to solve all of the problems attached to the project and get it funded in thirty days.

The stock market tanked in 2008 and my investments were shrinking. I was a Senior Vice President of Adventure Quest, and as he presented it to me, the project was close to getting funded. After meeting lawyers, producers, and other professionals attached to the project I cashed in most of my retirement money to get the one hundred thousand dollars needed to fund the project.

I was in a deep discussion about this with Marc one afternoon when we were cut off in mid-conversation. I tried to call back and couldn't reach him which was the first indicator of the problems I would be facing, but I gave him the benefit of the doubt because of our ten year friendship. I didn't hear anything from him for a couple of days and he was nowhere to be found.

When I finally did hear from him he said his phone had died. I couldn't understand why it took him so long to get back to me and I was stunned a few weeks later when he said that I cost him two thousand dollars by delaying my withdrawal because he was the one who had been irresponsible. I could understand a phone dying, especially the way we were cut off in mid-conversation, but I couldn't understand why it took him so long to get back to me.

FORTY TWO

Homeless Bound

In spite of the snafu, based on his word I trusted Marc with my life savings and gave him everything he needed to get the project funded and brought in one of my best friends who I knew could solve Marc's legal problems. In that same time frame I rescued him from a hotel room that he had no money to pay for and took him into my home to give him a place to stay.

Through my years of research into shamanism I have accumulated many items considered powerful and I had the ones that meant the most on a table that served as an altar. Altars are considered powerful and sacred spaces to be treated with the utmost respect.

Marc came in drunk one night and knocked a bottle of red wine all over my altar. Everyone fell silent and I had a bad feeling because this could be seen as a bad omen. I covered how shocked I felt inside, but I sensed *big* trouble coming.

One of my best friends was a fellow writer and a criminal defense attorney who I set Marc up with to take on the DUI issues. My lawyer friend arranged a hearing which would clear everything up. I expected Marc home on the eve of the hearing, but he didn't show up, so I figured he was staying with his brother for the night.

The following morning I received a phone call from my friend asking if I knew where Marc was. He was before the judge and Marc was a no show. Puzzled, I called Marc's brother and was stunned to discover that Marc was in jail. He had gotten drunk the night before and smashed up his car. His brother was in the process of hocking his guitars for bail money. I had a little bit of money, so I took what I had and bailed Marc out.

Marc blamed his brother and the people who worked at the restaurant where he had gotten drunk, but in truth there was no one to blame but himself. I was now committed with pretty much everything I had so I resigned myself to facing the music.

Penny lost faith at this point and became antagonistic toward me and the project. Marc needed a place to stay so I rented a U-Haul and spent a few back breaking days helping him move into a rental a few houses up the street. He wrote me two checks for the bail money and some of the money he owed me.

Both checks bounced.

Penny didn't know the financial details of what was happening, but Marc's irresponsibility proved to be too much for my already fragile relationship and she blew up in late July of 2009 and insisted that I move out of the house that I had put the down payment on. I could have made her move but she pulled her kids into it, so I left to ensure that they had a place to stay. I was shocked at her behavior which made a bad situation far worse than it needed to be, and I was disappointed and heartbroken at her readiness to end our nine year relationship so abruptly. She wasted no time getting approved for a loan, so I sold the house to her for the appraised value. I should have put it on the market and gotten more but I wanted what was best for the kids.

To make matters worse we had moved there because Julie, a good friend of ours had lived in the neighborhood for some time. Her two kids were the same age as Penny's and we had spent a lot of time together. The older girls were in Girl Scouts together and the boys hung around the neighborhood with a group of other boys. Julie lived a few houses away from us and Marc had moved in a couple of houses on the other side of her, all on the same side of the street.

Penny went out of town one weekend while the house sale was being finalized and I spent that Friday night at Marc's working to complete some paperwork. He was literally falling down drunk and changed from a blissful state to unhappiness every few minutes, then back again in rapid succession displaying bipolar behavior that had been hidden from me. Looking back, I suspect that this had been the reason for his earlier phone disconnect and two day disappearance. I couldn't believe he was still drinking after all the grief he caused me, not to mention the impact it had on his own life and the project.

We had a blow up and he ordered me out of his house. I said, "Fine, Fuck you! Have another drink. I'm out of here!"

I woke up the next morning numb, in an emotional fog. I had given all my money to a drunk, I was losing the "story book" home that I had given up everything else for and Penny was leaving me. I could barely think straight and decided to go for a swim at the pool in the greenbelt, hoping the water, sunlight, and exercise might clear my head a little.

When I went to the pool I saw crime scene tape surrounding the back of Julie's house and a cop sitting out back. I didn't know what to think and pushed ahead with my swim. When I finished, I left the pool, puzzling over the police presence when a neighbor approached me.

"Did you hear what happened?"

"No, I've been wondering."

"Julie's boyfriend cut her throat all the way through to her spine and her son and his best friend found her dead by the front door."

Everything went from dark to darker with still more darkness to come.

FORTY THREE

Torn Between Two Narcissists

Marc and I had to drive from Southern California to meet with a group of investors in Colorado. My credit card was declined in Colorado Because of Marc's bounced checks, forcing me to dip into money I didn't have. On our first night on the road we stopped in Vail. I thought he might have learned something from his DUI bust and all the grief it caused, but I was wrong. He stayed out all night drinking and getting in a barroom fight.

On our second night, after hours of pounding down shots in a meeting with investors he went out and met the "woman of his dreams"; a porn actress. A couple of days later she arrived in Southern California where her true colors came out and needless to say, Marc's love affair ended abruptly.

Numb and heartbroken from my split with Penny and Julie's death, I had no escape from Marc's insanity. I felt doubly trapped when I had to go home and deal with Penny who became increasingly hostile. With no escape either way, I was at a loss to understand how two people who I had helped the most were taking turns treating me worse than I had ever been treated by anyone in my entire life.

While I was trying to move out in an orderly way Penny exploded in front of her son and tried to force me out faster by screaming, grabbing my things, and pushing them out the door. I worried that she might assault me like she had in the past and I did not want that to happen in front of her son. She threw my clothes all over the ground and tossed my things into the garage breaking some of them. The defining moment of that unbearable pain was seeing the watch my dying mother gave me on the walkway in front of the house.

If I hadn't spent so much time in the jungle doing inner work with Ayahuasca and the other plants I don't think I could have survived her abuse and would have killed myself, but in the midst of her insanity I realized she was equating money to security and Julie's death had amplified her madness. I also knew that no matter how surreal and painful the moment might be, it would pass, so in this darkest moment of my life I let go.

At first it felt terrifying, followed by a sense of freedom and release, and I thought, she can have the house, the furniture, the stereo, the big screen TV, the refrigerator, washer, dryer, the rebuilt fountain, the new fence and everything else I bought and paid for.

Nothing is permanent.

I didn't know where to go and there was lots of activity on the project due to the funds I had contributed, so I ended up on Marc's couch, thinking it only temporary until the project got its legs, and at this point it was all I had left. I needed help moving, but Marc locked himself in his room. I had spent three full days moving him, but after one load he abandoned me, leaving me in a dangerous situation where I had to move myself. He blamed his withdrawal on a group of investors under the pretense that his feelings were hurt because they didn't believe in his integrity, yet his actions showed a total lack of any.

Determined to move the project forward after putting most of what I had into it along with the other investors I gave him half the money from my house sale to keep things moving. When I knocked on his bedroom door to take him to an appointment with his lawyer he threw a fit and screamed at me when I was there to help him.

I was at my wit's end, so I left to get away from him and stay with out of town friends. He had sucked me dry financially and refused to take any responsibility, and he stayed in his room refusing to talk to anyone.

I was at a loss for what to do and looked for a way to deal with the impossible situation I had gotten myself into. Literally in mid-sentence while talking about my impasse on a walk with a friend, a hawk feather appeared and in that moment I flashed on using it as a talking stick to disarm the emotional outbursts and interruptions that Marc used to derail anything he didn't want to hear.

With the help of his brother and Tran, the other Senior Vice President of Adventure Quest, we planned a surprise meeting where we agreed to use the hawk feather as a talking stick so everyone could be heard without interruption. This created a powerful turning point for us and a brief bounce up out of the abyss, but we were a long way from escaping the darkness. I had no place to live until some friends offered me a place to stay, but the reality was that it was an imposition to them and they didn't want me there which made it uncomfortable for me.

Throughout all of the madness which had gone on for six months, Marc made hundreds of promises he never honored. For months he told me, "I'll have some money for you in a few days. I'm getting you a gym membership. I'll scan the documents that need to be scanned."

He promised my brother who gave us valuable aid that he would have the scanning for him in two weeks, but it never happened. We owed my brother $1200.00 for work he had done and as a result of Marc's inaction and lack of integrity Marc lost credibility and put me in an awkward position with my brother. Marc also didn't keep his appointments with my attorney friend who had been trying to help, so my friend dropped him as a client.

Marc continued setting up meetings, then didn't follow through, all the while getting upset and wondering why people didn't believe in him. I lost track of how many times I hustled to get him for meetings, knocking and yelling through his door because he wouldn't answer his phone or the door. I almost called the cops one time when he set up a meeting with a bunch of investors and blew them all off with no explanation. He screwed up my personal plans repeatedly when I moved my life around to accommodate him only to have him drop out. One time I drove him to Riverside for meetings and dropped him off because he didn't want me in his meeting with an investor. Two days later I had to drive up there again to pick him up because of some stupid drunken confrontation he had gotten into. He wanted me to make phone calls and talk to people to try to clean up the mess caused by his drunken ignorance, but I refused.

The deceptions, evasions, and half-truths overwhelmed me. He rarely did what he said he would and he seldom kept his word. I couldn't believe anything he said because it usually never happened and he told me what he thought I wanted to hear instead of the truth.

In spite of the lies, deceptions, broken promises, and the long periods of time he refused to answer his phone, I kept showing up, paying bills, and floundering at the mercy of his drunken escapades.

More often than not his actions and words were at cross purposes until I came to the realization that in spite of all the lawyers, producers, and other professionals he didn't know what he was doing.

We had a rally at the end of 2009 and he finally agreed to talk to my coach who also coached me on how to coach him, but when I offered to do that he said that he knew how to handle everything, so I let it drop.

During this time for the better part of a year he drove me crazy about creating a web page. I got everything together and waited for content from him, but he never came up with it. Tran and I offered to take the scanning my brother needed off of his hands, but he wouldn't let go of the documents and wouldn't let go of any control, then he complained that Tran and I needed to step up to the plate and take things off his hands.

I set up a meeting with my web master and Marc was a no show so my web master and I worked on the web page by ourselves and once more I paid out of pocket. We spent a lot of time on it and I asked Marc for some scanned items because we needed content. He lied to me about putting them on a thumb drive. We finally went to a meeting with my web master that turned into an awkward and embarrassing situation. After the meeting Marc promised to send the content, but he never did.

I had been carrying him for a year after putting everything in his lap and he was about to get evicted, so I paid two months of his rent and had to pay back a substantial amount of the money I had given him that had not been mine to lend. I also had major tax problems because he had promised to pay the taxes and penalties from cashing my retirement in early. I couldn't expect any help from him and finally admitted to myself.

I was on my own.

When I raised my issues with him he said he didn't want to hear about my problems and didn't want me to add to his even though he had created mine. He asked me to drive him to Phoenix to get some money. When I asked about specifics he got defensive and evasive and didn't want to talk about it.

After arguing with me over the route my GPS plotted I drove him there expecting to go into a meeting to learn something, but that never happened. If he had been honest with me about the money I could've met with a friend who owed me money, but nothing was the way he presented it.

Amidst the insanity that my life had become I knew on some level that I was complicit in what happened with him and Penny, and no matter what anybody else did, my own choices and actions put me where I was and I had to take responsibility for that.

What I found fascinating from my own dysfunctional co-dependent perspective is that he continued to project his shortcomings onto me, refusing to take responsibility for what he did; the exact same thing that Penny did. I got hammered from both sides like a tag team ping-pong game in a no win situation.

What did that say about me?

I had committed my life's assets and managed to keep the project alive through a barrage of madness and I had no recourse. If I had taken any legal action it would have destroyed the project, not to mention the other investors who had collectively put in over a million and a half dollars.

I told Marc and Penny that I would no longer be the brunt of their anger and I refused to be the target for their faults, projections, and inability to take responsibility for what they said and did. A big part of my problem had been my lack of boundaries which they both took advantage of. Now I had drawn a line.

After the Phoenix debacle, I spent eighteen hours writing a letter that laid everything out to Marc in an effort to establish honest communication with him and he refused to read it.

After an uncomfortable few months of having no place to live I rented a small house with a good friend which gave me temporary stability. Marc left his rental unit and moved in with his brother and I continued driving him to meetings.

In February of 2010 we had to bring our Costa Rican associates to town. I footed a large part of the first meetings with our Costa Rican attorney to get things in motion to get the necessary permits for our expedition. Four months later we brought him and our new Costa Rican public relations man we had hired on our lawyer's recommendation up to meet the expedition team. I spent the last of my retirement money to make this happen, which was about $30,000. Marc never attended the meeting after telling me he would be there, so I felt embarrassed and at a loss about how to explain his absence, but between his brother and our international attorney the meeting worked out.

On a Friday, a couple of weeks before Marc had to go to jail he and his brother went to a meeting in Hollywood with a film studio. Penny and I wanted to go to the beach while I waited to hear about the meeting. At the last minute I decided to go to a part of the beach that we didn't usually go to, to walk along some cliffs while Marc and his brother drove back from Los Angeles. After we walked back and forth along the cliffs we picked a spot and sat.

While sitting there I acknowledged elemental forces of nature that were in play and did an internal prayer. Thinking through with a conscious intention, I drew on the energies of my heart, mind, and body, asking, "Are we doing the right thing with this project? Are we supposed to be doing this? Will it benefit the greatest good? It would be great to get some kind of a sign from spirit that let me know that I was doing the right thing.

A few moments later Penny said, "There's Marc!"

I stood and turned around to see him standing next to where we sat. We looked at each other stunned. They had been driving South on the freeway and his brother Mike wanted to pull over and stretch, so they left Interstate 5 and came South on Highway 101, pulling over at the spot where Penny and I sat. Not ten feet to the right or ten feet to the left, but the *exact* spot. He had been talking with Mike about calling me to let me know that the meeting had gone great.

It not only got my attention, it visibly rattled Marc, his brother, and Penny in a lightning flash of synchronicity.

Marc had to go to jail in August of 2010 for a two month stint to serve his time for the DUI's and the accident that totaled his car. I was broke, but it was a relief to be free of him for a couple of months. Soon after he went away his brother and I visited with a couple of high powered Beverly Hills entertainment attorneys he had found. One of them very generously gave his time and advice, giving us a good sense of the possibilities we had and some insights that helped fine tune our approach.

Soon after Marc was in jail he begged me to send him $120.00 so he could get a few things in the jail commissary. I couldn't afford it, but he promised me he would pay it back as soon as he got out. The San Diego City Jail allowed one email a day, limited to 34 lines, so I wrote when I could, knowing that everything would be read by the authorities before Marc got to see it. Throughout all the madness I joked with him about the fact that I had given him everything I had, hoping he would move beyond being possibly brilliant, because if we lost everything, I was no doubt the dumbest mother fucker on the planet, but if we could make it happen, then not only would he be brilliant, it would make me brilliant, so my fate as a moron or a brilliant visionary lay in his hands.

I hoped that his forced time out and distance from drinking would give him time to get his mind right. I sent him a few books to help him figure himself out; ***The Dark Side of the Light Chasers*** by Debbie Ford, ***Power vs. Force*** by David Hawkins, and ***The Anger Trap*** by Les Carter. I tried to complement what he was reading with things I said in my emails, and like I told Marc, I literally had a captive audience. More than anything, I hoped that in his sober time he would finally learn something and change his behavior.

FORTY FOUR

From Bad to Worse

When Marc was released from jail he finagled $2000.00 from another investor and bought himself a big screen television. He didn't tell me he had gotten any money and hired someone else to work with him and paid them $700.00 a week because he thought they could find more investors while I struggled to make ends meet. When he ran out of money he called me for a meeting and complained about how broke he was. He never once addressed the $120.00 I had put in the commissary for him which I could have used.

In my efforts to reconcile with Penny, she talked me into moving back in with her to give things another try. We had been dating again and things seemed to be going well between us while living apart. She refinanced the house and offered me half in November of 2010 while I still shared a rental. Thinking that Marc had learned his lesson in jail, I arranged for him to move in to the rental by leaving the $1000 deposit with the landlord while my room mate made plans to move out. I also left him a bed I had bought for $2500.00 and put it on his tab.

In January of 2011 Marc told me we needed to have another meeting with our Costa Rican partners. I was out of money, but we managed to get them up here for three days of meetings. Marc wanted to have a banquet with the Costa Ricans and our investment partners. At the last minute he said that we didn't have the money and begged me to put it on my credit card, promising me he would pay me back right away.

I told him I needed it back right away because I didn't have the resources to pay the bill. I was struggling to keep up with monthly tax payments to the state and the feds, let alone basic necessities like food and rent. He planned the meeting and put four of us down as the main speakers on an agenda sheet that he handed to the attendees.

The morning of the banquet I went to pick him up and knew something wasn't right when he didn't come to the door and I knew that he had been drinking. I had to get our Costa Rican attorney, publicist, and our international attorney, and bring them for breakfast. Marc showed up later saying he had been up drinking until three in the morning.

Later that evening at the banquet when the time came to speak he rambled drunkenly before calling up the other speakers. I had been the only one in all of the meetings with him and our Costa Rican team and I had charged the banquet to my credit card. When the time came for me to speak he called someone else who was not even involved with the project which embarrassed me. I had told a lot of people I would be speaking and I was on the printed agenda and could not explain why I had been skipped. I had a potential investor there and I am pretty sure they didn't invest after seeing Marc's slurred ramblings and my omission.

It took me some time to finally figure out that Marc was intimidated by me and the reason he set me up for failure and didn't have me speak is because he was envious and in fear of me stealing his thunder.

Classic narcissistic behavior.

I didn't talk to him for the following week. He wouldn't answer his phone and he wouldn't come to the door. After hearing concerns from other partners and discussing it with his brother, I went and banged on his bedroom window. He was deep in a depression and wouldn't communicate with anybody, and he had no money for me.

In February another rude surprise came in a phone call from my former landlord telling me that he was evicting Marc and putting a negative rating on my credit record. After a few high stress days Marc moved out and left behind a large number of his possessions, including the bed I had sold him.

None of this sat well with Penny who I had mistakenly moved back in with. Once again she became impatient and judgmental. The pressure built up in March and having no money didn't help matters any. Toward the end of March she told me she couldn't live with me and that she wanted me to move out, but I had nowhere to go.

One of the last things I did before ending up homeless was attend an Ayahuasca session in early April with a friend working with someone I had not worked with before in a tradition I had not worked in. I ended up practically leading the session with him by singing icaros, drumming, rattling, and other contributions. While integrating the following morning a sharp pain hit me in my lower back that I first thought was a muscle spasm until it came in waves that nearly incapacitated me. I managed to struggle through the last of the integration and one the last things I did was to gift the facilitator with a copy of **Land Without Evil**.

I suffered through an agonizing ride back to my friend's house from Los Angeles to Palm Springs, stopping to piss blood and a few chunks of kidney stone amidst wave after wave of crippling pain. I spent a miserable night tossing and turning on her couch before driving back to San Diego. The pain in and of itself was hard enough to deal with, but seeing the expression on people's faces reacting to me wincing in pain bothered me more. I had no money and no medical coverage, so I hoped to ride out the pain until it passed, but it continued with no relief amidst brief moments of fitful sleep for days on end.

Still fresh from the tragedy of Julie's murder, Penny was now fully psychotic in her heartless efforts to force me out of the house. I pleaded with her, telling her I was in no position to move at that moment and was in tremendous pain while she harassed and threatened me. Among other cruelties, she jabbed lit incense toward my face saying I was evil and I now understood too late why she had been ordered into court ordered therapy from her last marriage. I found a number of pictures of us she had taken from albums and burned my face off of, which concerned me so I saved them in case something happened to me.

While I was bedridden she packed some of my things without telling me. After breaking my things the last time she forced me out, combined with the fact that I had no place to go and was in no shape to move, I told her not to touch my things without asking me. She flew into a rage, accused me of being a bully, and demanded that I get out immediately while threatening to call the cops.

When I foolishly agreed to move back in she told me half of the house was mine. I had been paying half of the mortgage and half of the bills for years and her daughter, her boyfriend, and her son were also staying there. Now she was demanding for me to, "Get out of *my* house!"

I didn't have any money, but after bickering and threats from her I agreed to leave if she gave me $2000 for the furniture and appliances I bought as well as all the improvements I paid for. She had me sign a paper saying that I would never set foot in the house again. I didn't know it at the time, but she told me she had been barricading herself in her daughter's room because I was a bully, when the reality was that she was the one acting out the role and projecting it onto me.

I was not fully recovered from the kidney stones, but the shrillness of her threats made me worry that she might do something dangerous so I found a storage unit. She hired two Mexican laborers to help me move while she packed my things. It took a day and half to move out and put everything in storage.

After a long day of packing she tried to lock me out of the house and make me stay in the garage while threatening to call the cops. I was tired, sweaty, and dirty from moving and wanted to shower, so I did, feeling exposed while she lurked outside the bathroom door with a big knife while the shower scene from Alfred Hitchcock's "Psycho" kept flashing through my mind.

When I came out of the shower I saw that she had a full set of big kitchen knives. When I asked her what she was doing, she said that she was protecting herself from me because I was dangerous, then she barricaded herself in another room, again saying that I was dangerous, which was melodramatic and absurd. In the nine years we had been together, I had never once made an aggressive move toward her; in fact the opposite was true. She had verbally and physically assaulted me a number of times.

I don't know where I found the energy to move, but I considered her to be a danger not only to me, but to herself as well, as she had been suicidal in the past. She also went as far as having the locks changed, which was a total waste of money. If anyone needed protection, I did.

In my years on the shamanic path I discovered that the truth can come from anywhere. No matter what your religious orientation, every source of spiritual belief or religion contains some degree of truth, even what many consider to have no basis in "reality" like channeled information. I read and listen to whatever comes my way and run the information through my heart filter to see if it rings true, regardless of the source.

Tom Kenyon is a respected sound healer who has been channeling entities who refer to themselves as the Hathors since the late nineteen eighties. The Hathors say that they are a group of interdimensional, intergalactic beings who were connected to ancient Egypt through the Temples of the Goddess Hathor, as well as several other prehistoric cultures. I have done extensive research on ancient Egyptian cultures and have always been fascinated with them as well as the Maya and the Inca.

The more I have embraced the shamanic path and the more integrated I have become, the more synchronicities have occurred for me which I think of as signposts that confirm that I am heading in the right direction. What I have heard from the Hathors through Tom Kenyon has always rung true for me, sometimes in an uncanny manner that reflects my inner and outer reality, creating powerful synchronicities.

I was driven from my home while suffering unbearable pain so quickly that I had no time to plan, no idea of where to go, and no idea of what to do. Amidst all the chaos I experienced in my exterior reality as well as my inner and emotional worlds as well as with my kidney stones, on the day I moved out I checked the internet one last time while I still had access and found a timely email from Tom Kenyon that seemed like a life preserver that addressed me directly.

Transition States of Consciousness
A Hathor Planetary Message Through Tom Kenyon

Definitions

Chaotic Nodes are clusters of chaotic events. According to the Hathors, Earth has entered a Chaotic Node and, as a result, we can expect ever-increasing levels of chaos—including but not limited to earthquakes, volcanic activity, aberrant weather patterns, ecological distress, as well as economic, social and political turmoil.

Transition States of Consciousness are what the Hathors call the in-between places when a major loss has occurred and we find ourselves temporarily poised between an old reality that has passed away and a new reality that has not yet fully formed.

Perceptual markers are a term the Hathors use to describe how we make sense of our world and navigate through our lives using our five senses.

The Message

By their very nature Chaotic Nodes tend to generate transition states of consciousness. *Transition states of consciousness* emerge when *perceptual markers* disappear. And when this occurs you enter a *null zone* in which your old reality no longer exists, or has changed radically, while your new reality has not yet come into existence.

Due to the fact that you have entered an even more intense phase of the Chaotic Node, we wish to share with you our views regarding transition states, in the hopes that you will be able to utilize this knowledge for your own benefit.

For our purposes we can divide transition states into three primary categories: 1) personal transition states, 2) collective transition states and 3) physical death.

Personal Transition States

Let us turn our attention to personal transition states first, for your personal perception is the pivotal point around which your perceived reality operates.

Your perception of reality is fundamentally a personal creation. It is influenced by the collective perception of your culture, time, place and circumstance, but fundamentally your perception of what is real and not real is a creation—your creation.

Your perception of reality depends upon *habits of perception*, if you are like most persons. You are used to experiencing certain realities in your life and these tell you where you are, so to speak. You wake up in the morning and you look to the clock and the collective perception of time is immediately before you. Your choice to engage this illusion, or not, is a personal one. Indeed, one of the signs of spiritual mastery is the ability to navigate cultural illusions successfully while clearly understanding their nature.

When a situation in your personal life shifts dramatically there is a tendency for the perceptual markers to disappear or re-organize themselves.

Let us present one possible scenario. If you have worked at the same job for many years you have built your life around the demands of this position. You eat lunch at a certain time. You return home at a certain time. You interact with others in specific ways, tailored to fit the demands of your job.

If that job were suddenly removed, unexpectedly, those perceptual markers would disappear. There would be no need to get up at a certain time, eat at a certain time, return home at a certain time, and the people you interacted with for the bulk of your waking hours would no longer be available to you.

This situation is inherently disorienting for most people. Again, the perceptual markers have disappeared.

The same phenomenon occurs when any radical shift in your personal life takes place. If a relationship that is important to you suddenly ends the perceptual markers of that relationship disappear, and you enter the transition state of consciousness.

If you have a health crisis and your physical life is affected in radical ways the perceptual markers disappear, and this can be disorienting. You have entered a transition state of consciousness.

As the Chaotic Node increases in its intensity more and more persons will experience the shock waves of their old reality crumbling before them. What was certain in their lives is now uncertain. What was solid ground is seen to be no longer solid. We mean this both figuratively and literally.

There is another wave of transition states that is emerging from this Chaotic Node. It is already affecting many persons, but its affects will spread out in consciousness much like a tsunami.

This particular transition state has to do with the collapse of the collective lies of your culture. Increasingly more and more of you will see behind the shadow play; you will sense the puppet masters, and although their identities may elude you, you will see with increasing reality that aspects of your culture are a manipulation, a limitation, and in many cases, downright lies.

The lie that we are speaking to here is not the lie of economics, the lie of wars, or the lie of confining religions, but the lie of your identity—a lie that ensures your imprisonment. This lie is the belief and cultural assertion that you are nothing more than a physical human being and that there are, in fact, no other realms of being beyond your earthly experience.

The recognition of this lie is a harbinger of personal freedom, but in its beginning stages it can be quite disorienting. This is because multidimensional experiences are so different from your earthly day-to-day experiences. If you find yourself marooned between your earthly and multidimensional life, you have entered a transition state of consciousness.

Our purpose in sharing this information is to suggest a practical course of action during transition states of consciousness.

When you personally enter a powerful transition state you might, like many human beings, remain stuck in overwhelm. Many individuals find the shock of realizing that their perceptual markers have disappeared, along with the reality that they assumed to be real, deeply disturbing.

Due to the fact that time is accelerating—and by this we mean more events taking place in less time—remaining in a state of shock or overwhelm is a psychological indulgence which you cannot afford. The essential point we wish to convey here is that regardless of the nature of the transition state, whether it is personal in nature having to do with changes in your personal life, or due to recognizing your cultural manipulation—you are the creator of your reality.

You may have stories to explain why suddenly your life is bereft, but these are just stories. You may blame other persons, situations, or institutions for your problem, but this is misplaced responsibility. Your stories may be true and there may be other persons, situations or institutions to blame, but when you have entered a transition state of consciousness, you are at the central vortex of a powerful creative process. There is no reason or need to cry over "spilt milk" as one of your folk sayings goes. What is lost is lost. What is gone is gone.

Now the central question becomes, "What will you do?"
Will you remain stunned, in shock, in overwhelm, anger and sadness? Or will you step into your identity as a creator of your life?

To those of you who choose to remain in lower states of consciousness, we have no comment.

Our comments are for those of you courageous enough and bold enough to step into your identity as creators. If you are one of these, here is what we suggest.

When everything disappears, meaning the perceptual markers of your former reality, understand that you have entered into a *void point*.

A void point is a critical transition between an old reality and a new one. That which was, has ended. Instead of regretting the loss, you accept the void. This is, for many persons, a challenging undertaking, because in the void point there is nothing that can be done. You must simply be a witness to it, and to yourself, for in *this no-man's land* there are no perceptual markers.
Be careful what new markers you put into place, for these ideas and beliefs will be the stars in the new sky of your mind, and you shall navigate your way into these new times by the stars (thoughts and beliefs) that you have placed in the heavens of your own consciousness. So be wise when you go about creating new stars, our fellow navigators of the Mystery.

Collective Transition States of Consciousness

The human collective, from our perspective, is currently like an immense cosmic serpent shedding its old skin, writhing and twisting, scraping off old encumbrances. Some of these take the form of economic turmoil. Some of them are political in nature. Some of them are the collapse and transformation of cultural institutions. And some of these writhings and twistings are related to earthquake and volcanic activity, as well as aberrant weather patterns.

As natural and manmade disasters increase, more and more of you will find yourselves entering transition states of consciousness. Obviously those who experience an earthquake, volcano or destructive weather directly are the most prone to enter transition states, but those of you who are empathic in nature can experience the brunt of a natural or manmade disaster as if you were physically present.

Indeed as the veil that separates human consciousnesses from one another dissolves, more and more of you will experience the changes taking place in the world at a visceral level.

We now wish to address the question of a new creation for those of you who may find yourself in the aftermath of a natural or manmade disaster, such as an earthquake, a volcanic eruption, or destructive weather patterns.

If the destructive force is strong enough, the perceptual markers of your former reality may no longer exist. Your home or place of business may no longer be there. You may find yourself dealing with shortages of food and water, and there are any number of variables that can come together to create a state of shock and overwhelm.

We wish to be very clear in what we are about to say. Shock and overwhelm in the face of disasters are a natural mammalian response, and if you are to transcend and transform the moment you must reach upward to higher dimensions of your own existence, your own being, to those realms of consciousness that are beyond time and space.

To the extent that you are able to incorporate the transcendent aspects of your being as part of the equation for your survival, you will be able to mitigate the shock and overwhelm.

The central feature that needs to be identified in the midst of chaos, any form of chaos, is *the portal of opportunity*.

This opportunity for survival or for a new life may present itself in ways you do not expect. This is because the perceptual markers are no longer in place and your consciousness may not recognize an opportunity when it presents itself.

There is a deep-seated human habit, or tendency, that wishes to conform new realities to those of the past. This would be an unfortunate habit to engage in these situations.

There is much we could say about the hyper-dimensional realities involved in choice making during chaotic events, but we wish to "cut to the chase" and give that which will be most practical. Perhaps some other time we can share with you our philosophical musings about your infinite nature and the infinite possibilities that reside within you. However, for now, let us be a little simplistic and give you a formula to recognize and create opportunities for new life and a new destiny when they present themselves to you.

Assuming that you have entered a transition state of consciousness and that you have befriended the void point and are more or less comfortable with the great uncertainty of your situation, this is what we suggest.

Be curious and expect miracles.

By entering a state of curiosity you engage an aspect of your mind that is free to move unfettered by expectation. It becomes very much like the mind of a child, and it is this innocence—which is not the same as childishness—that allows you to enter a vibratory state of consciousness, which greatly benefits you.

By holding the expectation of miracles you release the power of creation within you, and to the extent that you accomplish this you will find increasing incidences of serendipity, coincidences of benefit and unexpected treasures, whether they be physical in nature or mental and emotional.

This combination of curiosity about what will happen next joined with an expectation of miracles will move you rapidly from the void point to a new life, a new creation, regardless of what might be happening for those around you.

During collective transition states of consciousness it is helpful to remember that each person is the creator of his or her own reality, and in the midst of chaos people will make different choices and enter different personal realities.

Do not be swayed by those who enter lower vibratory realms. You cannot save them from themselves. Look upward and live upward with curiosity and an expectation of miracles, and even in the gravest of situations miracles can, and will, occur for you.

Physical Death

One of the greatest difficulties for embodied beings is the transition state of consciousness you call death. This is due to the fact that all perceptual markers, including the five senses, disappear. If a person identifies solely with his/her material existence, he or she will find this transition state to be most difficult. This is because what she or he identified with no longer exists.

Although the physical world continues on, there is no input into consciousness from the five senses. It is as if the world has vanished and the body along with it. The great I Am, the central feature of transcendent consciousness, no longer receives information from the body, the five senses, or the external world. This can be deeply disturbing and disorienting for someone who has not directly experienced the other realms of his or her being.

Metaphorically speaking, you are like a vast tree, a *Tree of Life*, with many branches and many, many leaves and blossoms, and your current physical existence is just one of these leaves and one of these blossoms.

When a person passes through the transition state of consciousness you call death there are several options. If you are in a spiritual tradition the central figure of which is a guru, avatar or savior, you can follow the path of this being into the vibratory realm of his/her consciousness. In some religions this is known as heaven.

If you follow the path of a guru, avatar or savior understand that you are entering into his/her heaven, her/his vibratory attainment, and by necessity you enter also into his/her limitations in consciousness.

From our perspective the universe is infinite in nature, and by this we refer not to external space but to the interdimensional realities of your universe, and there is no single being in existence, from our experience, who understands and embraces all that is.

If, however, you wish to join your guru/avatar/savior in the death realms we have a few suggestions. One is to mentally call upon his/her name. This is an ancient understanding encapsulated in the Egyptian term *Ren*, meaning name. When you call upon the name of a spiritual being an aspect of him/her is compelled to move toward you. If, in that moment of encountering your guru/avatar/savior, he or she deems you worthy, you will be taken by him/her into his/her heavenly realm. For those of you in eastern spiritual traditions there are mantras connected with specified deities. Chanting these mantras mentally during death, or in the death realms, has the same effect.

For those of you who are not part of a spiritual tradition that follows a guru, avatar or savior, then the transition state of consciousness called death offers other possibilities.

As with the other two transition states of consciousness, the death realm has a void point, and its dominant features are stillness (silence) and darkness. All possibilities exist within the Void, but no actuality is in existence. It is like the acorn of an oak tree. The oak, the giant tree itself, is potentially within the acorn, but it does not yet exist.

So when you find yourself in the Void, which you will recognize by the fact that you are utterly alone in darkness and utter stillness, know that you are in the central nexus of your creative powers.

What you choose to create next will determine the course of your destiny and what worlds you will inhabit or realms of existence you will reside in. This is a critical juncture.

Many persons frightened by the darkness move to the light prematurely. And what they do not realize is that in their yearning they create the light. A portal opens before them, like a tunnel, and they can move into this tunnel of light, encountering those they have known before, thereby entering back into embodiment or other vibratory realms of existence without having fully understood the consequences. This is certainly one option open to you, and one that is often taken.

Another option, however, is to remain at the void point, residing in the Void itself, becoming aware of your Self as *pure consciousness*— transcendent to all phenomena. If you reside in this state of awareness long enough without the need to create something, you will discover your identity as the great I Am. And from this point of awareness you can choose the circumstances of your embodiment. You can choose the worlds you will inhabit or the realms of consciousness where you will reside.

This latter method gives you the greatest opportunities, though it is the most difficult for most people. And the reason for this difficulty has to do with the fact that most humans find it uncomfortable to not have a body. The yearning for a body and the experience of the material world often draws a person from the Void prematurely.

In summation, due to the intensifying phases of the Chaotic Node many of you will find yourselves in transitional states of consciousness. Regardless of what level you find yourself engaged in, whether it be your personal life, the collective experience, or the transition state you call death, know that you are the creator of your reality.

The Hathors
April 20, 2011

http://tomkenyon.com/

FORTY FIVE

Embracing the Void

I was undoubtedly in a chaotic node as defined by the Hathors as well as a transition state of consciousness in an in-between place where a major loss occurred. The perceptual markers that described how I made sense of my world using my five senses had literally disappeared and I was entering a null zone in which my old reality no longer existed while my new reality had not yet come into existence.

I understood my perception as a personal creation that depended on my habits of perception and the situation in my life had shifted dramatically made evident by the fact that my perceptual markers were disappearing and what had been certain in my life was now uncertain.

I also understood that in entering a transition state I was the central vortex of a powerful creative process and there was no reason to cry over "spilt milk". What was lost was lost. What was gone was gone. I entered a void point which I accepted, knowing that nothing could be done except witness it. In the midst of my chaos I hoped for a portal of opportunity and felt quite blank so I was heartened by the Hathor's advice to, "Be curious and expect miracles."

Witnessing the void my life had become and expecting miracles became the guiding principles I used to face the unknown that enveloped me. I accepted the fact that no matter what anyone said or did I had come to this point in my life through my own choices and it was up to me to take responsibility for them.

I bought a Toyota Prius in 2006 and for some reason, before I purchased it, I determined that it was big enough for me to sleep in. Little did I know the foresight I had figuring that out. The back and front seats fold down, making a relatively flat surface big enough to stretch out on and sleep in. I kept a duffle bag of clothes, my sleeping bag, extra blankets, a pillow, a small cooler, a couple of bags of food, water, and a sleeping mat in my back seat. When it was time to sleep I folded down the seats, stored my necessities in the front seats, put up my sun screen, laid out my mat and sleeping bag, and hung jackets over the side windows to keep out the light and give myself limited privacy.

I lived in my car for four and a half months. I'll never forget that first Sunday night sleeping in it parked alongside a school. I slept deep and soundly for nine hours, the most sleep I had in weeks and spent the next day emotionally numb, not knowing where to go or what to do. I told myself I was free and needed to concentrate on staying in the moment, embracing the void, and dealing with one thing at a time.

I didn't want to sleep in the same spot the next night. Kids would be showing up for school on Monday which would not look good. I found a spot that seemed safe on another street in front of someone's house, out of view of their front door. When I woke up in the morning a man taking out his trash looked suspiciously at me so I hustled out of there.

I was forced out into the street in such a rush that I had no time to prepare for anything to take care of my basic needs. When Monday morning rolled around I took things one at a time. I went to a camp ground to shower, but needed a token to get in the bathrooms, so I found an outdoor shower at the beach that I had to walk to and took my first homeless shower there among kayakers and surfers.

My next priority was to get a post office box. While driving to it I passed a twenty four hour health club. I inquired and got a free week long trial membership which took care of my immediate needs. They had weights, a lap pool, steam, sauna, free wireless internet and a big parking lot. I slept in my car there and woke up at the club where I worked out every morning, brushed my teeth, showered, and shaved, creating a morning routine followed by a stop at a hotel to get ice for my cooler. I spent most afternoons at the library using their free wireless internet and when the library closed early I went to coffee shops. In this limbo time I managed to eke out an existence editing and teaching at writer's conferences.

At night I set up my laptop on the passenger seat, lowered the seat back and watched DVD's from the back seat with an audio cable from the headphone output of my computer to the car's MP3 audio input and had surround sound in my own mini drive-in theater.

While shopping at Costco I discovered a special offer for a two year membership at the twenty four hour club for two-hundred-ninety-nine dollars so I took advantage of that.

Living in my car made me limited in what I could buy and store, so I lived Spartan, ate healthy, and trained hard. My diet consisted of trail mix, nuts, crackers, maca, super green powder full of vegetables, grasses, algae, etc., apples, rice milk, whey powder, granola, coconut oil, and supplements. On nights when I felt a craving I allowed myself a chicken burrito for dinner.

Things worked out great for a few weeks until I was rousted from a sound sleep at 3:30 in the morning by a cop banging on my window telling me I couldn't sleep in the parking lot. It didn't matter that I was a member of the club. I remembered seeing campers parked across the street from a waste treatment plant, so I went there. That spot lasted a few weeks before the cops hassled me again.

I found what I thought was a great spot in an industrial area and was watching a movie when the cops showed up again. I didn't know where to go so I went back to the health club and parked on the street that led to it. That lasted a couple of weeks until I woke up one morning to see a cop checking the line of cars behind me. He was a car or so away when I drove off. By this time I felt frustrated. I didn't mind sleeping in the car, but the harassment made me uneasy.

I went back to the fitness center and parked in the lot closest to the main building. I knew when the guard left for the day and timed my parking so that I went to bed after he left and woke up before another one came back in the morning.

A good friend who I had on board to help with technical support for the expedition offered to cash in some of his retirement money to invest in the project. I had been protecting him from investing because I didn't want him ending up on the street like me, let alone the inconsistencies from Marc, but we were in danger of losing the whole project because we owed money to one of our critical Costa Rica partners who threatened to sabotage it if we didn't pay up promptly. I contacted my friend and he immediately kicked in, saving the project. We had to wait for a harrowing few weeks before we heard that this Costa Rican partner was satisfied and would not sabotage the project. I should have gotten a finder's fee for bringing in these funds but I was willing to let it go to help the project as best I could.

Soon after getting these funds I got into a severe financial pinch with state and federal tax agencies as well as a looming threat of bouncing checks. Marc promised to meet with me implying that he would help but when the day came to meet he wouldn't answer his phone, leaving me in a bad situation. I had helped him numerous times in the past with rent, lawyers, bail money, etc., and now in my time of real need he turned his back on me.

It wasn't the fact that he didn't help me when I needed it, it was the fact that he led me to believe that he would. If he had simply shown some character and told me he didn't have the money it wouldn't have been so difficult, but he led me to believe that he would help, then ignored me which made matters far worse than they needed to be.

At this point I had to admit that Marc hadn't learned anything in jail which was not a comforting thought after giving up everything and working for two and half years for nothing, so I stopped calling him. If something did happen with the project he could call me. I was in a tough spot and had to scramble to survive.

Some family members found out about my situation which I had managed to keep hidden and took me in for a few weeks here and there which I would rather not have done. I did not feel welcome which made me feel uncomfortable and in the end I couldn't stay in either place due to situations that were out of my control after being pressured to move in from a family member who I had sheltered for months years earlier when they were in need.

When I no longer had a place to stay I was prepared to move back into my car, but my best friend Rob who had also been my manager in the company we worked for that screwed us both over who I had lined up to be in charge of the expedition's technical support and his wife insisted that I come stay with them rent free. When I resisted he reminded me that I had given him a place to stay when he divorced his first wife. They fell all over themselves making me feel welcome. I had not felt as comfortable as I did living with them in years and saw clearly that when things get tough you discover who your real friends are.

We did a Skype call with a Hollywood producer's people in March of 2014. On that call Tran introduced himself as second in command. When it was my turn to speak I also introduced myself as second in command, as my title was Sr. Vice President. Marc insisted on that title when I came on board and we went back and forth over it. I told him I should be simply vice president, not senior, but he was adamant about it.

On April 11th, 2014 we were called in to the producer's offices in Hollywood to do an audition tape for a possible reality show around the treasure hunt. In a meeting prior to going there Marc very rudely stated, "Tran is second in command!" in front of everyone.

All I ever did was try to help him and Marc "threw me under the bus" more times than I can count. I never wanted to outshine him. All I ever wanted was to show up and take care of business. The irony of this is that all I have to do is show up, take care of business, and I did outshine him, just by being myself!

In my video audition I did outshine him and he was so upset that they gave me more attention that he was envious and stopped communicating with me. I understood this and all the other incidences of this disgraceful treatment as envy and classic narcissistic behavior, but at least now I knew what I was dealing with and didn't care anymore.

FORTY SIX

Purificada

Throughout all the madness and financial ruin I magically continued my dietas with a lot of help from friends who sponsored me with generous donations, including my troubled sister who put up the money for me without hesitation when I became homeless. This brief summary of those journeys occurred in parallel with my ongoing treasure hunting drama and its aftermath. The details of those seven years of journeys involved the ongoing drama of my life and I did not see any benefit in recording any of them except for a brief recording from 2011.

In 2008 Yoda decided to change things up and go to the Andes for five Ayahuasca ceremonies. Although I preferred the jungle dietas, the intense inner work, isolation, and variety of teacher plants I felt loyal to the group and revisited Urubamba in the Sacred Valley where I had done Huachuma ceremonies a few years earlier.

When we finished our ceremonies there we visited places in and around Cusco, among them Ollantaytambo where I had been with my two year group a few years previous and Machu Picchu where we had to arrive at dawn because they limited the number of visitors to four hundred a day. On this my second visit I climbed Huayna Picchu, the mountaintop that rises over Machu Picchu where the Urubamba River bends. The Incas built this trail up its side and built temples and terraces on its top. The peak of Huayna Picchu is 8,835 feet above sea level, 850 feet higher than Machu Picchu. According to locals, the top of the mountain was the residence for the high priest and the temple virgins. Every morning before sunrise, the high priest with a small group would walk to Machu Picchu to signal the coming of the new day. While on that hike I visited The Temple of the Moon, one of the three major temples in the Machu Picchu area nestled on the side of the mountain at an elevation lower than Machu Picchu.

We also visited Moray, an archaeological site about 31 miles northwest of Cuzco on a high plateau at 11,500 feet, west of the village of Maras, known for being the site of over 5,000 salt evaporation ponds which have been used since Inca times. Moray contains unusual Inca ruins mostly consisting of terraced circular depressions, the largest being 98 feet deep.

One highlight of this adventure was parasailing 19,000 feet over the sacred valley sponsored by and insisted on by my great friend we called Wild Bill, a retired New York City Parole officer who had also contributed financially to this trip as well as some of my previous jungle dietas.

In 2010 we returned to the jungle for my eighth plant dieta where Ronaldo gave me a daily mixture of Chuchuwasi, Cumaseba, and Clavohuasca which were energizing, fortifying, and brought clarity. Once again I did two Ayahausca sessions alone in my tambo in addition to the five group ceremonies in the maloca. I have a vivid memory of being startled awake one morning by a loud thunk sound after an intense, energy draining ceremony the night before followed by a loud voice from one of the older helpers.

"Mateo, café!"

I crawled out from under my mosquito net half awake feeling hung over from the night before with a burgeoning headache and an uneasy stomach. The thought of drinking that dose first thing in the morning made me gag. It took everything I had to overcome the rising nausea that trapped it in my throat for a few agonizing seconds before I managed to choke it down.

Reluctant to move with the intense physical discomfort of keeping the brew down without vomiting I stretched out in my hammock and suffered. In one of those inexplicable moments of jungle magic it started to rain with a growing intensity that tracked with the escalating effects of the dose. My whole body shook hard in the hammock as the rainfall increased, pounding my tambo with so much force that it shook independent of me and I spent a few mind boggling minutes with me and the tambo shaking together while the voice of Scotty from Star Trek reverberated through my head with the words, "She can't take anymore captain!"

When things settled some the thunder and lightning raged shaking everything with its power every time it erupted. I felt sweaty and uncomfortable alongside the all encompassing power of the loud rolling thunder, but it thrilled me deep in my primal core. Its burgeoning energy drove me out into the downpour and down the steep muddy embankment into the raging waters. I worked my way out to the middle of the river where I submerged myself under the water amidst crashing thunderclaps and popped back up out of the water over and over again with fists clenched shouting "*Purificada!*"

It wasn't the brightest thing to do and I could have easily drowned or been electrocuted, but I felt so connected to everything on an elemental level that this mindless, instinctive act of thrilling passion and abandonment turned out to be one of my greatest peak life experiences of all time, and in my mind a rare, privileged blessing of a pure jungle baptism.

As if to reinforce this death defying, convoluted Ayahuasca instinctual "logic", much later in my journey when the effects of the Ayahuasca mellowed I stretched out in my hammock remaining absolutely still while it rocked me in a wide arc as if of its own accord. There was no wind and I stopped myself once or twice to insure that I remained perfectly immobile and the swaying continued, making me feel like the infant that I was, rocked by a powerful, loving, invisible mother.

I returned to the jungle for my ninth dieta starting Tuesday morning October 11, 2011 and only recorded thirty four minutes of my experiences to catch their highlights without reiterating the specifics which were well established after eight years. Ronaldo asked me if I wanted something to strengthen, fortify, or open myself up more and I said both.

After some thought he prescribed a pitcher a day of Tahuari, a large tree that supports lots of life. Its bark is used for inflammation, bronchitis, arthritis, depression, candida, and it supports balance when dealing with diabetes, Lupus, tumors, degenerative issues, and cancer. It also helps promote regular periods, bowel function, balanced oxygen levels in the blood, body temperature, and the removal of fungal infections and bacteria.

Prior to starting the dieta Ronaldo treated us to a Yaguarpanga session where we drank a half a glass of an infusion made from its leaves and vomited every twenty minutes for five hours. In my case I had it coming out both ends. Each time I vomited I had to run to the latrine, so I timed everything; drink, puke, shit, repeat for five hours. I started getting severe muscle cramps in my stomach toward the end and finished tapped out and exhausted.

I am happy to report that I only had two mild purges during the course of seven separate Ayahuasca experiences. For my plant bath they first brought the usual Guyausa, then they switched to Ajo Sacha, known as forest garlic which is what it smells like.

We drank a brew made from an uncultivated wild vine in our first ceremony and it took me into some dark places where I got lost and swallowed in the darkness which I endured and worked through. I was in the throes of the Cocos Island madness and I was dealing with some dark energy. Aside from Marc's insanity I had been steeped in the horrific bloody history of piracy. Large bat-like creatures swooped down on me, attacking me in my visions as if trying to frighten me like the slavering beast outside of Iquitos. I was confused and a little off balance trying to understand how I had attracted such focused overwhelming darkness, then I thought, wow, I am really honored that you think I am worthy of so much of your energy and attention, and with the completion of that thought they disappeared.

One of my intentions was a wish to visit with the Hathors, and after passing through the darkness I found myself with them in a command center where they suited me up in a giant robot exoskeleton armored suit to go out into the world and do what I needed to do. It felt very empowering and they came across as very efficient. They answered my questions in a telepathic manner and pumped me up in the best way, telling me they were preparing me for my purpose. I felt like I was one of them chosen and blessed by them to perform sacred tasks, one of which I thought at the time was the treasure hunt and the other was to get information out about sacred geometry and all of its aspects in regards to art, quantum physics, mathematics, and more. This second task became real three years later when I published *The Infinity Zone*.

I dreaded waking up first thing in the morning after a few hours of sleep for a solo dose after my challenging first ceremony and didn't know how I was going to do it. I took three quarters of a dose and braced myself for a solid ass kicking, but in the end I had an amazing, blissful day. Before I left for the jungle my roommate picked an animal card for me which was the jaguar, and the day before I left I watched Lion King with my grand niece and nephew. Once in the jungle a friend mentioned that I was there to be swallowed by a jaguar, referring to what I had written in *Spirit Matters* that he had just read.

In the jungle the bugs are most active between 11:00 in the morning and 3:00 in the afternoon and they drove me crazy so I spent most of the day under my mosquito net where I slipped into a gentle journey which I think was partly due to the Yaguarpanga purges. I did a lot of inner work, resolving some personal issues and moving on. At one point in the journey I sat up and looked down on myself to see freckles and liver spots on my arms, then I saw them all over my body and realized I was a jaguar. I didn't growl or anything like that, I just felt feline, like I had been inhabited by a jaguar. It made me think about my shamanic teachings, and for me this meant that I had come to the jungle to claim my power. It felt right, good, and empowering, like I had finally arrived, but I reminded myself you can never rest on your laurels. In my case I felt like I had found some semblance of balance.

I laid there for a long time feeling blissful until I went to the latrine and found masses of big biting black ants all over my shoes, clothes, and everything else. I went to war against them sweeping away like crazy with a broom, clearing them out. There was a long lasting ebb and flow to the battle, but I wasn't giving up.

Soon after that a helper came back to offer me more Ayahuasca. I took another quarter of a dose which sent me off gently again with no colors or fireworks, just a gentle blissful experience that left me peaceful, happy, and exhausted.

I audio journaled at 2:00 in the morning on Thursday after my second session and third time drinking reporting a great journey that opened up a lot of doors for me. As part of my evolution and experience I had become José and Ronaldo's official brew tester which was a deep honor for me, and on this night I had a different brew than everyone else which did not hit me as hard as the first night's brew.

I had a hard time choking the dose down and it got stuck in my throat, but after struggling with nausea for the first couple of hours I had some beautiful colors followed by some insights. After some time the colors were gone which I was okay with, then Ronaldo started singing icaros. Each time he called in a different plant spirit, each one showed itself through a display of its own unique, distinctive colors and patterns that washed through me, overwhelming me with their power.

I also had a vision that I thought came courtesy of the Hathors where I caught and saw what I characterized as rats, which were negative emotions that tried to work their way in and make something out of nothing. I saw them everywhere like a rash, but I felt protected by the "armor" the Hathors gave me which kept them out.

After the challenge of getting the night's dose down I was not looking forward to drinking again in the morning but they were going to give me the same brew everyone else had that night.

I did an audio check in at 9:15 on Thursday night October 13th after a long, challenging day. I didn't drink until around 11:30 that morning for my second solo, and my fourth journey. Some beautiful colors came but they didn't stay for long. I was processing a lot of information and figuring things out while clearing up a lot of inner issues. I spent most of the day under my mosquito net to avoid the annoying bugs and lost track of time, then I remembered we were supposed to meet so I struggled, finding myself a little incapacitated. The simplest things like putting my shoes on, tying them, and working a clasp on my neck chain became challenging ordeals. After all of my fussing I hustled to the meeting only to discover that I was three hours early.

Our next session came on Friday night and in this one Yoda told us a story about dealing with demons from the story of Ulysses, hero of the Odyssey. When Ulysses was going on his journey a witch came to him and said, "Whatever you do, don't go near the Strait of Messina because there is a six headed hydra monster there called Scylla. No matter what you do, you can't land there or Scylla will eat six of your crew and there is nothing you can do about it, so whatever you do, don't go there!"

Ulysses, being the adventurer, explorer, and conquering hero he was, went there, going along the strait and before he realized it, Scylla came up out of the water and gobbled up six of his men, one for each head. Ulysses was helpless, but after giving it some thought he ordered his men to get six cows and told them to make a bunch of giant fish hooks the size of the boat's anchor, as Scylla was that big. He butchered the cows and laid them out on the deck of his ship and hid the hooks in them with chains attached to the mast of the ship.

Scylla rose again and all six heads gobbled up the six cows with the chain attached. Ulysses ordered his men to set full sail ahead while Scylla tried to dive with all of the hooked cows inside each one of the heads. Eventually Ulysses pulled Scylla up out of the water and chopped all the heads off with his sword.

The last head was a feminine one that pleaded with him, saying, "I have been neglected and abandoned and I have been made into this creature on this earth and nobody ever wants to have anything to do with me. This is my lot in life and I have rued the day that you would come because I was told early on in my life by a witch that my miserable life would end the day that Ulysses came to finish me off.

This dieta came a few months after I became homeless and broke when Penny had erupted in full psychosis and the story about dealing with demons as a multi-headed beast became the defining metaphor of that experience for me.

I checked in again at 3:00 on Saturday morning from a sweet third group session with no major insights or darkness. I had a good time singing and drumming with Ronaldo, and looked forward to the coming night, my fourth group session and my sixth session overall.

My next check in came the following Sunday morning. In Saturday night's session I got disoriented, but I got some good inner work done. I sang and rattled with Ronaldo, but somewhere in the middle of it I stopped singing and rattling and totally forgot what I was doing, then I remembered and started singing and rattling again. Later in the ceremony I did a drum solo on the floor which Ronaldo loved.

We had our last session on Monday which turned out to be an amazing night from a very powerful brew. This was our fifth group session and the seventh ceremony for me as well as my fiftieth journey in that maloca, and counting my tambo solos, fifty five sessions overall in the jungle there.

In this last session my disorientation came with a vengeance and I kept getting lost when I went to the latrine. At one point I looked down and saw something weird on my shoe, eventually recognizing it as a fist sized slug. I had no idea how it got there and threw it off.

Other than a few rough spots, compared to other dietas, this one had been relatively gentle and I have no doubt that Yaguarpanga is what made all the difference.

FORTY SEVEN

The Peace Of Zen Emptiness

Prior to the year 2012 many people believed that disastrous or transformative events would occur on or around December 21st of that year. This date was regarded as the end date of a 5,126 year long cycle in the Mesoamerican Long Count calendar. Celebrations took place on December 21st to commemorate the event in Mexico, Guatemala, Honduras, and El Salvador, the countries that were part of the Maya civilization with main events at Chichén Itzá in Mexico and Tikal in Guatemala.

A number of astronomical alignments and numerological formulae were proposed for this date and a New Age interpretation said that it marked the start of a period when the Earth and its inhabitants would undergo a positive physical or spiritual transformation that would mark the beginning of a new era. Others thought it marked the end of the world or a similar catastrophe. Scenarios suggested for the end of the world included the arrival of the next solar maximum, an interaction between Earth and the supermassive black hole at the center of the galaxy, or Earth's collision with a mythical planet called Nibiru.

Mayan scholars stated that no classic Mayan accounts forecast impending doom and the idea that the Long Count calendar ended in 2012 misrepresented Mayan history and culture. Additionally astronomers debunked the doomsday scenarios with astronomical observations.

I found all of this excitement fascinating and did my own research. Though I didn't buy into the hype of anything in particular I kept an open mind. December 21st is the shortest day of the year which starts the winter represented by North on the medicine wheel. This is the time when the leaves have fallen from the trees, seeds holding their potential are settled underground, and animals hibernate, all waiting for the new life to come with their spring awakening.

I was at a standstill in my life. My old life was gone and I was broke, staying with good friends, barely making ends meet. I was open to any possibilities and knew that regardless of what happened, there wasn't anything I could do about it. Whatever did happen, if anything, was beyond my control. I accepted that and stayed in the moment to see how the mystery would unfold. In this state of open receptivity I received a peak life experience of what I think of as a Cosmic gift of rebirth as a reward for my acceptance of things bigger than me and quite possibly one of the miracles the Hathors said to expect after passing through that surreal, painful moment in the darkest moment of my life when I let go of everything and fully grasped the realization that nothing is permanent.

The seed of this magical celebration of death, transformation, and rebirth was planted in the middle of that very passage in early April in the form of *Land Without Evil*, my historical novel I had gifted to the facilitator of that fateful Ayahuasca session that triggered my kidney stone as if announcing my life as I had known it was over. This literal and figurative passage thrusted me into the chaos that precedes birth, or in this case a rebirth midwifed by the brilliant unstoppable producer, breath-taking aerialist, Creative Director, and Multi-media Storyteller, Sarah "Agent Red" Johnston who read the novel I gifted at the suggestion of a friend.

Agent Red called me in August of 2012 to tell me that she had fallen in love with *Land Without Evil* and wanted to adapt, direct, and produce an ambitious stage performance based on it in association with *Sky Candy*, a renowned aerial group in Austin Texas. There was no money in it, but she said I would get good exposure and credits, and we would be filmed as an episode of a KPBS documentary series called *Arts In Context*.

I agreed to collaborate on the script and said I wanted to go to Austin well in advance of the show to do everything I could to help make it happen, so if she could find me places to stay I would come and contribute whatever I could. Red and I met in Los Angeles soon after that first discussion and were filmed as part of the Arts In Context show, then we sketched out a battle plan. In the months that followed leading up to the show we kept in close touch and passed the script back and forth, refining it between us.

The **Land Without Evil** show ran from December 8 – 16, 2012, which in the bigger scheme of cosmic events ended on the week of December 21, 2012 at the historic Stateside at the Paramount theater in Austin Texas. The show sold out opening night and the last two performances. PBS filmed our rehearsals and performances for the **Arts in Context** episode which premiered nationally in January 2013.

Land Without Evil is a coming of age historical story based around rebirth, transformation, and shamanism. The story centers on a boy's conflict between the spiritual beliefs of life in a Jesuit Mission in Paraguay and the visions of his father, the shaman of the threatened Guarani tribe who are forced into a perilous cross continent journey in a quest for the mythical Land Without Evil. Told through aerials and acrobatics, dance, capoeira, flow arts, spoken word, ASL, music and singing our visually dynamic show featured stirring new music by local artists and ground-breaking video mapping. The subsequent **Arts In Context** episode was nominated for a 2013 Lonestar Emmy for best Cultural Documentary. **Land Without Evil** became a cutting-edge collaboration of creative multimedia and multidimensional artists counted among some of the brightest talents in Austin to craft an unforgettable journey of a dream within a dream.

The magic of it all flabbergasted me for a number of reasons. How many novels, much less historical novels get turned into stage shows? This coupled with the fact that my mother was a famous child acrobat made me feel exceptionally blessed to sit front and center through every performance as if she had given me this gift. I would have loved for her to see it, but the next best thing was my brother flying in from San Diego for the last three performances.

Agent Red, myself, and the rest of the cast and crew worked feverishly for weeks with minimal sleep to put on the show and I did everything I could, including building sets, running errands, picking up supplies, editing the show program, and anything else I could contribute and made myself sick with exhaustion. My brother put me up in a double Sheraton hotel room where I collapsed into a deep, extended sleep after weeks of couch surfing.

Aside from my brother, my publisher drove for four hours to come see the show and I choked up every time I watched it, feeling deep gratitude that the fifty people in the cast and crew worked so hard with their incredible array of talents that made the story come to life in ways

I never could have imagined thanks to the vision of Agent Red.

I returned to the jungle in October of 2013 for my tenth dieta and drank a daily pitcher of Chuchuwasi, Cumaseba, and Clavohuasca, the same combination I drank in 2010, which were energizing, fortifying, and brought clarity. Once again I did two Ayahausca sessions by myself in my tambo in addition to the five group ceremonies in the maloca. After less than forty minutes of recording in 2011 I felt no need to record anything this time and focused on my own ongoing, evolving issues.

My eleventh dieta in October 2014 was similar to 2013 with two Ayahausca sessions by myself and five group ceremonies working with daily pitchers of a Shihuahuaco, Cumaceba, and Bobinsana combination with Ajo Sacha for my plant baths.

I participated in my last three dietas through the generosity of friends and family along with any scant remaining funds I had and resigned myself to the fact that I wouldn't be able to continue participating until Yoda called to tell me I was going to the jungle again in October of 2015. I protested, but my words fell on deaf ears. He insisted that I was going because this would be his last year. He was well into his eighties and his heart was weak, but he was sponsoring me. I felt deeply touched that he wanted me there and though I had no money, I managed to cobble together the remaining funds needed to cover my travel.

2015 marked my twelfth dieta and my sixtieth ceremony in that maloca, and as fate would have it this happened just before my sixtieth birthday. Unlike the two previous *dietas*, this one hit me exceptionally hard and rooted out some deep seated frustrations. For this ordeal, along with my five group and two solo sessions, my daily pitcher consisted of Chuchuwasi, Cumaceba, Ipururu, Clavohuasca, and Estoraque. This powerful combination sent me over the edge leaving me with spectacular results.

As my dieta progressed my energies intensified and my mind, thoughts, and entire being spun out of control, as if my mental volume and brightness had been turned up full blast. I spun hard for days in chaotic dreams and fitful sleep, and the incessant buzz persisted through dreaming, waking, visions, and discussions with friends, which looking back on now, were quite insane. I experienced total madness in the true sense of the word and my full throttled, obsessive, out of control rage was all directed at Marc.

I became hopelessly swept up in the same indisputable certainty of absolute truth without any awareness of the possibility of a glaring discrepancy with a more grounded reality, lost in the one third uncertainty of Ayahuasca. Scenarios spun endlessly in my mind like a continuous loop of bad commercials where I exposed Marc at the moment of worldwide recognition, on the island, on television, at a lecture series, and countless other situations, the common theme of them all being exposing him and revealing the truth in his moment of glory. I have been spun up in the past, particularly in my younger days, but never this hard, this fast, and for as long.

I arrived at the airport in Lima for my flight back to Los Angeles exhausted from my ordeal and tried to check in on the internet now that I was in cell phone range, but none of my passwords worked. After a few half-hearted attempts I gave up and boarded my all night flight.

I walked out of the LAX international terminal around 7:30 the following morning and turned on my cell phone, finding eight messages from my credit union fraud department, my credit card fraud department and others. My identity had been stolen while I was in the jungle out of touch with civilization and over the course of the two weeks I was gone they had gotten to my checking account, ran up my American Express card, and made minimum payments to it from my credit union to get even more money.

All of that fraud not only wiped out what little I had in my checking account, but it put me thousands of dollars into debt. I was beyond broke, putting me into a deep sense of disbelief because this disastrous news after one of my most challenging Ayahuasca ordeals ever carried no emotional charge for me.

I accepted it all with a calm Zen-like emptiness that stayed with me throughout that long day and through all of the phone calls, office visits, verifications and other follow ups in the following days and weeks needed to make everything right and bring me back to ground zero financially.

Now that I had experienced this peace of nonattachment in what could have been habitually reactionary emotional chaos, the door to the possibilities that this skill brought continues to benefit me now that I know it exists.

FORTY EIGHT

My Hidden Empath

Little did I know when I embarked on the most hellish part of my life's journey with the intention of taking care of everybody that I would become trapped between two text book narcissists. In the beginning, whenever I saw or dealt with Marc he always put his best face on, and in doing so deceived me. I found out much too late that he was bipolar and hid his dark side from me. Penny did her own version of the same thing and over time her narcissism emerged in the escalating physical and verbal abuse that she couldn't contain.

My friend who had not listened to my guidance had her own psychotic break after becoming severely dehydrated from overindulging in MDMA and had to see a court ordered psychiatrist. When Penny became the subject of their conversation, the psychiatrist pointed out that she was a textbook narcissist and recommended a book, which our friend passed on to me. I already knew Marc was a narcissist, which was confirmed when I read the book.

Penny fit the same profile.

Narcissistic Personality Disorder is characterized by a long-standing pattern of grandiosity, an overwhelming need for admiration, and a lack of empathy toward others. Narcissists believe they are of primary importance in everybody's life or to anyone they meet and often display snobbish, disdainful, or patronizing attitudes.

Personality disorders are enduring patterns of inner experience and behavior that deviates from cultural norms. These patterns are seen in the areas of cognition, affect, interpersonal functioning, and impulse control. The enduring pattern is inflexible and pervasive across a broad range of personal and social situations and typically leads to distress or impairment in social, work, and other areas. This pattern is stable, long lasting, and its onset can be traced back to early adulthood or adolescence.

From a psychiatric perspective a person diagnosed with narcissistic personality disorder has to meet five or more of the following symptoms. Marc and Penny displayed all of them at different times.

- A grandiose sense of self-importance that exaggerates achievements and talents and expects to be recognized as superior without commensurate achievements
- A preoccupation with fantasies of unlimited success, power, brilliance, beauty, or ideal love
- A belief that he or she is "special" and unique and can only be understood by, or should associate with, other special or high-status people or institutions
- Requires excessive admiration
- Has a very strong sense of entitlement and unreasonable expectations of favorable treatment or automatic compliance with his or her expectations
- Is exploitative of others and takes advantage of others to achieve his or her own ends
- Lacks empathy and is unwilling to recognize or identify with the feelings and needs of others
- Is often envious of others or believes that others are envious of him or her
- Regularly shows arrogant, haughty behaviors or attitudes

The relationship between narcissists and the empaths is parasitic. Motivated by the desire to seek love and heal the wounded narcissist, empaths become the perfect host to the parasitic narcissist, and in my case, in my classic kamikaze style, one wasn't enough.

I had two.

Being preoccupied with emotionally feeding off of others to supply their egotistical needs, narcissists use tactics of manipulation to control the relationship. Often the narcissist remains in power and the empath feels victimized and powerless. Once the parasite has used up all the resources from the host, it moves on to a new host.

In less conscious states empaths and narcissists need each other and both partners are equally responsible for the imbalance. While an empath may feel powerless in the relationship, a narcissist cannot exist within it without the engagement of the well intentioned empath. If an empath sets boundaries and walks away, refusing to internalize the projected feelings of the narcissist, the abusive dynamic ceases to exist which is what happened with me when I lost everything.

A narcissist views others as objects rather than people who they see as sources that supply them with attention, admiration, and idealization to maintain a concealed fragile sense of self. Narcissism exists on a continuum, with hallmarks that include, but are not limited to a lack of empathy, inflated sense of self-importance, sense of entitlement, and a need for admiration. These characteristics start in early adulthood and occur in a range of situations. Narcissists have difficulty feeling their pain so they project their feelings onto their partner.

Due to their inability to relate to others as more than mere objects, narcissists lack the ability to love their partner. When seeing that their partner has withdrawn their love and care, the narcissist knows how to manipulatively regain the love of an empath by providing what feels like authentic love and connection. It can be confusing for an empath who feels heightened levels of bonding and "love" from the narcissist at times.

Empaths are highly sensitive people who can feel the emotional needs of others and often put the needs of others before their own. Their acute sensitivity allows them to truly feel and absorb another's pain. They are driven by a need to help and heal others. Empaths' hyper awareness of their partner's feelings often leads them to hold their partner's feelings, allowing their narcissistic partner to not have to feel the painful emotions themselves.

As a general rule empaths hope to be truly seen and loved by narcissists and their sense of worth is tied to being loved by their narcissistic partner. If they can make the person who is incapable of love, love them, then they are truly worthy of love. They try to heal the wounded narcissist, hoping that once healed, they in turn will provide the empath with the love and validation they so desperately desire.

Underlying their unconscious desire to seek love from the unloving narcissist is an acting out of a childhood relationship dynamic where they have felt unlovable or rejected by a primary caregiver, in my case, my father who abandoned us. The empath was unable to receive the unconditional love that every child needs and in their adulthood empaths seek validation and feel the worth they did not feel as a child, but the stakes are higher. In their mind it is only by turning the unloving narcissist into the loving and accepting "parent" that their self-worth can be restored.

Empaths, due to unavailability from their primary attachment figures associate love with pain and become tolerant of mistreatment from their narcissistic partner. The empath pours all of their energy into the relationship often tolerating high levels of mistreatment, hoping they can receive the love they desperately want and need, but as long as the empath holds the narcissist's disavowed feelings, the narcissist will not need to feel their own feelings, and without feeling the depth of their own feelings, they cannot change.

Empaths thrive on helping people and giving to others, but problems arise when the empath ignores their own needs in the process. Often empaths can be more aware of the feelings of others and what is going on in their environment than they are of their own internal state, a pattern that leads to the suppression of painful feelings and a lack of awareness about how to protect themselves from others. The more disconnected the empath is from their own feelings the more likely it is that they will pour all of their love and attention into the relationship and try to fix their partner and the more love and care the empath provides in the relationship, the more controlling and powerful the narcissist becomes leading to a vicious cycle of the demoralization of the empath. In this downward spiral the empath is blamed for the dysfunction of the relationship by the narcissist.

Empaths have the choice to remain in the abusive dynamic with the narcissist or take responsibility for their contribution to the dysfunctional relationship and focus all the attention and focus they put on "fixing" the narcissist on healing their own inner wounds.

In order for an empath to no longer be available for invasion by a narcissist they have to fully inhabit themself. According to Jung, "one does not become enlightened by imagining figures of light, but by making the darkness conscious." The empath has to create a relationship with the pain inside themself that they have not embraced. It is only through making the hidden and previously ignored pain within conscious that they can process their own wounds and begin healing.

It took me losing virtually everything I had before I woke up to this.

Although empaths see clearly that the narcissist is wounded they are often unable to connect to their own darkness. Empaths can dismiss their own psychic pain and minimize their feelings while overlooking the impact of early traumatic life experiences. The first stages of healing come when the empath understands their role in the relationship with the narcissist and seeks self awareness. Along with exploring their emotions, the empath can develop their sense of self and their own individuality. Empaths have the potential to flourish and deeply transform from their dysfunctional relationship with a narcissist.

According to narcissistic abuse recovery expert Kim Saeed, "When the empath and narcissist enter into a relationship together, it creates a magnetic, yet dysfunctional union because the empath gives to the point of complete and utter exhaustion. Profoundly disoriented, the empath is often destroyed by the relationship. This experience is painful and overwhelming but ultimately the empath undergoes a soul awakening. The narcissist remains the same."

Amen.

Breaking away from a narcissist brings tremendous pain and deep longings, but eventually the empath will look back and question how they ever tolerated being in a relationship with a narcissist. As empaths inhabit themselves and strengthen their sense of self, a sense of healthy boundaries develops and this emerging sense of self will be protective of their old self, placing strong boundaries that prevent future parasitic relationships with narcissists.

Other than a few personal items this hard won lesson cost me everything I had, including my financial security and my home, but as strange as it may sound, I am in deep gratitude for the lessons gained from solving this most difficult life puzzle and the freedom from a lifetime of those many hells I passed through.

Working and looking so hard to ferret out *my* narcissist which I thought had to be severe due to the way it was reflected back to me in the impossible situation I created trapped me between two predatory parasites, never once recognizing myself as the empath caught between them to drive the lesson home in my typical head on extreme kamikaze style.

Times two!

FORTY NINE

Freedom

In the years preceding the onslaught of the covid pandemic I hustled for income doing odd jobs, house cleaning, editing, publishing, teaching, book sales, and anything else that brought in income. Throughout that passage I managed to pay the IRS and the state of California $100 a month each. In the last couple of years of it I eventually got food assistance from the state and health care for the first time in ten years, then my tax man negotiated an Offer in Compromise which the government agreed to because I had made a continued effort to pay. I had to go back into debt for a few thousand dollars, but it was worth it for ten cents on the dollar and I worked to pay that off as fast as I could.

In the lean times I managed to publish a few books, among them the Santa Barbara Writers Conference Scrapbook and I produced and directed a no budget documentary of the same name.

I also did two cross country stints with the Mysteries of The Amazon tour with students of Pablo Amaringo, the legendary painter of Ayahuasca visions where I lectured about shamanism, writing, and creativity, and I participated in sound healing and other musical performances with my Peruvian friends.

I tried for years to find steady employment but nothing ever panned out until I put an application in to the 2020 U.S. Decennial Census on the suggestion of a friend. Largely because I am an Air Force Vietnam Era Veteran I landed a job as the IT Manager for the San Diego office which allowed me to save up a nest egg and get my health care and other neglected issues in order, leaving me with no debt and no obligations other than to myself.

In the aftermath of my emptiness my sister and my youngest niece had a bitter falling out for a number of years stemming from all the abuse they suffered at a young age. They had a lifelong history of feeding off of each other and turning different family members against each other through sabotage for imagined slights that had no justification.

I paid for a number of sessions with my coach for my youngest niece who I had come to the aid of for most of her life and spent thousands of dollars over the years including considerable fees for a lawyer with money I didn't have when things spun out of control with child support from her ex, but in the end she fell victim to a confused, angry self-perpetuating compulsion.

After a lifetime of protecting and often providing for her, she literally said, "Fuck you!" in her mid-forties and cut me off because I would not contribute to the delusional drama she created over and over again. At this time she and my sister who she had alienated herself from for five years prior to that decided to make peace and both of them turned their back on me and shut me out for imagined slights after I had sacrificed still more for them, making me the bad guy.

I have no judgment against their emotionally disturbed misconceptions and they are always welcome into my life as long as they are not trying to thrust me into the middle of their angry fear based emotional dramas. They are free to live by their choices in the reality of their own creations, a right everyone is entitled to, but I will not contribute to any baseless fear driven creations.

Fear is contraction and love is expansion, and in the words of the best karate I ever learned, no opponent, no game.

After a life time of rushing to their aid to "save the day", I realized that they were damaged beyond repair and I was not going to save anybody. My niece is an adult and if she and my sister cannot help themselves and want to blame and punish me for their sorrows when all I ever did was help, then that is their choice. My life time eye opening lesson is that nobody can save anybody else or change their mind. We all have to take responsibility for ourselves and our actions and no one else can do that for us but ourselves.

Now it's time to look out for me.

I spent most of my life trying to help everyone, running to their aid in times of need and "saving the day", riding in on my white horse like a good, noble mindless empath looking for the love and approval that I did not feel worthy of at my core.

Now I love myself too much to be subjected to any further abuse, especially when I have never been the aggressor, never spouted any insults, and never once acted out of unprovoked anger. As the madness increased and people asked me why I stayed with Penny I told them she was a worthy opponent which carried some truth. At this point on my journey I am at peace with myself because throughout all of it I maintained my integrity, and to be honest, I no longer care what anybody thinks about me.

It boggles my mind how the terrifying act of self abandonment and letting go is what opened the door to unconditional self love for me as all agendas were released, freeing me from any attachments. I had let it *all* go in that one act of surrendering to the very thing I feared the most.

My coach always told me to tell my secrets which I did to the best of my abilities in hopes that this version of Truth might light the path for those who choose to follow their way home to their heart and the fullness of being.

The irony of the blessing of freedom they gave me from my not worthy of being loved trap proves that the Universe has a wicked sense of humor. All of the people I sacrificed everything for the benefit of, especially those I had helped the most turned on me, unwittingly blessing me with the priceless gift of total freedom and at this juncture I have no obligation to anybody but myself.

Nothing is permanent.

I am literally and figuratively fully living the dream in the indigenous sense of there being no difference between sleeping, waking, dreaming, or visionary experiences. They are all parts of one and the same infinite continuum that I am passing through like an ongoing E-ticket ride of unfolding mystery that I find fascinating, yet have no attachment to. I find great joy knowing that the expanding spiral path going forward is infinite in every sense of the word, reinforcing those timeless words of wisdom that have been sung to me from as far back as I can remember.

"Row, row, row your boat gently down the stream.
Merrily, merrily, merrily, merrily, life is but a dream."

Recommended Reading

Abrams, David, *The Spell Of The Sensuous: Perception And Language In a More-Than -Human World*, (New York: Random House, 1996)

Berggren, Karen, *Circle of Shaman: Healing Through Ecstasy, Rhythm, and Myth*, (Rochester: Destiny Books, 1998)

Calvo, César, *Three Halves of Ino Moxo: Teachings of the Wizard of the Upper Amazon*, (Rochester: Inner Traditions, 1999)

Campbell, Joseph, *The Hero With A Thousand Faces*, (Novato: New World Library)

Campos, Don José, *The Shaman and Ayahuasca: Journeys to Sacred Realms*, (San Francisco: Divine Arts, 2011)

Dispenza, Joe, *Evolve Your Brain*, (Deerfield Beach: Health Communications, 2007)

Doreal, Dr. M., *The Emerald Tablets of Thoth The Atlantean*, (Nashville: Source Books, 2002)

Eliade, Mircea, *Shamanism, Archaic Techniques of Ecstasy*, (Princeton: University Press, 2004)

Friedman, Robert L., *The Healing Power of the Drum*, (Philadelphia: White Cliffs Media Co, 2000)

Hanson, Rick, Buddha's Brain: *The Practical Neuroscience of Happiness, Love, and Wisdom,* (Oakland: New Harbinger Publications, 2009)

Haule, John R., *Taking Direction from the Spirit in Shamanism and Psychotherapy,* (Shamanic Applications Review 1997)

Havelock, Eric A., *The Muse Learns to Write,* (New Haven: Yale University Press, 1988)

Jenny, Hans, *Cymatics: A Study of Wave Phenomena and Vibration,* (Newmarket: MACROmedia, 2001)

Jung, Carl, *The Portable Jung,* (New York: Penguin, 1976)

Jung, Carl, *The Psychology of the Transference,* (Princeton: Princeton University Press, 1959)

Jung, Carl, *The Undiscovered Self,* (New York: Signet Books, 2006)

Jung, Carl, *Symbols of Transformation,* (New York: Pantheon, 1956)

Kenyon, Tom, *The Hathor Material: Messages From an Ascended Civilization,* (Baltimore: Orb Communications, 2012)

Lawlor, Robert, *Sacred Geometry: Philosophy & Practice,* (London: Thames & Hudson, 1982)

MacLean, P., *The Triune Concept of Brain and Behavior,* (Toronto: University of Toronto Press, 1973)

MacLean, P., *The Triune Brain in Evolution,* (New York: Plenum Press, 1990)
McKee, Robert, *Story,* (New York: Regan Books, 1997)

McKenna, Terence, *Food of the Gods,* (New York: Bantam Books, 1992)

McNeley, James K., *Holy Wind in Navajo Philosophy,* (Tucson: University of Arizona Press, 1981)

Merkur, Dan, *Becoming Half Hidden: Shamanism and Initiation Among the Inuit*, (New York: Garland Publishing, 1992)

Merleau-Ponty, Maurice, *Phenomenology of Perception*, (London: Routledge & Kegan Paul, 1962)

Ouspensky, Pyotr D., *In Search of the Miraculous*. (San Diego: Harcourt Brace, 1949)

Pallamary, Matthew, J., *Spirit Matters*, (San Diego: Mystic Ink Publishing, 2007)

Pallamary, Matthew, J., Mayberry, Paul, *The Infinity Zone*, (San Diego: Mystic Ink Publishing, 2012)

Pallamary, Matthew, J., *Phantastic Fiction*, (San Diego: Mystic Ink Publishing, 2015)

Pallamary, Matthew J., *The Center Of The Universe Is Right Between Your Eyes But Home Is Where The Heart Is,* (San Diego: Mystic Ink Publishing, 2017)

Pallamary, Matthew J., *Death:(A Love Story),* (San Diego: Mystic Ink Publishing, 2020)

Schwaller de Lubicz, R. A., *The Temple in Man*, (Rochester: Inner Traditions, 1981)

Schwaller de Lubicz, R. A., *The Temple of Man*, (Rochester: Inner Traditions, 1998)

Sheldrake, Rupert, *Morphic Resonance: The Nature of Formative Causation*, (Rochester: Park Street Press, 2009)

Steiner, Rudolph, *The Fourth Dimension: Sacred Geometry, Alchemy, and Mathematics*, (Great Barrington: Anthroposophic Press, 2001)

Stevens, José, *Earth to Tao*, (Santa Fe: Bear and Company, 1994)

Stevens, José, *Transforming Your Dragons: How to Turn Fear Patterns into Personal Power*, (Santa Fe: Bear and Company, 1994)

Talbot, Michael, *The Holographic Universe,* (New York: Harper Perennial, 2011)

Vogler, Christopher, *The Writer's Journey: Mythic Structure For Writers,* (Studio City: Michael Wiese Productions, 2007)

Winkelman, Michael, *Shamanism: The Neural Ecology of Consciousness and Healing,* (Westport: Bergin & Garvey, 2000)

ABOUT THE AUTHOR

Matthew J. Pallamary's works have been translated into Spanish, Portuguese, Italian, Norwegian, French, and German. His historical novel of first contact between shamans and Jesuits in 18th century South America, titled, **Land Without Evil** received rave reviews along with a San Diego Book Award for mainstream fiction. It was also adapted into a full-length stage and sky show, co-written with and directed by Agent Red and performed by Sky Candy, an Austin Texas aerial group. The making of the show was the subject of a PBS series, Arts in Context episode, which garnered an EMMY nomination.

His nonfiction book, **The Infinity Zone: A Transcendent Approach to Peak Performance** is a collaboration with professional tennis coach Paul Mayberry that offers a fascinating exploration of the phenomenon that occurs at the nexus of perfect form and motion. **The Infinity Zone** took 1st place in the International Book Awards, New Age category and was a finalist in the San Diego Book Awards.

His first book, a short story collection titled **The Small Dark Room Of The Soul** was mentioned in The Year's Best Horror and Fantasy and received praise from Ray Bradbury and has been released as an audio book.

His second collection, **A Short Walk to the Other Side** was an Award Winning Finalist in the International Book Awards, an Award Winning Finalist in the USA Best Book Awards, and an Award Winning Finalist in the San Diego Book Awards. It has been released as an audio book.

DreamLand a novel about computer generated dreaming, written with legendary DJ Ken Reeth won first place in the Independent e-Book Award in the Horror/Thriller category and was an Award Winning Finalist in the San Diego Book Awards. It has also been released as an audio book.

It's sequel, **n0thing** is titled after the main character, who in the real world is his nephew, an international Counter-Strike gaming champion. After winning what amounts to the Super Bowl of gaming, n0thing and his winning teammates, are recruited as a literal "dream team" whose mission is to go into the nightmares of battle scarred veterans and rescue them from their traumatic memories while becoming ambassadors for a gaming platform that exceeds virtual reality with an experience that pushes the boundaries of reality itself.

Eye of the Predator was an Award Winning Finalist in the Visionary Fiction category of the International Book Awards. **Eye of the Predator** is a supernatural thriller about a zoologist who discovers that he can go into the minds of animals.

CyberChrist was an Award Winning Finalist in the Thriller/Adventure category of the International Book Awards.

CyberChrist is the story of a prize winning journalist who receives an email from a man who claims to have discovered immortality by turning off the aging gene in a 15 year old boy with an aging disorder. The forwarded email becomes the basis for an online church built around the boy, calling him CyberChrist. It has also been released as an audio book.

Phantastic Fiction - A Shamanic Approach to Story took first place in the International Book Awards Writing/Publishing category. *Phantastic Fiction* is Matt's guide to dramatic writing that grew out of his popular Phantastic Fiction Workshop.

Night Whispers was an Award Winning Finalist in the Horror category of the International Book Awards. Set in the Boston neighborhood of Dorchester, *Night Whispers* is the story of Nick Powers, who loses consciousness after crashing in a stolen car and comes to hearing whispering voices in his mind. When he sees a homeless man arguing with himself, Nick realizes that the whispers in his head are the other side of the argument.

His memoir *Spirit Matters* detailing his journeys to Peru, working with shamanic plant medicines took first place in the San Diego Book Awards Spiritual Book Category, and was an Award-Winning Finalist in the autobiography/memoir category of the National Best Book Awards. *Spirit Matters* is also available as an audio book.

The Center Of The Universe Is Right Between Your Eyes But Home Is Where The Heart Is was an Award Winning Finalist in the International Book Awards. Based on a lifetime of research into shamanism, visionary states, the evolution of written communication and the roots of storytelling, award-winning author, editor, and shamanic explorer Matthew J. Pallamary takes those with open minds courageous enough to question the illusions that most of us think of as real on an expansive journey that pierces the veil of reality itself.

AfterLife: The Adventures of a Lost Soul was inspired by real life events, William Peter Blatty's ***The Exorcist***, and the dynamics of demonic possession.

Matt has also produced and directed ***The Santa Barbara Writers Conference Scrapbook*** documentary film and co-wrote the book of the same title in collaboration with Y. Armando Nieto, and conference founder Mary Conrad.

Death: (A Love Story) a first person narrative spoken by the omniscient voice of Death itself, who says, "I'm here to tell you stories and share some science, history, and myths, all of which are your creations that I want to share to help you understand me more. You have seen me as Satan, Anubis, Mot, Thanatos, God, the Devil, loving, punitive, dark, light – the list goes on and on! It is my sincerest hope that our friendly reintroduction here will change the way you think of me, and maybe in some small way reflect the depth of the love I have for you.

Matt's work has appeared in Oui, New Dimensions, The Iconoclast, Starbright, Infinity, Passport, The Short Story Digest, Redcat, The San Diego Writer's Monthly, Connotations, Phantasm, Essentially You, The Haven Journal, The Hurricanes & Swan Songs Anthology, The Santa Barbara Literary Journal, The Closed Eye Open, The Montecito Journal, and many others. His fiction has been featured in The San Diego Union Tribune which he has also reviewed books for, and his work has been heard on KPBS-FM in San Diego, KUCI FM in Irvine, television Channel Three in Santa Barbara, and The Susan Cameron Block Show in Vancouver. He has been a guest on the following nationally syndicated talk shows; Paul Rodriguez, In The Light with Michelle Whitedove, Susun Weed, Medicine Woman, Inner Journey with Greg Friedman, and Environmental Directions Radio series. Matt has appeared on the following television shows; Bridging Heaven and Earth, Elyssa's Raw and Wild Food Show, Things That Matter, Literary Gumbo, Indie Authors TV, and ECONEWS. He has also been a frequent guest on numerous podcasts, among them, The Psychedelic Salon, Black Light in the

Attic, Third Eye Drops, C-Realm, Psychedelics Today, Voices in the Dark, Adventures Through the Mind, Beyond the Veil, and many others.

Matt received the Man of the Year Award from San Diego Writer's Monthly Magazine and has taught a fiction workshop at the **Southern California Writers' Conference** in San Diego, Palm Springs, and Los Angeles, and at the **Santa Barbara Writers' Conference** for over thirty years. He has lectured at the Greater Los Angeles Writer's Conference, the Getting It Write conference in Oregon, the Saddleback Writers' Conference, the Rio Grande Writers' Seminar, the National Council of Teachers of English, The San Diego Writer's and Editor's Guild, The San Diego Book Publicists, The Pacific Institute for Professional Writing, The 805 Writers Conference, The College of Central Florida, Yakima Valley College in Washington, The Yakima Public School System, and he has been a panelist at the World Fantasy Convention, Con-Dor, and Coppercon. He is presently Editor in Chief of Mystic Ink Publishing.

Matt was a featured lecturer and performer at the **Mysteries of the Amazon** exhibit at the Appleton Museum in Ocala Florida and The Larson Gallery in Yakima Washington. He frequently visits the mountains, deserts, and jungles of North, Central, and South America pursuing his studies of shamanism.

WWW.MATTPALLAMARY.COM

BOOKS BY MATTHEW J. PALLAMARY

THE SMALL DARK ROOM OF THE SOUL

LAND WITHOUT EVIL

SPIRIT MATTERS

DREAMLAND (WITH KEN REETH)

THE INFINITY ZONE (WITH PAUL MAYBERRY)

A SHORT WALK TO THE OTHER SIDE

CYBERCHRIST

EYE OF THE PREDATOR

PHANTASTIC FICTION

NIGHT WHISPERS

THE SANTA BARABARA WRITERS CONFERENCE SCRAPBOOK
(WITH MARY CONRAD & Y. ARMANDO NIETO)

n0THING

AFTERLIFE: THE ADVENTURES OF A LOST SOUL

THE CENTER OF THE UNIVERSE IS RIGHT BETWEEN YOUR EYES
BUT HOME IS WERE THE HEART IS

DEATH: (A LOVE STORY)

Made in the USA
Las Vegas, NV
16 January 2022

41599147R00189